FamilyCircle®

Quick&Easy
Cooking

Meredith® Consumer Marketing
Des Moines, Iowa

Family Circle® *Quick & Easy Cooking*

Meredith® Corporation Consumer Marketing
Vice President, Consumer Marketing: David Ball
Consumer Product Marketing Director: Steve Swanson
Consumer Marketing Product Manager: Wendy Merical
Business Director: Ron Clingman
Senior Production Manager: George Susral

Waterbury Publications, Inc.
Contributing Writer: Deborah Wagman
Editorial Director: Lisa Kingsley
Associate Editor: Tricia Bergman
Creative Director: Ken Carlson
Associate Design Director: Doug Samuelson
Contributing Copy Editors: Terri Fredrickson, Gretchen Kauffman, Peg Smith
Contributing Indexer: Elizabeth T. Parson

Family Circle® Magazine
Editor in Chief: Linda Fears
Creative Director: Karmen Lizzul
Food Director: Regina Ragone, M.S., R.D.
Senior Food Editor: Julie Miltenberger
Associate Food Editor: Michael Tyrrell

Meredith Publishing Group
President: Tom Harty
Vice President, Manufacturing: Bruce Heston

Meredith Corporation
President and Chief Executive Officer: Stephen M. Lacy

In Memoriam: E.T. Meredith III (1933–2003)

Pictured on the front cover:
Turkey Saltimbocca
(recipe page 94)
Photography by Jason Donnolly

First Edition.
Printed in the United States of America.
ISSN: 1942-7468
ISBN: 978-0-696-30090-5

All of us at Meredith® Consumer Marketing are dedicated to providing you with information and ideas to enhance your home. We welcome your comments and suggestions. Write to us at: Meredith Consumer Marketing, 1716 Locust St., Des Moines, IA 50309-3023.

Quick as a wink. Easy as pie. If these phrases do not exactly describe the way you perceive meal making, turn the page.

Whether you're looking for fast and fabulous feasts to kick off a special celebration or searching for recipes that lead to healthful family meals that come together in a hurry, you'll find them here.

Each one of the innovative, interesting recipes on these pages is custom-made to keep pace with today's fast-lane family and to give a little octane boost to you—the "pedal to the metal" cook that keeps your family speeding along.

And here, "quick and easy" does not mean bland and boring. This collection of more than 300 recipes—from soothing soups, stick-to-the-ribs meat dishes, and budget-stretching meatless meals to sensational side dishes and delightful desserts—proves that creativity and convenience can drive side by side.

The great-tasting and healthful recipes in *Quick & Easy Cooking* were created for time-pressed cooks who want to feed their families well. With easy-to-find ingredients and short start-to-finish times, most of these recipes can be on the table in 30 minutes or less from the time you walk in the door.

So get going—you're on your way to some fabulous food. Happy cooking!

Because health and time-saving features are paramount these days, look for the following icons throughout the book:

 Healthy: The "healthy" icon means that the recipe meets certain calorie, fat, and sodium guidelines. See page 336 for more information.

One-Pan: The "one-pan" icon means that the recipe uses a single pan in its preparation, and that translates to easy cleanup.

TABLE OF CONTENTS

189

283

309

54

Meat—it's what's for dinner. Choose from this savory selection of sensational, stick-to-the ribs suppers any night of the week—every one delivers big flavor for little effort.

11

19

43

MEATY MAIN DISHES

32

Beef Stroganoff 🍲

If you would like to trim a few calories and fat grams from this rich recipe, feel free to substitute reduced-fat—but not no-fat—sour cream for the full-fat version.

MAKES 4 servings **PREP** 20 minutes **COOK** 10 minutes

- 12   ounces boneless beef sirloin steak
- 1   8-ounce carton sour cream
- 2   tablespoons all-purpose flour
- ½   cup water
- 2   teaspoons instant beef bouillon granules
- ¼   teaspoon black pepper
- 2   tablespoons butter or margarine
- 2   cups sliced mixed fresh mushrooms (button, cremini, and/or shiitake)
- ½   cup chopped onion (1 medium)
- 1   clove garlic, minced
- 2   cups hot cooked noodles

① If desired, partially freeze beef for easier slicing. Trim fat from meat. Thinly slice meat across the grain into bite-size strips. In a small bowl stir together sour cream and flour. Stir in the water, bouillon granules, and pepper; set aside.

② In a large skillet melt butter over medium-high heat. Add meat, mushrooms, onion, and garlic; cook and stir about 5 minutes or until meat is desired doneness. Drain off fat.

③ Stir sour cream mixture into meat mixture in skillet. Cook and stir until thickened and bubbly. Cook and stir for 1 minute more. Serve over noodles.

PER SERVING 486 calories; 30 g total fat (15 g sat. fat); 108 mg cholesterol; 573 mg sodium; 30 g carbohydrate; 2 g fiber; 24 g protein

Beef and Vegetable Stir-Fry

Why go to the expense of Asian takeout when you can whip up this colorful, crunchy dinner in a matter of minutes?

MAKES 4 servings **START TO FINISH** 25 minutes

- 1   tablespoon vegetable oil
- 1   16-ounce package frozen stir-fry vegetables (any combination)
- 1   pound purchased beef stir-fry strips
- ¾   cup lower-sodium beef broth
- ¾   cup purchased peanut sauce
- 2   3-ounce packages ramen noodles, broken (any flavor)
- ¼   cup chopped peanuts

① In a very large skillet heat oil over medium-high heat. Add vegetables; cook and stir for 5 to 6 minutes or until crisp-tender. Remove from skillet.

② Add half of the beef to skillet (add more oil if necessary). Cook and stir for 2 to 3 minutes or until desired doneness. Remove from skillet. Add remaining beef to skillet; cook and stir for 2 to 3 minutes or until desired doneness. Return all beef and vegetables to the skillet.

③ In a small bowl stir together broth and peanut sauce. Add to skillet. Bring to boiling; add noodles (save seasoning packets for another use). Reduce heat. Cook, covered, for 3 to 4 minutes or until noodles are tender, stirring twice. Transfer to dinner plates; sprinkle with peanuts.

PER SERVING 609 calories; 26 g total fat (7 g sat. fat); 54 mg cholesterol; 1,630 mg sodium; 55 g carbohydrate; 8 g fiber; 41 g protein

« Fast, affordable, and fantastic— this one-pan, Asian-inspired dish hits all three bases. »

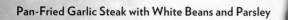

Pan-Fried Garlic Steak with White Beans and Parsley

Pan-Fried Garlic Steak with White Beans and Parsley 🍲

All you need to make this protein-packed dish into a magnificent meal is a crisp green salad tossed with balsamic salad dressing.

MAKES 4 servings **START TO FINISH** 20 minutes

- 4   4- to 5-ounce beef ribeye steaks, cut ½ inch thick
-     Olive oil
-     Salt and black pepper
- 6   cloves garlic, peeled and thinly sliced
- 2   tablespoons butter
- 1   15- to 19-ounce can cannellini beans (white kidney beans)
- ¼   cup snipped fresh parsley

① Drizzle steaks lightly with olive oil; sprinkle with salt and pepper.

② Heat a very large heavy skillet over medium-high heat. Add steaks and reduce heat to medium. Cook steaks for 3 to 4 minutes per side or until desired doneness (145°F for medium-rare). Remove steaks from skillet; cover and keep warm. Add garlic slices to pan. Cook and stir for 1 minute or until softened; remove from pan.

③ Add butter and beans to skillet; heat through. Add parsley and cook 1 minute more. Top steaks with garlic and serve with beans.

PER SERVING 326 calories; 18 g total fat (7 g sat. fat); 81 mg cholesterol; 415 mg sodium; 16 g carbohydrate; 5 g fiber; 29 g protein

quick tip   When choosing wine for cooking use, check the sale bins—it is never necessary to pay more than $8 to $10 for a bottle that is worthy of your dish as well as your glass. Generally, blended red wines—wines made from two or more kinds of grapes—are the most flavor-balanced bet.

Easy Beef Burgundy

Beef Burgundy is—without a doubt—one of the world's most aromatic dishes. When you leave this sumptuous supper to your slow cooker, your nose will have a happy homecoming.

MAKES 6 servings **PREP** 15 minutes **COOK** 8 to 10 hours (low) or 4 to 5 hours (high)

- 1   10.75-ounce can condensed cream of onion soup
- 1   10.75-ounce can reduced-fat and reduced-sodium condensed cream of mushroom soup
- ¾   cup Burgundy or other dry red wine
- 1½   pounds beef stew meat, trimmed and cut into 1-inch cubes
- 8   ounces fresh mushrooms, quartered (3 cups)
- 1   medium onion, sliced
- 8   ounces whole wheat pasta or multigrain pasta, cooked and drained

① In a 3½- or 4-quart slow cooker combine onion soup, mushroom soup, and Burgundy. Stir in beef stew meat, mushrooms, and onion.

② Cover and cook on low-heat setting for 8 to 10 hours or on high-heat setting for 4 to 5 hours. Serve over hot cooked pasta.

PER SERVING 354 calories; 9 g total fat (2 g sat. fat); 73 mg cholesterol; 647 mg sodium; 33 g carbohydrate; 2 g fiber; 30 g protein

Easy Beef Burgundy

Peppery Steak with Bordelaise Sauce

Bordelaise [bor-duh-LAYS] is one of France's most famous sauces. The French fuss for hours over it—but with this streamlined recipe, you don't have to.

MAKES 4 servings **START TO FINISH** 25 minutes

- 1¼   cups water
- 1   cup packaged sliced fresh mushrooms
- ½   cup finely chopped onion (1 medium)
- 1   0.87- to 1.2-ounce package brown gravy mix
- ¼   cup dry red wine
- 4   beef ribeye, top loin, or tenderloin steaks, cut ¾ inch thick (about 1½ pounds)
- 2   teaspoons garlic-pepper seasoning
- 2   tablespoons olive oil

① For sauce, in a medium saucepan bring the water to boiling. Add mushrooms and onion. Reduce heat. Cook, covered, for 3 minutes. Stir in dry gravy mix and red wine. Cook, uncovered, about 3 minutes or until thickened, stirring occasionally. Cover; keep warm.

② Meanwhile, trim fat from steaks. Rub garlic-pepper seasoning into both sides of each steak. In a large skillet heat oil over medium-high heat. Add steaks; reduce heat to medium. Cook to desired doneness, turning once halfway through cooking. Allow 7 to 9 minutes for medium-rare (145°F) to medium (160°F). Serve the steaks with the sauce.

PER SERVING 366 calories; 18 g total fat (5 g sat. fat); 81 mg cholesterol; 954 mg sodium; 7 g carbohydrate; 1 g fiber; 39 g protein

Spinach-Stuffed Flank Steak ♥

To serve this steak—and all steaks—at their juicy best, always allow the meat to rest at room temperature for about 5 minutes before slicing.

MAKES 4 servings **PREP** 25 minutes **BROIL** 10 minutes

- ⅓   cup dried tomatoes (not oil-packed)
- ¼   cup chopped fresh parsley
- 3   tablespoons chopped fresh basil or 2 teaspoons dried basil, crushed
- 1½   teaspoons finely shredded lemon peel
- 2   cloves garlic, minced (1 teaspoon minced)
- 1   teaspoon extra virgin olive oil
- 1   1-pound beef flank steak or top round steak
- ¼   teaspoon kosher salt
- ¼   teaspoon freshly ground black pepper
- 1   10-ounce package frozen chopped spinach, thawed and well drained
- 2   tablespoons grated Parmesan cheese

① In a small bowl place dried tomatoes; cover with boiling water. Let stand for 10 minutes. Drain. Snip into small pieces.

② Meanwhile, in another small bowl combine parsley, basil, lemon peel, garlic, and oil. Set aside.

③ Trim fat from steak. Score both sides of steak in a diamond pattern by making shallow diagonal cuts at 1-inch intervals. Place steak between 2 pieces of plastic wrap. Working from center to edges, pound with the flat side of a meat mallet into a 12 x 8-inch rectangle. Remove plastic wrap. Sprinkle steak with ⅛ teaspoon of the kosher salt and ⅛ teaspoon of the pepper.

④ Sprinkle parsley mixture over the steak; top with spinach. Sprinkle with the remaining ⅛ teaspoon kosher salt and ⅛ teaspoon pepper, the softened tomatoes, and Parmesan cheese. Starting from a short side, roll up steak. Secure with wooden toothpicks at 1-inch intervals, starting ½ inch from an end. Cut between the toothpicks into eight 1-inch slices.

⑤ Place slices, cut sides down, on the unheated rack of a broiler pan. Broil 3 to 4 inches from the heat until desired doneness, turning once. Allow 10 to 12 minutes for medium rare (145°F) or 12 to 16 minutes for medium (160°F). Before serving remove toothpicks.

PER SERVING 235 calories; 10 g total fat (4 g sat. fat); 48 mg cholesterol; 367 mg sodium; 7 g carbohydrate; 3 g fiber; 30 g protein

Steaks with Pan Sauce

Steaks with Pan Sauce 🍲

Beef broth packaged in resealable cartons tastes much fresher than beef broth packed in cans.

MAKES 2 servings **START TO FINISH** 20 minutes

- 5 tablespoons cold butter
- 2 beef steaks, such as top loin, ribeye, or tenderloin, cut about ¾ inch thick
- ⅓ cup dry red wine or apple juice
- ¼ cup reduced-sodium beef broth
- 2 tablespoons finely chopped shallots or 1 clove garlic, minced
- 1 tablespoon whipping cream (no substitutes)
  Salt
  Ground white pepper

① In a large skillet melt 1 tablespoon of the butter over medium-high heat (if possible, do not use a nonstick skillet). Reduce heat to medium. Add steaks and cook about 6 minutes or until medium-rare (145°F), turning once. Transfer steaks to a platter; cover tightly with foil to keep warm (steaks will continue to cook as they stand). Drain fat from skillet.

② Add wine, broth, and shallots to the hot skillet. Using a wire whisk, stir and scrape the bottom of the pan to remove browned bits. Continue to cook over medium heat about 3 to 4 minutes or until liquid is reduced to about 2 tablespoons. Reduce heat to medium-low.

③ Stir in whipping cream. Stir in remaining 4 tablespoons butter, 1 tablespoon at a time, whisking until butter melts and sauce thickens slightly. Season to taste with salt and white pepper. Serve sauce at once over steaks.

PER SERVING 599 calories; 52 g total fat (28 g sat. fat); 163 mg cholesterol; 325 mg sodium; 3 g carbohydrate; 0 g fiber; 23 g protein

Stovetop Lasagna 🍲

Forget about all the lengthy layering required for oven-baked lasagnas. Here you get that same robust Italian flavor in an expedited skillet meal.

MAKES 6 servings **START TO FINISH** 30 minutes

- 1 pound lean ground beef
- 1 cup chopped onion (1 large)
- 1 clove garlic, minced
- 3 cups dried mini lasagna noodles or dried extra-wide noodles
- 1 24- to 26-ounce jar tomato and basil pasta sauce
- 1 cup water
- 1 cup low-fat cottage cheese or ricotta cheese
- 1 cup shredded Italian-blend cheeses or mozzarella cheese
- ¼ cup grated Parmesan cheese
- 1 tablespoon snipped fresh parsley (optional)

① In very large skillet cook and stir ground beef, onion, and garlic over medium-high heat until meat is browned and onion is tender. Stir in noodles, pasta sauce, and the water. Bring to boiling; reduce heat. Cook, covered, for 15 minutes or until noodles are tender and liquid is absorbed.

② Meanwhile, combine cottage cheese, Italian-blend cheeses, Parmesan cheese, and, if desired, parsley. Drop by spoonfuls over meat mixture. Simmer, covered, for 5 minutes more or until cheese melts.

PER SERVING 532 calories; 19 g total fat (8 g sat. fat); 69 mg cholesterol; 736 mg sodium; 54 g carbohydrate; 4 g fiber; 34 g protein

Skillet Pot Roast with Mushrooms and Cherries ♨

This cherry-flecked pot roast is sensational with hot buttered noodles.

MAKES 4 to 6 servings **START TO FINISH** 30 minutes

1 12-ounce package frozen unsweetened, pitted dark sweet cherries

1 8-ounce package fresh button mushrooms, halved (3 cups)

1 medium red sweet pepper, cut into bite-size strips

1 cup chopped onion (1 large)

2 teaspoons dried sage or thyme, crushed

1 tablespoon olive or vegetable oil

2 16- or 17-ounce packages refrigerated cooked beef pot roast with juices

2 tablespoons balsamic vinegar

① Place frozen cherries in colander. Run cold water over cherries to partially thaw. Set aside; drain well.

② In a very large skillet cook mushrooms, sweet pepper, onion, and 1 teaspoon of the sage in hot oil for 7 minutes or until tender. Add pot roast and juices, cherries, and balsamic vinegar to skillet. Bring to boiling; reduce heat. Simmer, uncovered, for 10 minutes or until heated through and juices thicken slightly, stirring occasionally. Stir in remaining sage.

PER SERVING 451 calories; 18 g total fat (7 g sat. fat); 120 mg cholesterol; 727 mg sodium; 27 g carbohydrate; 4 g fiber; 49 g protein

Skillet Pot Roast with Mushrooms and Cherries

Cowboy Steak Tacos

In ranch country in the American West, there is always coffee on the campfire, and leftover brew makes its way into wonderful, rustic gravies like this.

MAKES 4 servings **START TO FINISH** 30 minutes

1 pound eye of round, thinly sliced

¼ teaspoon salt

1 cup strong coffee

2 tablespoons ketchup

2 teaspoons chili powder

2 teaspoons vegetable oil

1 small red onion, thinly sliced

1 red or green sweet pepper, thinly sliced

12 6-inch tortillas (flour, corn, or whole wheat)

¾ cup prepared corn relish

Fresh cilantro leaves (optional)

① Sprinkle steak slices with salt; set aside. For sauce, in a small bowl whisk together coffee, ketchup, and chili powder.

② In a very large skillet cook and stir beef in hot oil for 2 to 3 minutes or until browned on all sides. Add sauce, onion, and sweet pepper. Cook 6 to 8 minutes or until vegetables are tender and sauce is thickened.

③ Meanwhile, wrap tortillas in paper towels. Warm in microwave on high for 30 seconds. Spoon steak and vegetable mixture on tortillas. Top with corn relish and sprinkle cilantro.

PER SERVING 596 calories; 20 g total fat (6 g sat. fat); 74 mg cholesterol; 1,169 mg sodium; 71 g carbohydrate; 4 g fiber; 32 g protein

quick tip For slick slicing, place eye of round in the freezer for 20 minutes—partially frozen meats slice evenly and super-thinly.

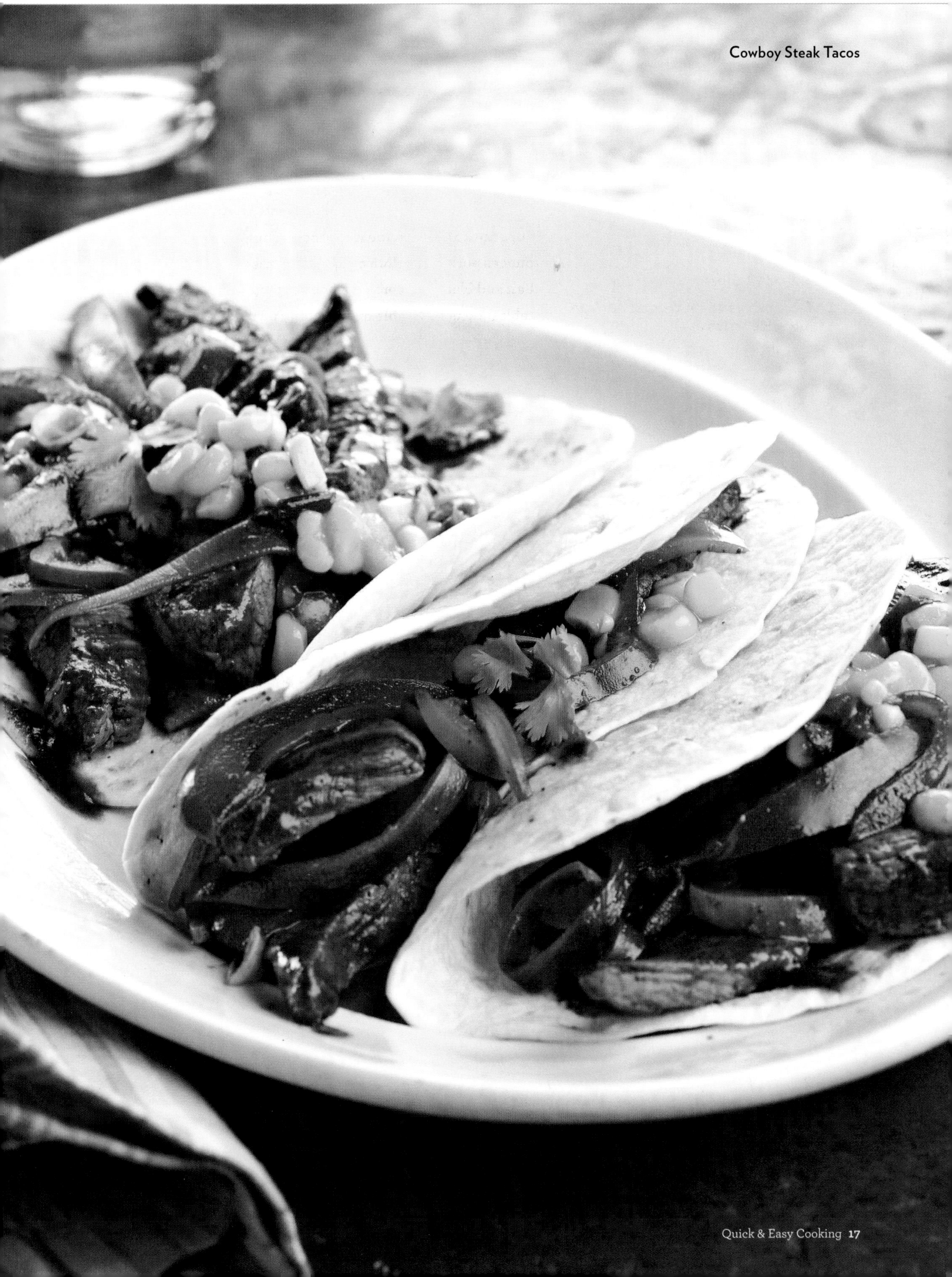

Cowboy Steak Tacos

Beef Sirloin Tips with Smoky Pepper Sauce

Beef Sirloin Tips with Smoky Pepper Sauce

Depending on which area of the country you live, tri-tip steak may also go by the names triangle steak, coulotte steak, and Santa-Rosa-style steak. Whatever its name, it is a nice, lean, and intensely flavorful cut.

MAKES 4 servings **START TO FINISH** 30 minutes

- 1¼ pounds boneless beef tri-tip steak (bottom sirloin)
- ½ teaspoon smoked paprika or regular paprika
- 1 tablespoon vegetable oil
- 1 12- to 16-ounce jar roasted red and/or yellow sweet peppers
- ½ cup hickory- or mesquite-flavor barbecue sauce
- ¼ cup coarsely snipped fresh parsley

① Trim fat from meat. Cut meat into 1- to 1½-inch pieces; sprinkle with paprika. In an extra-large skillet cook meat in hot oil over medium-high heat until brown. Remove from skillet.

② Meanwhile, drain roasted peppers, reserving liquid. Cut up peppers. Measure ½ cup of the reserved liquid (if necessary, add enough water to equal ½ cup).

③ Add roasted peppers and the reserved liquid to the skillet. Stir in barbecue sauce. Cook, uncovered, for 5 to 10 minutes or until mixture is slightly thickened, stirring frequently. Return meat to the skillet; heat through. Sprinkle with fresh parsley.

PER SERVING 318 calories; 16 g total fat (5 g sat. fat); 91 mg cholesterol; 494 mg sodium; 13 g carbohydrate; 2 g fiber; 30 g protein

Asian Beef Salad

To cut nice, thin steak strips, place the top loin in the freezer for about 20 minutes before slicing.

MAKES 4 servings **START TO FINISH** 25 minutes

- 1 9- to 10-ounce package chopped hearts of romaine
- 12 ounces beef top loin steak (about ¾ inch thick) or beef strips cut for stir-fry
- ¼ teaspoon salt
- ¼ teaspoon black pepper
- 1 tablespoon vegetable oil
- 1 medium red sweet pepper, cut into strips
- ¾ cup packaged coarsely shredded fresh carrots
- ½ cup sliced green onions (4)
- ½ cup chopped dry-roasted peanuts
- ½ cup bottled sesame-ginger salad dressing

① Divide romaine among 4 plates; set aside. Thinly slice steak into bite-size strips. If using beef strips, cut any large pieces into bite-size strips. Season meat strips with salt and pepper.

② In a large skillet cook meat strips in hot oil over medium-high heat for 4 to 5 minutes or until brown. Add sweet pepper and carrots; cook and stir for 1 minute more. Remove skillet from heat; stir in green onions. Spoon meat mixture over romaine on each plate. Sprinkle with peanuts. Drizzle with dressing. Serve immediately.

PER SERVING 474 calories; 35 g total fat (8 g sat. fat); 48 mg cholesterol; 512 mg sodium; 18 g carbohydrate; 5 g fiber; 23 g protein

Asian Beef Salad

Ravioli-Vegetable Stacks

Why plum tomatoes? The flesh of plum—or roma—tomatoes is extra meaty, so there is less tomato juice to dilute the flavor of these savory stacks.

MAKES 4 servings **START TO FINISH** 25 minutes
OVEN 425°F

- 1 pound frozen sausage- or meat-filled ravioli
- 2 small zucchini
- 4 plum tomatoes, thinly sliced
- 3 tablespoons olive oil
- ½ cup small fresh basil leaves
- 1 8-ounce package shredded Italian-blend cheese (2 cups)
  Salt and black pepper
  Fresh basil (optional)

① Preheat oven to 425°F. Cook ravioli according to package directions. Trim ends from zucchini; slice each zucchini lengthwise. Add zucchini to ravioli during the last 3 minutes of cooking time. Drain but do not rinse.

② In a 2-quart square baking dish layer half of the tomato slices. Drizzle with 1 tablespoon of the olive oil. Sprinkle with ¼ cup of the basil leaves. Using tongs, layer with half of the ravioli and half of the cheese. Add a layer of zucchini slices; drizzle with 1 tablespoon oil. Layer with remaining ravioli, ¼ cup basil leaves, remaining cheese, and remaining tomato slices; drizzle with remaining 1 tablespoon oil. Sprinkle with salt and pepper.

③ Bake, uncovered, for 9 to 10 minutes or until cheese is melted and begins to brown. To serve, cut into squares. If desired, sprinkle with fresh basil.

PER SERVING 571 calories; 33 g total fat (12 g sat. fat); 114 mg cholesterol; 1,258 mg sodium; 48 g carbohydrate; 8 g fiber; 29 g protein

Beef and Three-Cheese Tortellini Salad

Add a loaf of warm garlic bread and you'll have a wonderful summer supper.

MAKES 4 servings **START TO FINISH** 30 minutes

- 2 cups refrigerated or frozen cheese-filled tortellini (about 9 ounces)
- 8 ounces cooked beef or cooked ham, cut into thin strips (1½ cups)
- 1 cup packaged Colby Jack or cheddar cheese cubes
- 1 cup packaged broccoli florets
- 1 small yellow summer squash or zucchini, halved lengthwise and sliced (1 cup)
- ½ cup bottled Parmesan Italian salad dressing
- 3 to 4 cups torn leaf lettuce
  Cherry tomatoes, quartered (optional)

① Cook tortellini according to package directions. Drain tortellini. Rinse with cold water; drain again.

② In a large bowl combine tortellini, meat strips, cheese, broccoli, and squash. Drizzle salad dressing over beef mixture; toss gently to coat. Quick-chill in the freezer for 10 minutes or until ready to serve (or chill in the refrigerator for 4 to 24 hours).

③ To serve, divide leaf lettuce among salad plates. Place meat mixture on lettuce. If desired, garnish with cherry tomatoes.

PER SERVING 498 calories; 28 g total fat (12 g sat. fat); 97 mg cholesterol; 822 mg sodium; 30 g carbohydrate; 3 g fiber; 31 g protein

> ⟨ Cool and crunchy main-dish salads are just the thing for revving up sagging summertime appetites. ⟩

Beef and Three-Cheese Tortellini Salad

Chili Burgers

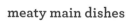

Chili Burgers

Keep a supply of ready-to-go beef or turkey patties in your freezer—these burgers will be such a hit that you'll want to make them often.

MAKES 4 servings **START TO FINISH** 30 minutes

- 4   4-ounce purchased uncooked ground beef or turkey patties
- ½   teaspoon salt
       Dash black pepper
- 1   tablespoon vegetable oil
- ¼   cup chopped onion (1 small)
- 1   clove garlic, minced
- 1   15-ounce can chili with beans
- 1   14.5-ounce can diced tomatoes, undrained
- 4   slices Texas toast, toasted
- ½   cup shredded cheddar cheese (2 ounces)

① Sprinkle patties with salt and pepper. Heat a very large skillet over medium-high heat. Add patties; reduce heat to medium. Cook, uncovered, for 6 to 8 minutes or until juices run clear (160°F), turning once. Remove patties from skillet and keep warm. Drain fat from skillet; discard. Carefully wipe out skillet.

② Add oil to skillet. Return skillet to heat. Add onion and garlic; cook over medium heat until tender. Stir in chili and undrained tomatoes. Bring to boiling; reduce heat. Simmer, uncovered, for 5 to 10 minutes or until desired consistency, stirring occasionally.

③ To serve, place patties on toast. Spoon chili mixture over top. Sprinkle with cheese.

PER BURGER 676 calories; 43 g total fat (16 g sat. fat); 172 mg cholesterol; 1,419 mg sodium; 39 g carbohydrate; 5 g fiber; 36 g protein

Pork with Spaetzle and Braised Cabbage

Spaetzle [SHPEHT-sluh] means "little sparrow" in German. These tiny noodles are made by pushing dough through the holes of a colander into boiling water, which is a time-consuming process. Luckily you can buy them frozen!

MAKES 4 servings **START TO FINISH** 40 minutes

- 1   10.5-ounce package dried spaetzle
- 3   tablespoons butter
- 1   tablespoon chopped fresh parsley
       Salt and ground black pepper
- 2   tablespoons packed brown sugar
- 2   tablespoons cider vinegar
- 2   tablespoons water
- 3   cups shredded red or green cabbage
- 1   17-ounce package refrigerated cooked pork roast au jus

① Cook spaetzle according to package directions; drain. In a large skillet cook spaetzle in 2 tablespoons of the butter over medium heat for 8 to 10 minutes, gently stirring occasionally. Stir in parsley and season to taste with salt and pepper. Remove from skillet and keep warm.

② In the same skillet combine brown sugar, vinegar, the water, and the remaining 1 tablespoon butter. Bring to boiling over medium heat, stirring to dissolve brown sugar. Add cabbage. Return to boiling; reduce heat. Cook, covered, for 5 minutes or until cabbage is crisp-tender. Season to taste with salt and pepper.

③ Meanwhile, reheat pork roast according to package directions. Serve pork roast with spaetzle and cabbage.

PER SERVING 565 calories; 17 g total fat (8 g sat. fat); 152 mg cholesterol; 1,453 mg sodium; 64 g carbohydrate; 4 g fiber; 37 g protein

Pork Chops with Black Bean Salsa ♥

Corn relish is seldom shelved with other kinds of canned corn in the supermarket. You will most likely find it in one of the gourmet food aisles.

MAKES 4 servings **START TO FINISH** 25 minutes

- 4 pork loin chops, cut 1¼ inches thick (about 3 pounds)
- 1 teaspoon Jamaican jerk or Cajun seasoning
- ⅛ teaspoon black pepper
- ¾ cup canned black beans, rinsed and drained (½ of a 15-ounce can)
- ⅔ cup corn relish
- 1½ teaspoons lime juice
- ¼ teaspoon ground cumin
  Lime wedges (optional)

① Preheat broiler. Trim fat from chops. Rub Jamaican jerk seasoning and pepper onto both sides of chops. Place pork chops on the unheated rack of a broiler pan. Broil 3 to 4 inches from the heat for 16 to 20 minutes or until 160°F, turning once halfway through broiling.

② For salsa, in a small bowl combine black beans, corn relish, lime juice, and cumin. Serve chops with salsa and, if desired, lime wedges.

PER CHOP 442 calories; 9 g total fat (3 g sat. fat); 185 mg cholesterol; 457 mg sodium; 20 g carbohydrate; 2 g fiber; 66 g protein

Pork Chops with Black Bean Salsa

Peach-Glazed Chops

Pork takes to sweet and fruity accompaniments like no other meat, and this shiny glaze makes the chops as pretty as they can be.

MAKES 4 servings **START TO FINISH** 25 minutes

- 4 pork loin chops, cut 1 inch thick
  Salt and black pepper
- ¾ cup peach or apricot preserves
- 2 tablespoons lemon juice
- 1 tablespoon vegetable oil
- 2 teaspoons Dijon mustard

① Preheat broiler. Season chops with salt and pepper. Place chops on the unheated rack of a broiler pan. Broil 5 to 6 inches from the heat for 6 minutes. Meanwhile, for glaze, in a small bowl combine preserves, lemon juice, oil, and mustard; brush or spoon some over chops. Turn chops. Broil about 6 minutes more or until done (155°F), spooning glaze over chops the last 3 minutes of broiling. Spoon any remaining glaze on chops before serving.

PER CHOP 591 calories; 16 g total fat (5 g sat. fat); 177 mg cholesterol; 393 mg sodium; 42 g carbohydrate; 1 g fiber; 63 g protein

Oven-Fried Pork Chops ♥

Chops are extra juicy when enclosed in this crunchy crust.

MAKES 4 servings **PREP** 10 minutes **BAKE** 20 minutes **OVEN** 425°F

- 4 pork loin chops, cut ¾ inch thick
- 2 tablespoons butter, melted
- 1 egg, beaten
- 2 tablespoons milk
- ¼ teaspoon black pepper
- 1 cup herb-seasoned stuffing mix, finely crushed

① Preheat oven to 425°F. Trim fat from chops. Pour butter into a 13 x 9 x 2-inch baking pan, tilting pan to coat the bottom. In a shallow dish combine egg, milk, and pepper. Place stuffing mix in a second shallow dish. Dip chops into egg mixture. Coat both sides with stuffing mix. Place in baking pan.

② Bake, uncovered, for 10 minutes. Turn chops. Bake for 10 to 15 minutes more or until 160°F and juices run clear.

PER CHOP 327 calories; 14 g total fat (6 g sat. fat); 147 mg cholesterol; 383 mg sodium; 13 g carbohydrate; 2 g fiber; 35 g protein

Bacon-Wrapped Pork and Beans

Bacon-Wrapped Pork and Beans

If bacon wrapped around the pork fillets does not cook up as much as you would like it to, simply hold a medallion in a pair of tongs and roll its bacon edges slowly over the hot fire.

MAKES 4 servings **START TO FINISH** 30 minutes

1	1½- to 1¾-pound center-cut pork loin fillet
	Salt and black pepper
8	slices center-cut bacon
16	green onions
1	pint cherry or grape tomatoes, halved
1	16-ounce can pinto beans, rinsed and drained
⅓	cup ketchup
2	tablespoons water
1	teaspoon yellow mustard

① Cut pork loin crosswise into 8 pieces. Sprinkle lightly with salt and pepper. Wrap 1 slice of bacon around each slice; secure with a small skewer or wooden pick. For a charcoal grill, arrange medium-hot coals around a drip pan. Test for medium heat above pan. Place pork on grill rack over pan. Cover and grill about 25 minutes or until pork is slightly pink in center and juices run clear (160°F), turning once halfway through grilling.

② Meanwhile, chop 4 green onions; set aside. Place remaining onions on grill rack over coals. Cook for 3 to 4 minutes or just until tender, turning occasionally.

③ In a saucepan combine the chopped onions, tomatoes, beans, ketchup, the water, and mustard. Bring to boiling; reduce heat. Cover and simmer until heated through. Serve with pork and green onions.

PER SERVING 452 calories; 11 g total fat (4 g sat. fat); 107 mg cholesterol; 1,147 mg sodium; 33 g carbohydrate; 8 g fiber; 55 g protein

quick tip To prevent wooden skewers or toothpicks from burning on the grill, soak them in cool water for 30 minutes before using.

Chili-Peanut Pork Chops with Carrot-Cucumber Salad

English cucumbers—also sometimes called hothouse cucumbers—are easy to find in the produce department. They are the long thin ones, usually wrapped tightly in plastic wrap. Since they do not have seeds, the waste-free cukes slice beautifully.

MAKES 4 servings **START TO FINISH** 20 minutes

1	cup dry-roasted peanuts
2	teaspoons chili powder
4	bone-in or boneless pork chops, cut ½ inch thick
2	tablespoons olive oil
¼	cup vinegar
1	tablespoon sugar
3	small carrots
1	small English cucumber
½	cup fresh cilantro leaves
	Chili powder

① In a food processor or by hand chop ¾ cup of the peanuts. In a shallow dish combine chopped peanuts and the 2 teaspoons chili powder. Press pork chops into peanut mixture, turning to coat on both sides.

② In an extra-large skillet heat oil over medium heat. Add chops; cook about 10 minutes or until slightly pink in center and juices run clear (160°F), turning once halfway through cooking time.

③ Meanwhile, in a medium bowl combine vinegar and sugar, stirring until sugar is dissolved. Using a vegetable peeler, cut carrots and cucumber lengthwise into ribbons. Add to bowl. Stir in the remaining ¼ cup peanuts and the cilantro leaves.

④ Serve chops with carrot-cucumber mixture. Sprinkle with additional chili powder.

PER SERVING 444 calories; 32 g total fat (6 g sat. fat); 52 mg cholesterol; 97 mg sodium; 17 g carbohydrate; 5 g fiber; 25 g protein

Maple-Glazed Pork Medallions ♥

Pure maple syrup is expensive, but it is worth the splurge. You only need a little bit, and the real stuff infuses flavor that maple-flavor pancake syrups can only dream of.

MAKES 4 servings **START TO FINISH** 30 minutes

1½	**cups water**
¾	**cup uncooked long grain white rice**
¼	**teaspoon salt**
1	**1- to 1¼-pound pork tenderloin, cut into ¾-inch slices**
2	**teaspoons vegetable oil**
1	**large red cooking apple, cored and cut into ½-inch wedges**
⅓	**cup pure maple syrup**
2	**tablespoons water**
¼	**teaspoon salt**
½	**teaspoon finely chopped canned chipotle peppers in adobo sauce (optional) (see quick tip, below)**

① In a large saucepan combine the 1½ cups water, rice, and ¼ teaspoon salt. Bring to boiling over high heat; reduce heat to low. Cook, covered, for 15 minutes or until rice is tender and liquid is absorbed.

② Meanwhile, in a large skillet cook pork in hot oil over medium-high heat for 6 to 8 minutes or until slightly pink (160°F). Remove meat from skillet; set aside.

③ Add apple wedges to skillet. Cook and stir for 2 minutes. Add maple syrup, the 2 tablespoons water, ¼ teaspoon salt, and, if using, chipotle peppers. Cook and stir until boiling; boil gently for 2 to 3 minutes or just until apples are tender. Return pork to skillet; heat through. Serve over rice.

PER SERVING 394 calories; 9 g total fat (2 g sat. fat); 75 mg cholesterol; 354 mg sodium; 52 g carbohydrate; 2 g fiber; 27 g protein

quick tip Because hot chile peppers, such as chipotles, contain volatile oils that can burn your skin and eyes, avoid direct contact with chiles as much as possible. When working with chile peppers, wear plastic or rubber gloves. If your bare hands touch the chile peppers, wash them well with soap and water.

Smoked Pork Chops with Mustard-Dill Sauce

Smoked loin chops are most often located near the bacon in your supermarket.

MAKES 6 servings **PREP** 10 minutes **BROIL** 9 minutes

6	**smoked pork loin chops, cut 1 inch thick**
3	**tablespoons packed brown sugar**
3	**tablespoons cider vinegar or white wine vinegar**
½	**cup Dijon mustard**
3	**tablespoons olive oil**
½	**teaspoon dried dill**
	Dash black pepper

① Preheat broiler. Place chops on the unheated rack of a broiler pan. Broil 3 to 4 inches from the heat for 9 to 12 minutes or until heated through, turning once halfway through broiling.

② Meanwhile, for sauce, in a small bowl stir together brown sugar and vinegar until sugar is dissolved. Using a wire whisk, beat in mustard, olive oil, dill, and pepper until well combined. Transfer warm chops to a serving platter. Drizzle smoked chops with some of the sauce. Pass remaining sauce.

PER CHOP 208 calories; 11 g total fat (2 g sat. fat); 45 mg cholesterol; 1,453 mg sodium; 7 g carbohydrate; 0 g fiber; 15 g protein

quick tip If you happen to have fresh dill in your garden or fridge, by all means toss it into this pork-perfect sauce. When substituting fresh dill for dried dill—or any fresh herb for its dried version—use three times more. In this recipe, for instance, use 1½ teaspoons of fresh dill to replace the ½ teaspoon of dried dill.

Pork Chops with Fennel Salad

Pork Chops with Fennel Salad

Fennel is a vegetable you will enjoy getting to know. Its crisp bulb has a refreshing, slightly sweet, licorice taste that sings in this salad.

MAKES 4 servings **START TO FINISH** 27 minutes

4	½-inch-thick pork loin chops
	Salt and black pepper
2	tablespoons olive oil
2	oranges
12	ounces young green beans, trimmed
1	tablespoon honey
1	red pear or apple, cored and thinly sliced
½	of a fennel bulb, cored and thinly sliced

① Sprinkle pork chops lightly with salt and pepper. In a very large skillet heat 1 tablespoon of the olive oil. Add chops; cook for 6 minutes. Turn chops and squeeze juice from half of one orange over chops. Cook for 6 to 8 minutes more or just until pink in centers.

② Meanwhile, in another skillet place green beans with enough water to cover. Bring to boiling; reduce heat and simmer, covered, 8 minutes or until tender. Drain.

③ For fennel salad, juice the remaining orange half in a bowl. Stir in honey, remaining olive oil, ¼ teaspoon salt and ¼ teaspoon pepper. Peel and slice remaining orange. Add orange, pear, and fennel to the orange juice-honey mixture.

④ Place chops on serving plates with beans; spoon any pan juices over beans. Serve fennel salad and top with fennel fronds.

PER SERVING 406 calories; 23 g total fat (6 g sat. fat); 68 mg cholesterol; 214 mg sodium; 27 g carbohydrate; 7 g fiber; 25 g protein

Peppered Pork Chops and Pilaf ♥

To make this one-pan supper even simpler, opt for one of the wonderful vegetable mixtures available in your market's freezer case.

MAKES 4 servings **START TO FINISH** 25 minutes

4	boneless pork loin chops, cut ¾ inch thick
2	teaspoons seasoned pepper blend
1	tablespoon olive oil
3	cups vegetables, such as broccoli, carrots, mushrooms, onions, and/or sweet peppers, cut into bite-size pieces
1	14.5-ounce can chicken broth
2	cups uncooked instant brown rice
¼	cup bottled roasted red sweet pepper, drained and cut into strips

① Trim fat from chops. Sprinkle both sides of meat with seasoned pepper. In a large skillet heat oil over medium-high heat. Add chops; reduce heat to medium. Cook chops for 8 to 12 minutes or until 160°F, turning once halfway through cooking. Remove chops from skillet, reserving drippings; cover chops to keep warm.

② Add vegetables, broth, and uncooked rice to skillet. Bring to boiling; reduce heat. Simmer, covered, for 5 to 7 minutes or until rice is done and vegetables are crisp-tender. Return pork chops to skillet; cover and heat through. Garnish with roasted red pepper strips.

PER SERVING 304 calories; 9 g total fat (2 g sat. fat); 47 mg cholesterol; 607 mg sodium; 31 g carbohydrate; 4 g fiber; 25 g protein

 Versatile pork—queen of quick cooking—is a blank canvas for a whole world of diverse flavors.

Cranberry-Sauced Pork and Sweet Potatoes ♥

Here tart cranberries temper the sweetness of the potatoes to create a perfect state of equilibrium.

MAKES 4 servings **START TO FINISH** 20 minutes

- 4 boneless pork loin chops, cut ¾ inch thick (about 1 pound)
  Salt and black pepper
  Nonstick cooking spray
- 1 17-ounce can sweet potatoes
- 1 tablespoon butter or margarine
- 1 cup orange juice
- ¼ cup dried cranberries

① Trim fat from chops. Sprinkle chops lightly with salt and pepper. Lightly coat an unheated large skillet with cooking spray. Preheat skillet over medium-high heat. Add chops; reduce heat to medium. Cook for 8 to 12 minutes or until chops are 160°F, turning once halfway through cooking.

② Meanwhile, place sweet potatoes in a medium saucepan. Mash with a potato masher. Stir in butter. Cook and stir over medium heat until potatoes are heated through. If desired, season to taste with salt and pepper.

③ Remove chops from skillet, reserving drippings; cover chops to keep warm. Add orange juice and cranberries to drippings in skillet. Bring to boiling; reduce heat. Simmer, uncovered, about 7 minutes or until liquid is reduced by half. Transfer chops to dinner plates; spoon sauce over chops. Serve with sweet potatoes.

PER SERVING 341 calories; 8 g total fat (4 g sat. fat); 78 mg cholesterol; 226 mg sodium; 38 g carbohydrate; 3 g fiber; 27 g protein

Thai Pork and Vegetable Curry ♥

Jasmine rice is a long grain variety of rice most often imported from Thailand. It possesses such a wonderful, nutty fragrance and flavor that once you've tasted it, you may not want to cook plain rice again.

MAKES 4 servings **START TO FINISH** 30 minutes

- 1⅓ cups uncooked jasmine rice (about 9 ounces)
- 12 ounces pork tenderloin or lean boneless pork
  Salt and black pepper
- 2 tablespoons vegetable oil
- 8 ounces green beans, bias-sliced into 1½-inch pieces (2 cups)
- 1 red sweet pepper, cut into thin bite-size strips
- 2 green onions, bias-sliced into ¼-inch pieces
- 1 14-ounce can unsweetened coconut milk
- 4 teaspoons bottled curry paste
- 1 teaspoon sugar
- ⅛ teaspoon crushed red pepper
- 1 lime, cut into wedges

① Cook rice according to package directions; drain. Keep warm.

② Meanwhile, thinly slice pork into bite-size pieces. Sprinkle with salt and pepper. In a large nonstick skillet heat 1 tablespoon of the oil over medium-high heat. Add pork; cook and stir about 4 minutes or until no pink remains. Remove from skillet.

③ Add the remaining 1 tablespoon oil to skillet. Add green beans; cook and stir for 3 minutes. Add sweet pepper and green onions; cook and stir about 2 minutes more or until vegetables are crisp-tender. Remove from skillet. Add coconut milk, curry paste, sugar, and crushed red pepper to skillet. Bring mixture to boiling; reduce heat. Simmer, uncovered, about 2 minutes or until mixture is slightly thickened. Stir in pork and vegetables; heat through. Serve over hot cooked rice with lime wedges.

PER SERVING 490 calories; 16 g total fat (5 g sat. fat); 47 mg cholesterol; 593 mg sodium; 63 g carbohydrate; 3 g fiber; 23 g protein

quick tip A 9-ounce package of frozen cut green beans, thawed, can be substituted for the fresh beans. Add them to the skillet along with the sweet pepper and onions; cook as directed.

Thai Pork and Vegetable Curry

Pierogies with Meat Sauce

Pierogies with Meat Sauce

Thank the cooks of Poland for these savory stuffed dumplings.

MAKES 4 servings **START TO FINISH** 25 minutes

- 1 12.8-ounce package frozen potato-and-onion-filled pierogies
- 8 ounces uncooked chorizo sausage or bulk Italian sausage
- 1 pint red and/or yellow cherry tomatoes, halved
- 1 8-ounce can tomato sauce
- 4 ounces watercress (4 cups)

① In a Dutch oven cook pierogies in 4 cups lightly salted boiling water according to package directions. Drain and cover to keep warm.

② Meanwhile, in a very large skillet brown sausage. Drain off fat. Reserve ½ cup tomatoes; add remaining tomatoes and tomato sauce to skillet. Cook, uncovered, 6 to 8 minutes or until tomatoes begin to soften.

③ Divide pierogies among plates. Spoon sauce over pierogies. Top with reserved tomatoes and watercress.

PER SERVING 419 calories; 24 g total fat (8 g sat. fat); 54 mg cholesterol; 1,331 mg sodium; 34 g carbohydrate; 3 g fiber; 20 g protein

Kielbasa and Kraut Skillet 🍲

To slice kielbasa on the bias, just cut the links at a 45-degree angle.

MAKES 4 servings **START TO FINISH** 25 minutes

- 1 pound cooked kielbasa, bias-sliced into 2-inch pieces
- 1 small red onion, thinly sliced
- 1 15-ounce can sauerkraut, undrained
- 1 tablespoon coarse-grain brown mustard
- ¼ to ½ teaspoon caraway seeds
- ¼ teaspoon salt
- ¼ teaspoon black pepper

① In a large skillet cook kielbasa and onion over medium heat just until onion is tender. Stir in undrained sauerkraut, mustard, caraway seeds, salt, and pepper. Cook, covered, over medium heat about 10 minutes or until heated through.

PER SERVING 392 calories; 34 g total fat (16 g sat. fat); 50 mg cholesterol; 1,755 mg sodium; 6 g carbohydrate; 2 g fiber; 14 g protein

Cowboy Bowls

If you have some heat-seeking palates at your table, feel free to substitute jalapeño jack cheese for the milder cheddar variety.

MAKES 4 servings **START TO FINISH** 20 minutes

- 1 24-ounce package refrigerated mashed potatoes
- 1 17- to 18-ounce package refrigerated cooked shredded pork with barbecue sauce
- 1 15- to 16-ounce can chili beans in chili gravy
- 1 cup frozen whole kernel corn
- ½ cup chopped red sweet pepper
- ¼ cup finely chopped onion
- ½ cup shredded cheddar cheese (2 ounces)

① Heat mashed potatoes according to package directions.

② Meanwhile, in a medium saucepan combine pork, undrained chili beans, corn, sweet pepper, and onion. Heat through.

③ Transfer mashed potatoes to shallow bowls or mugs. Top with pork mixture and sprinkle with cheese.

PER SERVING 600 calories; 21 g total fat (7 g sat. fat); 76 mg cholesterol; 1,125 mg sodium; 74 g carbohydrate; 8 g fiber; 31 g protein

Cowboy Bowls

Apple-Sausage Rigatoni 🍲

Fresh herbs that may be used to enhance the flavor of this recipe are chives, thyme, and parsley.

MAKES 4 servings **START TO FINISH** 25 minutes

6 ounces dried rigatoni pasta

8 ounces cooked smoked sausage links, halved lengthwise and cut into 1-inch pieces

1½ pounds McIntosh or Braeburn apples, cored and cut into ½-inch slices

½ cup whipping cream

½ cup crumbled Gorgonzola or other blue cheese (2 ounces)

Fresh herbs (optional)

① In a Dutch oven cook pasta according to package directions; drain in a colander.

② In the same Dutch oven cook sausage over medium heat until light brown. Add apples; cook about 5 minutes or until apples are light golden brown, stirring occasionally. Stir in cooked pasta, whipping cream, and cheese; heat through. If desired, garnish with fresh herbs.

PER SERVING 613 calories; 34 g total fat (16 g sat. fat); 92 mg cholesterol; 1,056 mg sodium; 56 g carbohydrate; 5 g fiber; 26 g protein

Apple-Sausage Rigatoni

Gorgonzola-Sauced Tortellini with Artichokes

Gorgonzola is an Italian blue-veined cheese. The variety is usually slightly sweeter than other blue cheeses, but any variety of blue cheese may be used here.

MAKES 4 servings **START TO FINISH** 30 minutes

1 9-ounce package refrigerated spinach cheese tortellini or three-cheese tortellini

8 ounces bulk sweet or hot Italian sausage

6 ounces cremini, stemmed shiitake, or button mushrooms, sliced (1½ cups)

1 small onion, cut into thin wedges

2 ounces Gorgonzola cheese, crumbled (½ cup)

1 14.5-ounce can diced tomatoes with basil, garlic, and oregano, drained

1 6-ounce jar marinated artichoke hearts, drained and quartered

1 tablespoon finely shredded Parmesan cheese

2 tablespoons thinly sliced fresh basil

① Cook tortellini according to package instructions; drain.

② Meanwhile, in a 3-quart saucepan cook sausage, mushrooms, and onion until sausage is no longer pink and onion is tender, breaking up sausage with a wooden spoon. Drain off fat.

③ Add Gorgonzola cheese; cook and stir over low heat until cheese melts. Gently stir in tortellini, drained tomatoes, and artichokes; heat through. Sprinkle with Parmesan cheese and basil.

PER SERVING 624 calories; 36 g total fat (13 g sat. fat); 96 mg cholesterol; 1,695 mg sodium; 52 g carbohydrate; 3 g fiber; 26 g protein

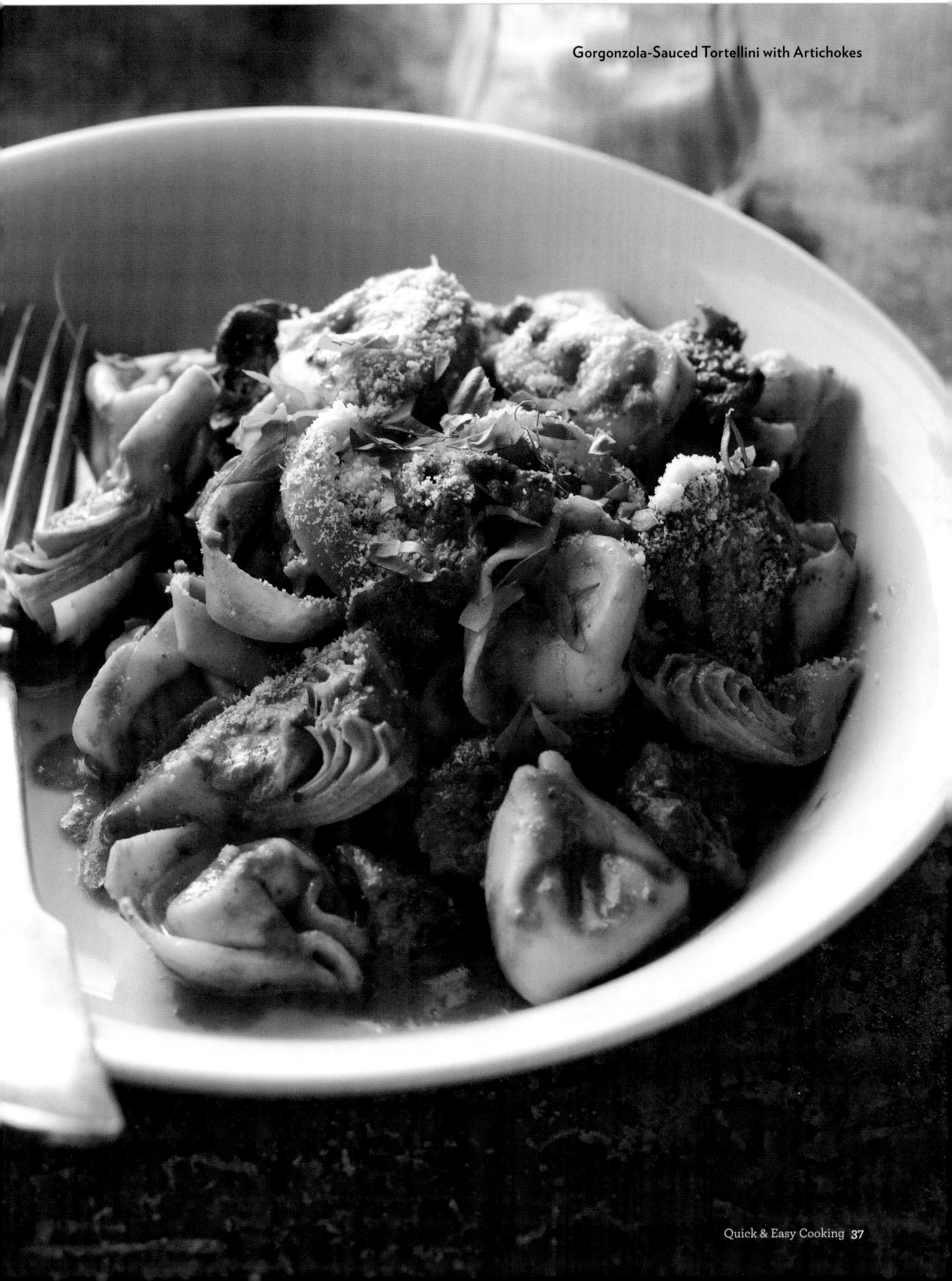

Gorgonzola-Sauced Tortellini with Artichokes

Vermicelli with Sausage and Spinach

Vermicelli with Sausage and Spinach

One of sausage's greatest assets is that—in almost any dish—one variety of sausage stands in well for another. Try this creamy-rich dish with all your favorite sausages to see which you like best.

MAKES 4 to 6 servings **START TO FINISH** 25 minutes

1   pound cooked smoked sausage, halved lengthwise and cut into ½-inch slices

¾   cup chopped onion (1 large)

2   large cloves garlic, chopped

2   teaspoons olive oil

2   14.5-ounce cans reduced-sodium chicken broth

¼   cup water

8   ounces packaged dried vermicelli or angel hair pasta, broken in half

1   9-ounce package fresh prewashed baby spinach

¼   teaspoon black pepper

⅓   cup whipping cream

① In a 4-quart Dutch oven cook sausage, onion, and garlic in hot oil over medium-high heat until sausage is lightly browned and onion is tender.

② Add broth and the water to Dutch oven; bring to boiling. Add pasta; cook for 3 minutes, stirring frequently. Add spinach and pepper; cook about 1 minute more or until spinach wilts. Stir in whipping cream. Serve immediately.

PER SERVING 689 calories; 43 g total fat (16 g sat. fat); 97 mg cholesterol; 1,470 mg sodium; 50 g carbohydrate; 4 g fiber; 26 g protein

quick tip To save time and effort from recipes calling for chopped garlic or onions, consider purchasing their convenience versions—jarred chopped garlic and frozen chopped onions. When using ready-to-go garlic, use 1 teaspoon of jarred garlic for every garlic clove the recipe calls for. Frozen chopped onions stand in for freshly chopped onions in equal amounts.

Spaghetti with Italian Sausage and Spinach

Often, hot Italian sausage is really, really hot. If you and your family do not like super-spicy foods, choose mild Italian sausage for this spaghetti.

MAKES 8 servings **START TO FINISH** 35 minutes

1   19- to 20-ounce package uncooked mild or hot Italian sausage links, cut into 1-inch pieces

2   medium yellow or green sweet peppers, cut into bite-size strips

1   small sweet onion, cut into wedges

1   14- to 16-ounce package dried multigrain, whole wheat, or regular spaghetti

1   teaspoon crushed red pepper

¼   teaspoon salt

½   cup chicken broth

6   cups packaged fresh baby spinach

2   to 3 ounces Asiago cheese, shaved

     Additional crushed red pepper (optional)

① In a very large skillet cook sausages for 15 minutes or until no longer pink, turning occasionally. Add sweet peppers and onion to skillet. Cook for 5 minutes more or until vegetables are tender, stirring occasionally.

② Meanwhile, in a large pot cook spaghetti according to package directions, adding crushed red pepper to the water. Reserve 1 cup pasta cooking water. Drain pasta; return to pan.

③ Toss sausage mixture and salt with spaghetti in pan. Stir in chicken broth and enough reserved pasta water to thin. Add spinach; toss just until combined and spinach is slightly wilted. Sprinkle each serving with Asiago cheese and, if desired, additional crushed red pepper.

PER SERVING 466 calories; 24 g total fat (9 g sat. fat); 59 mg cholesterol; 738 mg sodium; 40 g carbohydrate; 5 g fiber; 21 g protein

Sausage Pasta Skillet

If you purchase roasted sweet peppers in a can, be sure to transfer leftover peppers and their liquid to a glass or plastic container before storing them in the refrigerator.

MAKES 4 servings **START TO FINISH** 35 minutes

- 8 ounces dried campanelle or penne pasta
- 8 ounces bulk hot or sweet Italian sausage
- 1 medium onion, cut into thin wedges
- 1 26-ounce jar garlic pasta sauce
- ⅔ cup roasted red sweet peppers, cut into bite-size strips
- ¼ cup pitted kalamata olives, quartered
- 1 cup shredded Italian-blend cheeses

① Cook pasta according to package directions; drain.

② In a large skillet cook sausage and onion until sausage is browned and onion is tender; drain off fat. Stir in pasta sauce, roasted sweet peppers, and olives. Bring to boiling. Stir in pasta to coat. Top with shredded cheese.

PER SERVING 616 calories; 28 g total fat (11 g sat. fat); 63 mg cholesterol; 1,037 mg sodium; 65 g carbohydrate; 6 g fiber; 26 g protein

Sausage Pasta Skillet

Chorizo-Topped Mexican Pizzas

Chorizo is available in bulk, or the loose-ground, raw form used here—as well as in links.

MAKES 4 servings **START TO FINISH** 20 minutes

- 8 ounces chorizo sausage
- 1 cup chunky salsa with corn and beans (deli-style)
  Nonstick cooking spray
- 4 7- to 8-inch flour tortillas
- 1 cup shredded Mexican cheese blend (4 ounces)
- 1 avocado, halved, seeded, peeled, and sliced
- 4 green onions, chopped (½ cup)
- ¼ cup snipped fresh cilantro
  Lime wedges

① Preheat broiler. In a large skillet cook chorizo over medium heat until no longer pink, using a wooden spoon to break up meat as it cooks. Drain off fat. In a small saucepan heat salsa over medium heat until heated through.

② Lightly coat a large baking sheet with cooking spray. Arrange tortillas, 2 at time, on baking sheet; top each with ¼ cup of the cheese. Broil 3 to 4 inches from the heat for 2 to 3 minutes or until cheese is melted.

③ Top each pizza with some of the salsa, cooked chorizo, avocado, green onions, and cilantro. Pass lime wedges.

PER SERVING 588 calories; 41 g total fat (15 g sat. fat); 75 mg cholesterol; 1,242 mg sodium; 31 g carbohydrate; 6 g fiber; 24 g protein

Bucatini and Bacon

Bucatini and Bacon

Pecorino romano, an Italian grating cheese—is made from sheeps' milk. Its texture is similar to that of Parmesan cheese, but tastes a bit tangier.

MAKES 4 servings **START TO FINISH** 25 minutes

- 8 ounces dried bucatini or fusilli pasta
- 3 cups fresh baby spinach
- 1 28-ounce can whole peeled tomatoes with basil, undrained
- 6 slices bacon, crisp-cooked, drained, and crumbled
- 3 cloves garlic, minced
- ½ cup freshly grated Pecorino Romano cheese
  Salt
  Black pepper
  Freshly grated Pecorino Romano cheese (optional)

① In a Dutch oven cook pasta according to package directions; drain. Return pasta to hot Dutch oven. Stir in spinach; cover Dutch oven.

② Meanwhile, drain tomatoes, reserving liquid. Snip the tomatoes into bite-size pieces. In a medium saucepan combine tomatoes, bacon, and garlic. Bring to boiling; reduce heat. Simmer, uncovered, for 10 minutes, stirring occasionally.

③ Add tomato mixture to pasta mixture. Cook until heated through, tossing gently to coat and adding some of the reserved tomato liquid if mixture is dry. Stir in ½ cup cheese. Season to taste with salt and pepper. If desired, sprinkle each serving with additional cheese.

PER SERVING 355 calories; 9 g total fat (4 g sat. fat); 24 mg cholesterol; 845 mg sodium; 51 g carbohydrate; 4 g fiber; 17 g protein

quick tip Seeding a tomato is a snap. Simply halve the tomato crosswise to expose seed chambers and then hold the tomato over a bowl and give it a squeeze—the seeds will make a quick exit. If a seed or two remains, don't worry about it!

Bacon and Tomato Fettuccine

To save time, cut the raw strips of bacon into small strips, then stir and fry over medium-high heat until crisp.

MAKES 6 servings **START TO FINISH** 30 minutes

- ¾ cup butter, cut up and softened
- 1 pound dried fettuccine
- 1½ cups finely shredded Parmigiano-Reggiano cheese (6 ounces)
- ⅓ cup seeded and chopped roma tomato (1 medium) (optional)
- ¼ cup small fresh basil leaves (optional)
- 2 slices bacon, crisp-cooked, drained, and crumbled (optional)
  Finely shredded Parmigiano-Reggiano cheese (optional)
  Freshly ground black pepper (optional)

① Place half of the butter in a large bowl; set aside.

② Cook fettuccine according to package directions. Remove ½ cup of the pasta cooking water; set aside. Drain pasta slightly, leaving some water with the pasta.

③ Add cooked pasta to butter in bowl; toss to coat. Add the remaining butter and 1½ cups cheese. Toss to combine, adding enough of the reserved ½ cup pasta water to reach a creamy consistency. If desired, top with tomato, basil, and bacon.

④ If desired, sprinkle each serving with additional cheese and pepper.

PER SERVING 613 calories; 33 g total fat (20 g sat. fat); 83 mg cholesterol; 685 mg sodium; 58 g carbohydrate; 3 g fiber; 21 g protein

Four-Cheese Linguine with Prosciutto

To whip up a simple side dish to serve with this ultrarich pasta, simply halve a pint box of grape tomatoes and quickly saute them in a bit of olive oil over medium-high heat.

MAKES 8 servings **START TO FINISH** 30 minutes

1¼   pounds dried linguine
1   cup shredded Emmentaler or Swiss cheese (4 ounces)
1   cup shredded fontina cheese (4 ounces)
1   cup crumbled Gorgonzola or other blue cheese (4 ounces)
¾   cup finely shredded Parmesan cheese (3 ounces)
2   tablespoons all-purpose flour
2   cups whipping cream
8   ounces thinly sliced prosciutto, coarsely chopped
    Freshly ground black pepper

① In a Dutch oven cook linguine according to package directions; drain. Return linguine to hot Dutch oven.

② Meanwhile, for sauce, in a large saucepan combine Emmentaler cheese, fontina cheese, Gorgonzola cheese, and Parmesan cheese. Sprinkle with flour; toss gently to coat. Stir in cream and prosciutto. Cook and stir over medium heat just until mixture comes to boiling.

③ Pour sauce over cooked linguine; stir gently to coat. Sprinkle each serving with pepper.

PER SERVING 768 calories; 46 g total fat (24 g sat. fat); 133 mg cholesterol; 1,023 mg sodium; 58 g carbohydrate; 2 g fiber; 32 g protein

Bacon and Blue Cheese Dinner Pies

To prepare fresh thyme for the pies' tops, simply run your thumb and index finger firmly along the stem, working from the top to the bottom. This method will quickly strip the leaves from the stems.

MAKES 4 servings **PREP** 15 minutes **BAKE** 15 minutes **OVEN** 400°F

4   slices bacon
1   8.5-ounce package corn muffin mix
½   cup all-purpose flour
1   teaspoon chili powder
1   egg, lightly beaten
¼   cup milk
1   large Granny Smith apple, cored and thinly sliced
⅓   cup blue cheese crumbles
    Fresh thyme (optional)

① Preheat oven to 400°F. In a skillet cook bacon until crisp. Drain; reserve 2 tablespoon drippings. Chop bacon.

② Meanwhile, in a bowl combine muffin mix, flour, chili powder, egg, and milk with a fork. Divide dough into 4 portions. Place 2 portions on each of 2 greased baking sheets and press each portion to a 6- to 7-inch circle.

③ Top each circle with a layer of apple slices, leaving a 1-inch border. Fold edges around apple slices. Brush apples and crust with reserved bacon drippings.

④ Bake 10 minutes. Top with blue cheese and the bacon; bake 5 to 7 minutes more until edges are golden and center of crust is set. If desired, sprinkle with thyme, .

PER SERVING 524 calories; 19 g total fat (6 g sat. fat); 79 mg cholesterol; 890 mg sodium; 72 g carbohydrate; 3 g fiber; 15 g protein

quick tip   To trim cleanup tasks, consider lining your baking sheets with parchment paper rather than greasing them or spraying them with nonstick spray. When you're through with a parchment paper-lined pan, cleanup is just a matter of tossing away the paper—no scrubbing required.

BLT Salad with Warm Vinaigrette

BLT Salad with Warm Vinaigrette

Mark this recipe with a sticky note so you remember to make it when summer tomatoes are abundant.

MAKES 4 servings **START TO FINISH** 20 minutes

8	slices bacon
4	slices country Italian bread
1½	cups cherry tomatoes
8	cups torn romaine
⅓	cup blue cheese crumbles
¼	cup cider vinegar
¼	cup olive oil
1	teaspoon sugar
1	teaspoon Dijon mustard
	Salt and ground black pepper

① In a large skillet cook bacon over medium heat until crisp, turning occasionally. Remove bacon from skillet; drain on paper towels.

② Meanwhile, toast bread. Halve cherry tomatoes. Break bacon into 2-inch pieces. On plates layer toast, romaine, tomatoes, bacon, and blue cheese.

③ For vinaigrette, in screw-top jar combine vinegar, oil, sugar, and mustard. Shake well. Season to taste with salt and pepper. Drizzle vinaigrette on salads.

PER SERVING 375 cal; 26 g fat (7 g sat. fat); 31 mg chol; 923 mg sodium; 24 g carbo; 4 g fiber; 14 g pro.

Pasta with Ham, Dried Tomatoes, and Cheese

No bow tie pasta? Choose any variety of pasta made with folds or holes that will catch this tasty sauce. Rigatoni, corkscrew, and macaroni all make great substitutes.

MAKES 6 servings **START TO FINISH** 30 minutes

1	16-ounce package dried bow tie pasta
1¼	cups half-and-half or light cream
2	egg yolks
½	teaspoon garlic salt
6	ounces cooked ham, cut into bite-size strips
1	cup shredded Italian blend cheese
½	cup oil-packed dried tomatoes, well drained and chopped
2	green onions, thinly sliced (¼ cup)

① In a 4-quart Dutch oven cook pasta according to package directions. Drain pasta and return to pan; keep warm.

② Meanwhile, for sauce, in a medium saucepan whisk together half-and-half, egg yolks, and garlic salt. Cook and stir over medium heat just until bubbly. Pour sauce over hot cooked pasta. Add ham, cheese, and tomatoes. Stir to combine. Cook over medium-low heat until heated through. Stir before serving. Sprinkle each serving with green onions.

PER SERVING 473 calories; 15 g total fat (7 g sat. fat); 114 mg cholesterol; 719 mg sodium; 61 g carbohydrate; 3 g fiber; 23 g protein

《 When summer tomatoes are red, ripe, and juicy, try this BLT in a bowl. 》

Need a quick-fix dinner? Choose chicken or turn to turkey—both birds will fly terrific tastes to your table in no time at all.

53   77   94

QUICK POULTRY

73

Chicken Breasts with Mozzarella

The pretty colors and full flavors of this dish may lead people to believe that you spent more time on it than you really did.

MAKES 4 servings **START TO FINISH** 30 minutes

1 6-ounce package long grain and wild rice pilaf mix

1 cup packaged fresh broccoli florets

¼ cup thinly sliced green onions (2)

1 tablespoon olive oil or vegetable oil

4 Italian-style or butter-garlic marinated skinless, boneless chicken breast halves

1 medium tomato, cored, halved, and thinly sliced

4 slices mozzarella cheese (3 ounces)

① Prepare rice according to package directions, adding broccoli the last 5 minutes of cooking. Stir in green onions and set aside.

② Meanwhile, preheat broiler. In a large broilerproof skillet heat oil over medium-high heat. Add chicken; reduce heat to medium. Cook for 8 to 12 minutes or until no longer pink (170°F), turning occasionally to brown evenly. If necessary, reduce heat to medium-low to prevent overbrowning. Remove skillet from heat.

③ Arrange halved tomato slices on chicken breast halves. Top with cheese. Broil chicken 3 to 4 inches from heat about 1 minute or until cheese is melted and brown. Serve chicken with rice mixture.

PER SERVING 363 calories; 10 g total fat (4 g sat. fat); 73 mg cholesterol; 1,269 mg sodium; 38 g carbohydrate; 3 g fiber; 31 g protein

Apple-Dijon Chicken

Buttered spaetzle makes a terrific accompaniment for these creamy-rich chicken breasts.

MAKES 4 servings **START TO FINISH** 30 minutes

4 skinless, boneless chicken breast halves
Salt and black pepper

2 tablespoons butter or margarine

1 medium tart cooking apple (such as Granny Smith), thinly sliced

⅓ cup whipping cream

2 tablespoons Dijon mustard

① Butterfly-cut each chicken breast half by cutting horizontally from 1 long side of the breast almost to, but not through, the opposite long side of the breast. Lay the breast open. Sprinkle both sides of chicken breasts with salt and pepper.

② In a large skillet melt 1 tablespoon of the butter over medium-high heat. Add 2 of the chicken breasts; cook for 4 to 6 minutes or until no longer pink (170°F), turning to brown evenly. Remove chicken from skillet; cover to keep warm. Repeat with remaining chicken.

③ Melt remaining 1 tablespoon butter in skillet. Add apple; cook and stir about 3 minutes or until tender. Add whipping cream and mustard to skillet. Cook and stir until heated through and thickened slightly. Season to taste with additional salt and pepper. Serve sauce and apples over chicken.

PER SERVING 342 calories; 16 g total fat (9 g sat. fat); 142 mg cholesterol; 407 mg sodium; 6 g carbohydrate; 1 g fiber; 40 g protein

 Who says a plate must hold three things? Save time and bolster nutrition by skipping the starch.

**Chicken and Sausage
with Acini di Pepe**

Chicken and Sausage with Acini di Pepe

This one-dish meal couldn't be easier.

MAKES 6 servings **START TO FINISH** 30 minutes

- 1 pound skinless, boneless chicken breast halves, cut into 1-inch pieces
- 1 pound cooked smoked sausage links, cut into ½-inch slices
- 1 cup chopped sweet onion (1 large)
- ½ cup chopped red sweet pepper (1 small)
- 3 cloves garlic, minced
- 1 tablespoon butter
- 1 14-ounce can reduced-sodium chicken broth
- ¾ cup water
- 1 tablespoon balsamic vinegar
- ⅛ teaspoon cayenne pepper
- 1½ cups dried acini di pepe
- ½ cup sliced green onions (4)

① In a 4-quart Dutch oven cook chicken, sausage, onion, sweet pepper, and garlic in hot butter over medium heat for 5 minutes, stirring occasionally. Add broth, the water, vinegar, and cayenne pepper.

② Bring just to boiling. Stir in acini de pepe; reduce heat. Simmer, covered, about 10 minutes or until chicken is no longer pink and pasta is tender, stirring occasionally. Remove from heat. Stir in green onions.

PER SERVING 583 calories; 27 g total fat (9 g sat. fat); 97 mg cholesterol; 898 mg sodium; 49 g carbohydrate; 3 g fiber; 36 g protein

quick tip Acini di pepe, which means peppercorns in Italian, is a teeny round pasta, often used in soups. Any small pasta makes a good substitute for acini di pepe. Try orzo. Or substitute small alphabet-shape pasta for a child-friendly dish.

Quick Skillet Lasagna

This good-looking skillet should go straight to a trivet on the table—it's too handsome to dish up in the kitchen.

MAKES 6 servings **START TO FINISH** 30 minutes

- 8 ounces uncooked lean ground chicken or turkey
- ½ cup chopped onion (1 medium)
- 2 cups spaghetti sauce
- 1 cup water
- 2 cups dried extra-wide noodles
- 1½ cups coarsely chopped zucchini
- ½ cup fat-free ricotta cheese
- 2 tablespoons grated Parmesan or Romano cheese
- 1 tablespoon snipped fresh parsley
- ½ cup shredded mozzarella cheese (2 ounces)
  Snipped fresh parsley (optional)

① In a large skillet cook ground chicken and onion over medium heat until meat is browned, using a wooden spoon to break up meat as it cooks. Drain off any fat.

② Stir in spaghetti sauce and the water. Bring to boiling. Stir in noodles and zucchini. Return to boiling; reduce heat. Simmer, covered, about 10 minutes or until noodles are tender, stirring occasionally.

③ Meanwhile, in a small bowl combine ricotta cheese, Parmesan cheese, and 1 tablespoon parsley. Drop cheese mixture by spoonfuls into 4 mounds on pasta mixture. Sprinkle each mound with mozzarella cheese.

④ Cook, covered, over low heat for 4 to 5 minutes or until cheese mixture is heated through and mozzarella cheese is melted. If desired, sprinkle with additional parsley.

PER SERVING 186 calories; 3 g total fat (2 g sat. fat); 45 mg cholesterol; 519 mg sodium; 21 g carbohydrate; 2 g fiber; 17 g protein

...que

...hat bear the word veronique,
...es.

...**FINISH** 20 minutes

...ness, boneless chicken breast halves

¼ teaspoon salt

¼ teaspoon black pepper

¼ cup butter

1 cup seedless red grapes, halved

3 tablespoons sherry vinegar or red wine vinegar

¼ teaspoon dried thyme, crushed

① Sprinkle chicken with salt and pepper. In a large skillet cook chicken in 2 tablespoons of hot butter over medium-high heat for 8 to 10 minutes or until no longer pink (170°F), turning once. Transfer to a serving platter; keep warm.

② For sauce, add the remaining 2 tablespoons butter, grapes, vinegar, and thyme to the hot skillet. Cook and stir until slightly thickened, scraping up any browned bits on bottom of skillet. Serve sauce over chicken.

PER SERVING 301 calories; 15 g total fat (8 g sat. fat); 115 mg cholesterol; 348 mg sodium; 7 g carbohydrate; 0 g fiber; 33 g protein

Chicken Veronique

Chicken Fajita Pasta

The chile bin at the market can be so confusing. Anaheim chile peppers are narrow, elongated, and muted chartreuse in color. Their flavor is mellow and just a bit spicier than that of sweet peppers.

MAKES 6 to 8 servings **START TO FINISH** 35 minutes

12 ounces dried pappardelle or egg noodles

1 8-ounce carton sour cream

½ cup chipotle liquid meat marinade

2 tablespoons lime juice

1 teaspoon chili powder

1 teaspoon ground cumin

½ teaspoon crushed red pepper

1 medium onion, halved and thinly sliced

1 medium red sweet pepper, seeded and cut into thin bite-size strips

1 fresh Anaheim chile pepper, seeded and cut into thin bite-size strips (see quick tip, page 28) (⅓ cup)

2 tablespoons olive oil

1 to 1¼ pounds skinless, boneless chicken breast halves, cut into thin bite-size strips

1 tablespoon snipped fresh cilantro (optional)

Lime wedges (optional)

① In a 4- to 5-quart Dutch oven cook pasta in lightly salted boiling water according to package directions. Drain and return pasta to pan; keep warm. Meanwhile, in a medium bowl combine sour cream, marinade, lime juice, chili powder, cumin, and crushed red pepper. Set aside.

② In a large skillet cook onion, sweet pepper, and Anaheim pepper in 1 tablespoon of the olive oil over medium heat for 4 to 5 minutes or until crisp-tender. Remove vegetables from skillet; set aside. Add the remaining 1 tablespoon oil to skillet. Add half of the chicken; cook and stir over medium-high heat for 2 to 3 minutes or until chicken is no longer pink. Remove from skillet. Repeat with remaining chicken, adding additional oil if necessary.

③ Add chicken, vegetables, and sour cream mixture to pasta. Toss to coat. Cook over low heat until heated through. If desired, sprinkle with cilantro and serve with lime wedges.

PER SERVING 453 calories; 15 g total fat (6 g sat. fat); 60 mg cholesterol; 589 mg sodium; 53 g carbohydrate; 3 g fiber; 27 g protein

Chicken Lo Mein

Chicken Lo Mein

Convenient, ready-to-go stir-fry sauces make Asian-influenced meals a snap. Many flavorful varieties are on the market—try several until you find your favorite.

MAKES 4 servings **START TO FINISH** 25 minutes

- 8 ounces dried Chinese egg noodles, rice noodles, or udon (broad, white noodles)
- 2 tablespoons peanut oil or canola oil
- 1 16-ounce package frozen stir-fry vegetables
- 1 tablespoon finely chopped fresh ginger
- 1 pound skinless, boneless chicken breast halves, cut into ½-inch pieces
- ⅓ cup stir-fry sauce
   Sliced green onions or snipped fresh cilantro (optional)

① Cook noodles according to package directions; drain. Return noodles to hot pan.

② Meanwhile, pour 1 tablespoon of the oil into a large skillet; heat skillet over medium-high heat. Add frozen vegetables and ginger; cook and stir for 4 to 6 minutes or until vegetables are crisp-tender. Remove from skillet. Add the remaining 1 tablespoon oil to skillet; add chicken. Cook and stir chicken for 3 to 4 minutes or until chicken is no longer pink.

③ Return vegetables to skillet. Add cooked noodles and stir-fry sauce; stir all ingredients together to coat with sauce. Cook and stir until heated through. If desired, garnish each serving with green onions.

PER SERVING 455 calories; 8 g total fat (2 g sat. fat); 66 mg cholesterol; 907 mg sodium; 60 g carbohydrate; 2 g fiber; 30 g protein

quick tip When the watched pot never boils, speed it up! Water comes to boiling more quickly when the pot is covered with a tight-fitting lid. Measure water to make sure you are heating no more than you need.

Chicken with Cranberry Sauce

To use leftover cranberry sauce, spoon it onto steaming bowls of hot oatmeal.

MAKES 4 servings **START TO FINISH** 25 minutes

- 1 tablespoon butter, margarine, or olive oil
- 4 skinless, boneless chicken breast halves
- ½ of a 16-ounce can (1 cup) whole cranberry sauce
- 2 tablespoons honey
- ½ teaspoon ground ginger

① In a large skillet melt butter over medium-high heat. Add chicken; reduce heat to medium. Cook over medium heat for 8 to 12 minutes or until no longer pink (170°F), turning occasionally to brown evenly. If necessary, turn heat to medium-low to prevent overbrowning. Remove skillet from heat. Remove chicken from skillet, reserving drippings; cover chicken to keep warm.

② For sauce, add cranberry sauce, honey, and ginger to drippings in skillet. Cook and stir over medium-low heat until heated through. Serve sauce with chicken.

PER SERVING 330 calories; 5 g total fat (2 g sat. fat); 90 mg cholesterol; 127 mg sodium; 36 g carbohydrate; 1 g fiber; 33 g protein

Chicken with Herb Rub

You might consider doubling this recipe so you have four extra herbed chicken breasts to chop into soups or salads during the week.

MAKES 4 servings **START TO FINISH** 20 minutes

- ½ cup snipped fresh mint
- 2 tablespoons sesame seeds
- 2 to 4 teaspoons fennel seeds, crushed
- 2 teaspoons dried thyme, crushed
- 4 skinless, boneless chicken breast halves
- 1 tablespoon olive oil or vegetable oil

① For rub, in a small bowl combine mint, sesame seeds, fennel seeds, thyme, 1 teaspoon salt, and ¼ teaspoon black pepper. Sprinkle rub evenly over chicken; rub in with your fingers.

② In a large skillet heat oil over medium-high heat. Add chicken; reduce heat to medium. Cook for 8 to 12 minutes or until no longer pink (170°F), turning to brown evenly.

PER SERVING 228 calories; 8 g total fat (1 g sat. fat); 82 mg cholesterol; 662 mg sodium; 2 g carbohydrate; 1 g fiber; 34 g protein

Chicken with Greek Orzo Risotto

Adding chicken broth in small increments makes the orzo risotto extra creamy.

MAKES 4 servings **START TO FINISH** 30 minutes

- 4 skinless, boneless chicken breast halves (about 1¼ pounds total)
  Salt and freshly ground black pepper
- 2 tablespoons olive oil
- 3 cups reduced-sodium chicken broth
- 2 cloves garlic, minced
- 1 cup dried orzo pasta (rosamarina)
- ¾ cup quartered cherry tomatoes
- ½ cup crumbled feta cheese (2 ounces)
- ¼ cup sliced pitted ripe olives
- 1 tablespoon snipped fresh oregano

① Lightly sprinkle chicken with salt and pepper. In a very large skillet heat 1 tablespoon of the oil over medium heat. Add chicken; cook for 8 to 12 minutes or until chicken is no longer pink (170°F), turning once.

② Meanwhile, for risotto, in a medium saucepan bring broth and garlic to boiling; reduce heat and simmer. In a large saucepan heat the remaining 1 tablespoon oil over medium heat. Add orzo; cook and stir for 1 minute. Slowly add ½ cup of the hot broth to orzo, stirring constantly. Continue to cook and stir over medium heat until broth is absorbed. Continue adding broth, ½ cup at a time, stirring constantly until broth is absorbed and mixture is creamy. (This should take about 15 minutes.) Remove from heat.

③ Stir tomatoes, cheese, olives, and oregano into risotto. Serve chicken with risotto.

PER SERVING 451 calories; 14 g total fat (4 g sat. fat); 99 mg cholesterol; 952 mg sodium; 35 g carbohydrate; 2 g fiber; 44 g protein

Edamame-Chicken Stir-Fry ♥

Gingerroot grates easily if it is peeled and frozen before grating.

MAKES 4 servings **START TO FINISH** 30 minutes

- 8 ounces skinless, boneless chicken breast halves
- 3 tablespoons bottled hoisin sauce
- 1 tablespoon rice vinegar
- 1 tablespoon reduced-sodium soy sauce
- ¼ teaspoon crushed red pepper
- 3 teaspoons olive oil or canola oil
- 2 teaspoons grated fresh ginger
- 1 cup bias-sliced carrots (2 medium)
- 2 cups broccoli florets
- 1 cup ready-to-eat fresh or frozen, thawed, shelled sweet soybeans (edamame)
- 1 8.8-ounce pouch cooked whole grain brown rice

① Cut chicken into thin bite-size strips; set aside. For sauce, in a small bowl stir together hoisin sauce, rice vinegar, soy sauce, and crushed red pepper; set aside.

② Pour 2 teaspoons of the oil into a large nonstick wok or large nonstick skillet. Heat over medium-high heat. Add ginger; cook and stir for 15 seconds. Add carrots and stir-fry for 1 minute. Add broccoli and edamame and stir-fry 4 to 5 minutes more or until vegetables are crisp-tender. Remove vegetables from wok. Add remaining 1 teaspoon oil to the wok. Add chicken strips and stir-fry for 2 to 4 minutes or until chicken is no longer pink. Return vegetables to the wok. Add sauce to chicken mixture, tossing to coat. Heat through.

③ Meanwhile, heat rice according to package directions. Serve chicken mixture over rice.

PER SERVING 312 calories; 9 g total fat (1 g sat. fat); 33 mg cholesterol; 299 mg sodium; 35 g carbohydrate; 5 g fiber; 23 g protein

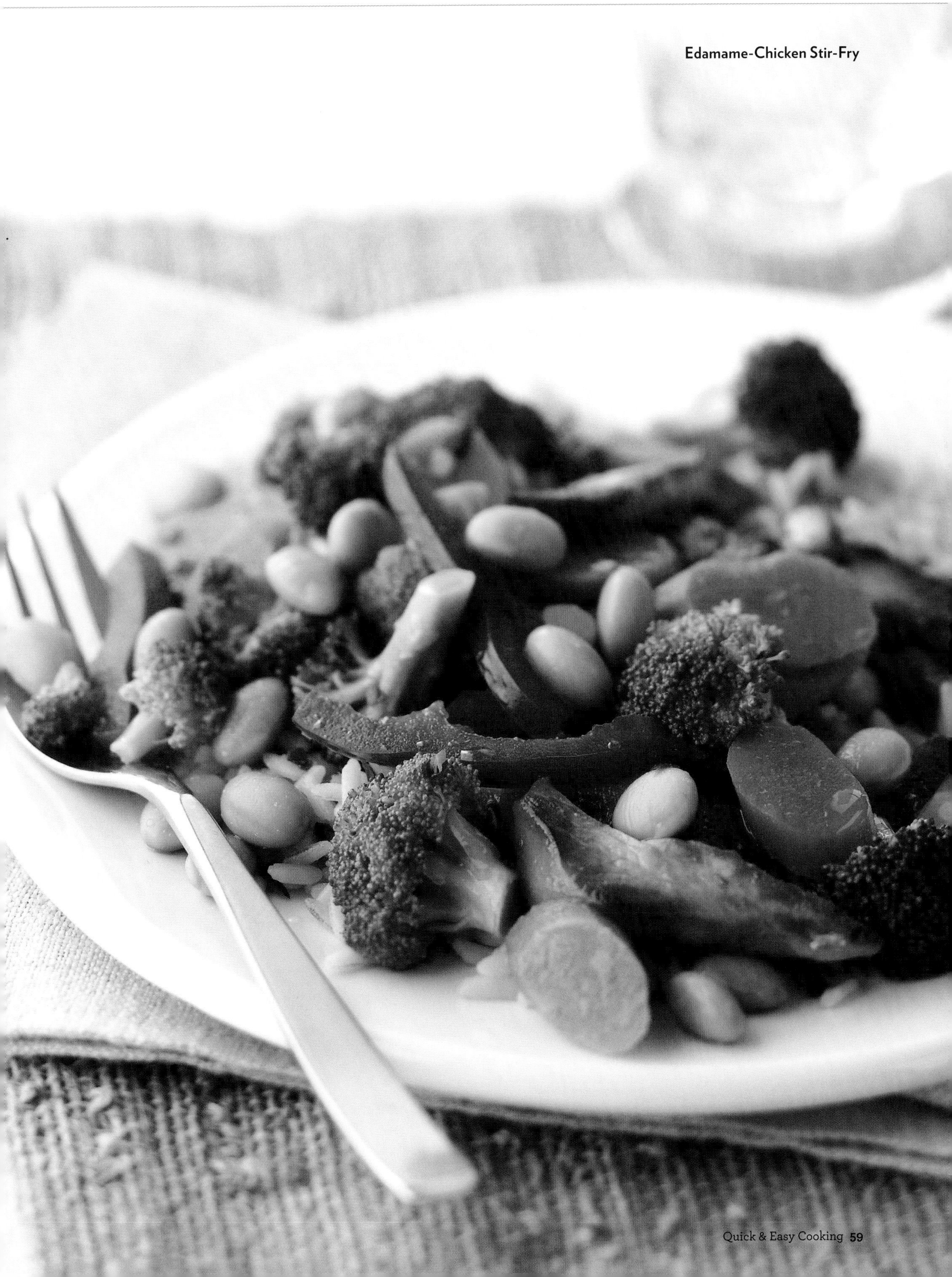

Edamame-Chicken Stir-Fry

Chicken-Veggie Pasta Toss

Chicken-Veggie Pasta Toss ♥

Generous portions of this light and lovely pasta toss weigh in at under 400 calories each!

MAKES 4 servings **START TO FINISH** 30 minutes

- 12 ounces skinless, boneless chicken breast halves
- 6 ounces dried multigrain penne pasta (2 cups)
- 1 tablespoon olive oil or canola oil
- 4 cloves garlic, minced
- ¼ teaspoon crushed red pepper
- 1 16-ounce package frozen broccoli stir-fry vegetable mix
- 1 15-ounce can no-salt-added cannellini beans (white kidney beans), rinsed and drained
- ½ to ¾ cup reduced-sodium chicken broth
- 1 tablespoon snipped fresh oregano

① Cut chicken into bite-size strips; set aside. Cook pasta according to package directions. Drain.

② Meanwhile, in an extra-large nonstick skillet heat oil over medium-high heat. Add garlic and crushed red pepper; cook and stir for 30 seconds. Add frozen vegetables; cook and stir for 5 minutes more. Remove vegetables from skillet.

③ Add chicken to the hot skillet; cook and stir for 3 to 4 minutes or until no longer pink. Return vegetables to the skillet. Add drained pasta, beans, and enough of the chicken broth to moisten. Cook, stirring occasionally, until heated through.

④ Serve in shallow bowls. Sprinkle with oregano.

PER SERVING 399 calories; 6 g total fat (1 g sat. fat); 49 mg cholesterol; 214 mg sodium; 50 g carbohydrate; 10 g fiber; 35 g protein

Chipotle Chile Chicken with Blueberry Pepper Salsa ♥

When fresh blueberries are inexpensive and plentiful, by all means use them for this gorgeous salsa. Simply smash a few of them with a fork to release some of their juices.

MAKES 4 servings **START TO FINISH** 25 minutes
OVEN 400°F

- Nonstick cooking spray
- 2 tablespoons honey
- 2 teaspoons finely chopped chipotle chile pepper in adobo sauce (see quick tip, page 28)
- 1 tablespoon butter, melted
- 1 teaspoon dried oregano, crushed
- ½ teaspoon salt
- 4 skinless, boneless chicken breast halves
- 1½ cups frozen blueberries, thawed, drained
- 1 11-ounce can mandarin oranges, drained
- 3 tablespoons finely chopped red onion
- 1 teaspoon finely shredded lime peel
- 2 teaspoons lime juice

① Preheat oven to 400°F. Coat a 13 x 9 x 2-inch baking pan with cooking spray; set aside. In a small bowl stir together 1 tablespoon honey, 1 teaspoon chipotle pepper, melted butter, oregano, and salt. Brush both sides of chicken with chipotle mixture. Arrange chicken in prepared pan. Bake 15 to 20 minutes or until no longer pink (170°F).

② Meanwhile, for salsa, in a medium bowl combine blueberries, oranges, red onion, the remaining honey and chipotle, the lime peel, and the lime juice. Serve salsa with chicken.

PER SERVING 279 calories; 5 g total fat (2 g sat. fat); 90 mg cholesterol; 420 mg sodium; 25 g carbohydrate; 2 g fiber; 34 g protein

‹ Keep dinner warm and wonderful by serving pasta dishes in heated bowls. **›**

Golden Skillet Chicken

With stalks of steamed broccoli on the side, this is a meal fit for company.

MAKES 4 servings **START TO FINISH** 20 minutes

- 4   skinless, boneless chicken breast halves
- 1   10.75-ounce can condensed golden mushroom soup
- ¾   cup reduced-sodium chicken broth
- ½   of an 8-ounce tub cream cheese with chive and onion
- 8   ounces angel hair pasta or thin spaghetti, cooked and drained

① Place each chicken breast half, boned side up, between 2 pieces of plastic wrap. Pound lightly until ¼ inch thick. Discard plastic wrap.

② Heat a large nonstick skillet over medium-high heat for 1 minute. Add chicken and cook about 4 minutes or until no longer pink (170°F), turning once. (If necessary, cook half the chicken at a time.) Remove chicken from skillet; keep warm.

③ For sauce, add soup, broth, and cream cheese to the hot skillet. Cook and stir over medium heat until combined and heated through. Serve chicken and sauce over hot cooked pasta.

PER SERVING 520 calories; 14 g total fat (8 g sat. fat); 113 mg cholesterol; 906 mg sodium; 51 g carbohydrate; 2 g fiber; 43 g protein

Cinnamon-Roasted Chicken with Pumpkin-Sage Grits

In American cuisine, cinnamon is most often used in sweet baked goods. But its warm spiciness adds intriguing taste to savory dishes as well.

MAKES 4 servings **PREP** 10 minutes **ROAST** 18 minutes **OVEN** 400°F

- 4   4- to 6-ounce skinless boneless chicken breast halves
- 1   tablespoon vegetable oil
- 1½   teaspoons salt
- 1   teaspoon ground cinnamon
- ½   teaspoon black pepper
- 1½   cups water
- ⅔   cup instant grits (two 1-ounce packages)
- ½   cup canned pumpkin
- 1   tablespoon snipped fresh sage
- ⅓   cup shredded cheddar cheese
     Sage leaves

① Preheat oven to 400°F. Arrange chicken breast halves in a 13 x 9 x 2-inch baking pan. Drizzle chicken with oil and sprinkle with 1 teaspoon of the salt, the cinnamon, and pepper. Rub the spices over all sides of the chicken. Roast in preheated oven for 18 to 20 minutes or until no longer pink and juices run clear.

② Meanwhile, in a medium saucepan bring the water to boiling. Stir in grits until combined. Stir in pumpkin, sage, and ½ teaspoon of the salt. Return to boiling; reduce heat. Cook, uncovered, for 5 to 7 minutes or until thickened, stirring frequently. Remove from heat; stir in cheese.

③ To serve, spoon grits onto dinner plates and top with chicken breast halves. Add sage leaves.

PER SERVING 253 calories; 8 g total fat (3 g sat. fat); 76 mg cholesterol; 1,162 mg sodium; 14 g carbohydrate; 2 g fiber; 30 g protein

Cinnamon Roasted Chicken
with Pumpkin-Sage Grits

Southwest Chicken Skillet

Southwest Chicken Skillet ♥

Another time make this skillet using turkey tenderloins.

MAKES 4 servings **START TO FINISH** 20 minutes

- 1 pound skinless, boneless chicken breast halves, cut into bite-size strips
- 1 tablespoon Southwest chipotle-flavor salt-free seasoning (such as Mrs. Dash)
- 1 tablespoon vegetable oil
- 1 medium yellow sweet pepper, coarsely chopped
- 1 small zucchini, bias-sliced and quartered
- ½ of a medium onion, cut into thin wedges
- ½ cup bottled salsa
- ½ cup frozen whole kernel corn
- ½ cup cooked or canned black beans, rinsed and drained
- 4 8-inch whole wheat flour tortillas (see quick tip, below) or hot cooked rice (optional)

  Chopped fresh cilantro (optional)

① Sprinkle chicken with seasoning. Heat oil over medium-high heat in a very large skillet. Add chicken; reduce heat to medium. Cook and stir about 2 minutes or until chicken is browned on all sides. Add sweet pepper, zucchini, and onion; cook and stir for 2 to 3 minutes more or until crisp tender.

② Add salsa, corn, and beans to skillet. Cook and stir for 1 to 2 minutes more or until heated through and chicken is no longer pink.

③ Serve with warm tortillas or rice, and sprinkle with cilantro, if desired.

PER SERVING 233 calories; 5 g total fat (1 g sat. fat); 66 mg cholesterol; 271 mg sodium; 17 g carbohydrate; 4 g fiber; 30 g protein

Pecan-Crust Chicken

With a simple spinach salad on the side, you'll be all set.

MAKES 4 servings **START TO FINISH** 35 minutes

- 2 tablespoons orange marmalade
- 2 tablespoons pure maple syrup
- 1 cup finely chopped pecans
- 3 tablespoons all-purpose flour
- ¼ teaspoon salt
- 4 skinless, boneless chicken breast halves
- 2 tablespoons vegetable oil
- 1 tablespoon butter

① In a small bowl stir together orange marmalade and maple syrup; set aside. In a shallow dish combine pecans, flour, and salt. Brush both sides of chicken breast halves with marmalade mixture. Dip chicken into pecan mixture to coat, pressing pecan mixture onto chicken if necessary.

② In a very large skillet heat vegetable oil and butter over medium heat until butter melts and mixture begins to bubble. Add chicken and cook for 6 minutes. Turn chicken. Cook for 6 to 9 minutes more or until golden brown and no longer pink (170°F). Watch closely and reduce heat if chicken browns too quickly.

PER SERVING 506 calories; 32 g total fat (5 g sat. fat); 90 mg cholesterol; 279 mg sodium; 21 g carbohydrate; 3 g fiber; 36 g protein

quick tip To heat tortillas, place 1 tortilla on a plate. Cover with a damp paper towel. Repeat, alternating tortillas and damp towels. Pop in the microwave and heat for 30 to 45 seconds.

Thai Chicken ♥

The most intense ginger flavor lies just beneath the root's beige skin. To remove, scrape the skin off gently with the back of a spoon.

MAKES 2 servings **START TO FINISH** 20 minutes

- 2 medium skinless, boneless chicken breast halves (8 to 10 ounces total)
- ⅛ teaspoon salt
- 1 teaspoon canola oil
- 1 teaspoon grated fresh ginger
- 1 clove garlic, minced
- ¼ cup unsweetened light coconut milk
- 2 tablespoons snipped fresh cilantro
- 1 tablespoon peanut butter
- ¼ teaspoon black pepper
- ¼ teaspoon crushed red pepper
- 1 tablespoon chopped dry-roasted peanuts (optional)

① Sprinkle chicken with salt. In a medium skillet heat oil over medium-high heat. Add chicken; reduce heat to medium. Cook for 8 to 12 minutes or until chicken is no longer pink (170°F), turning once halfway through cooking time. Remove chicken from skillet; cover to keep warm.

② For coconut sauce, add ginger and garlic to skillet; cook for 30 seconds or until fragrant. In a small bowl whisk together coconut milk, 1 tablespoon of the cilantro, peanut butter, black pepper, and crushed red pepper. Add coconut milk mixture to skillet. Cook and stir over medium-high heat until bubbly.

③ To serve, line 2 plates with coconut sauce. Top with chicken. Sprinkle with remaining 1 tablespoon cilantro and, if desired, peanuts.

PER SERVING 217 calories; 9 g total fat (2 g sat. fat); 66 mg cholesterol; 266 mg sodium; 4 g carbohydrate; 1 g fiber; 28 g protein

Chicken with Peanut-Coconut Milk Sauce

If you have leftover coconut milk, transfer the milk to a glass or plastic container. The milk keeps, refrigerated, for up to a week.

MAKES 4 servings **START TO FINISH** 20 minutes

- 4 skinless, boneless chicken breast halves
- 1 tablespoon vegetable oil
- ¾ cup unsweetened coconut milk
- ¼ cup peanut butter
- ¼ teaspoon ground ginger
- ¼ teaspoon black pepper
- 4 green onions, cut into 1-inch pieces
- ¼ cup honey-roasted peanuts, coarsely chopped
  Sliced green onions (optional)

① In a large skillet cook chicken in hot oil over medium heat for 8 to 12 minutes or until no longer pink (170°F), turning occasionally to brown evenly. Remove chicken from skillet; cover to keep warm.

② In a small bowl whisk together coconut milk, peanut butter, ginger, and pepper; set aside. Add green onions to skillet. Cook and stir about 2 minutes or until tender. Stir in coconut milk mixture. Cook and stir until bubbly. Spoon over chicken; sprinkle with peanuts and, if desired, sliced green onions.

PER SERVING 415 calories; 25 g total fat (11 g sat. fat); 82 mg cholesterol; 192 mg sodium; 8 g carbohydrate; 2 g fiber; 39 g protein

Thai Chicken

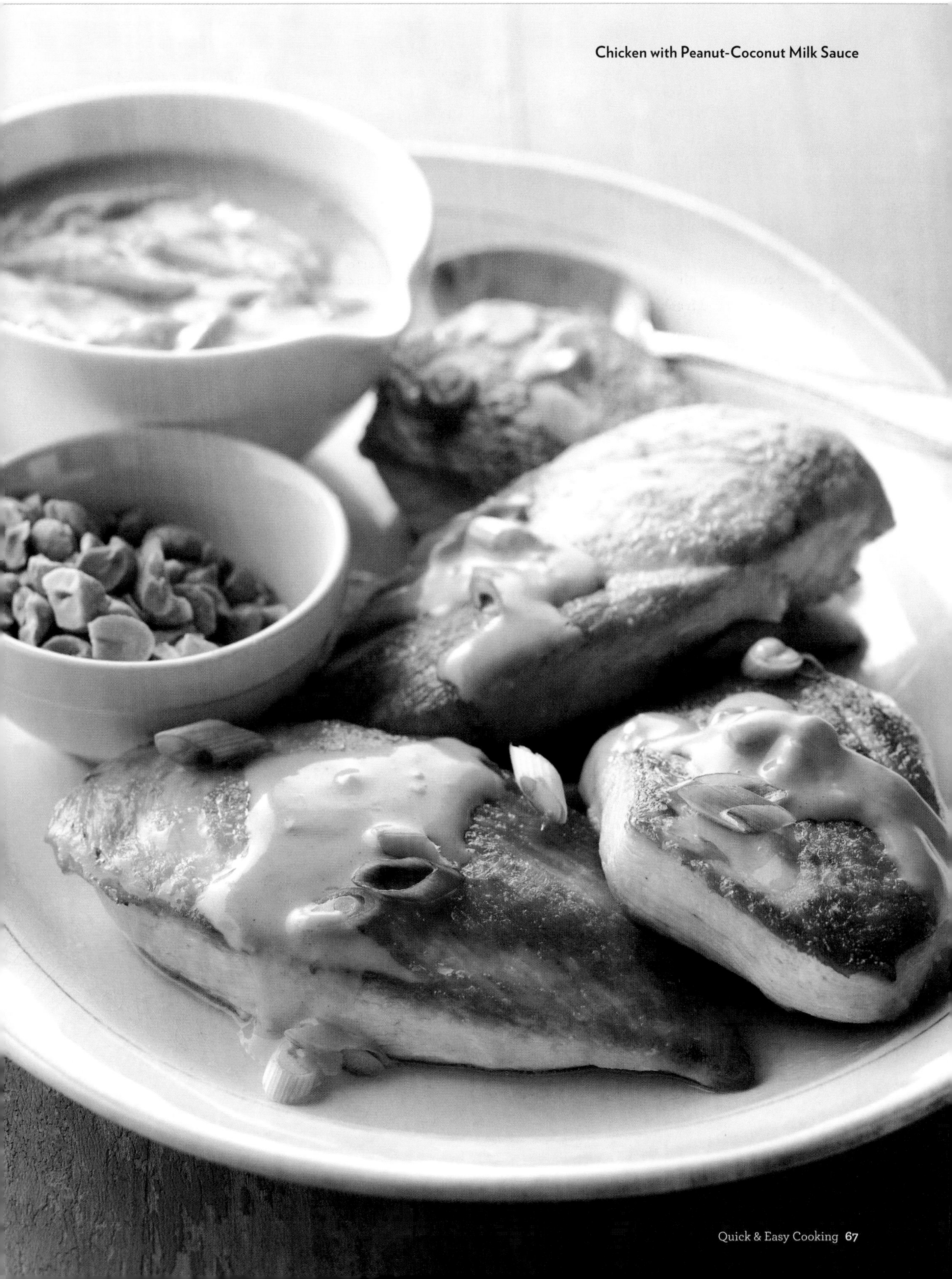

Chicken with Peanut-Coconut Milk Sauce

Thai Chicken Stir-Fry

Thai Chicken Stir-Fry

If you do not have rice wine, pale dry sherry makes an excellent substitute.

MAKES 4 servings **START TO FINISH** 35 minutes

- 1 pound skinless, boneless chicken breast halves
- ¼ cup rice wine
- 3 tablespoons reduced-sodium soy sauce
- 2 tablespoons water
- 1 tablespoon fish sauce (optional)
- 1½ teaspoons cornstarch
- ½ teaspoon crushed red pepper
- 1 tablespoon vegetable oil
- 1 teaspoon grated fresh ginger
- 2 cloves garlic, minced
- 1½ cups bias-sliced carrots (3 medium)
- 2 cups fresh pea pods, tips and strings removed, or one 6-ounce package frozen pea pods, thawed
- 4 green onions, bias-sliced into 1-inch pieces
- ⅓ cup dry-roasted peanuts
- 2 cups hot cooked rice
  Chopped peanuts (optional)

① Cut chicken into 1-inch pieces; set aside.

② For sauce, stir together rice wine, soy sauce, the water, fish sauce (if desired), cornstarch, and crushed red pepper. Set aside.

③ Pour oil into a wok or large skillet. (If necessary, add more oil during cooking.) Heat over medium-high heat. Add ginger and garlic to wok; cook and stir 15 seconds. Add carrots; cook and stir for 2 minutes. Add pea pods and green onions; cook and stir for 2 to 3 minutes or until vegetables are crisp-tender. Remove vegetables from wok.

④ Add half the chicken to hot wok. Cook and stir for 3 to 4 minutes or until chicken is no longer pink. Remove from wok. Repeat with remaining chicken. Return all chicken to wok. Push chicken from center of wok. Stir sauce; add to center of wok. Cook and stir until thickened and bubbly. Return vegetables to wok. Stir in the ⅓ cup peanuts. Cook and stir for 1 to 2 minutes more or until heated through. Serve with rice. If desired, sprinkle with additional chopped peanuts.

PER SERVING 406 calories; 11 g total fat (2 g sat. fat); 66 mg cholesterol; 1,020 mg sodium; 43 g carbohydrate; 3 g fiber; 34 g protein

Chicken Jambalaya

Jambalaya is one of the hallmarks of Creole cooking.

MAKES 4 servings **START TO FINISH** 23 minutes

- 8 ounce skinless, boneless chicken breast halves
- 2 teaspoons Cajun seasoning
- 8 ounces fully cooked spicy or mild link sausage, sliced
- 1 small red onion, cut in thin wedges
- 2 yellow, green, and/or orange sweet peppers, cut into bite-size strips
- 2 14.5-ounce cans no-salt-added stewed tomatoes
  Quick brown rice, cooked (optional)

① Cut chicken into 1-inch pieces; place in a small bowl and toss with Cajun seasoning.

② Heat a very large over medium-high heat. Add chicken and sausage to skillet; cook 3 to 4 minutes or until chicken begins to brown.

③ Add onion and sweet peppers to chicken mixture; cook, stirring frequently, for 2 minutes. Add stewed tomatoes; cover and cook 5 to 7 minutes or until chicken is no longer pink. If necessary, break up tomatoes with a spoon.

④ Ladle into bowls and serve with brown rice, if desired.

PER SERVING 355 calories; 18 g total fat (5 g sat. fat); 81 mg cholesterol; 637 mg sodium; 23 g carbohydrate; 3 g fiber; 29 g protein

Chicken Jambalaya

Penne Chicken in Red Sauce

Check Step 1 for the slickest way ever to cook spinach. You'll use this technique often!

MAKES 4 servings **START TO FINISH** 25 minutes

6   ounces dried penne pasta

1   9-ounce package fresh spinach

1½   pounds skinless, boneless chicken breast halves, cut into thin bite-size strips

2   tablespoons olive oil

¼   teaspoon salt

⅛   teaspoon black pepper

1   14-ounce jar red pasta sauce

1   cup shredded mozzarella cheese (4 ounces)

① Cook pasta according to package directions. Place spinach in a large colander set in the sink. When pasta is done, pour pasta and cooking water over spinach in colander. Set aside.

② Meanwhile, in a very large skillet cook chicken, half at a time, in hot oil over medium-high heat for 2 to 3 minutes or until no longer pink. Drain off fat. Return all of the chicken to skillet. Sprinkle with salt and pepper.

③ Add pasta sauce to skillet. Bring to boiling. Stir in pasta-spinach mixture; heat through. Remove from heat. Sprinkle with cheese. Let stand for 3 to 5 minutes or until cheese is melted.

PER SERVING 538 calories; 16 g total fat (5 g sat. fat); 114 mg cholesterol; 789 mg sodium; 42 g carbohydrate; 4 g fiber; 55 g protein

Mango Chicken Salad ♥

Mangoes are available year-round, but they are most plentiful and quite affordable in their peak season—from late April through late May.

MAKES 4 servings **START TO FINISH** 30 minutes
OVEN 350°F

3   skinless, boneless chicken breast halves

2   limes

1   cup unsweetened coconut milk

½   teaspoon crushed red pepper

1   tablespoon soy sauce

½   cup flaked unsweetened coconut

2   mangoes, seeded, peeled, and chopped

     Lettuce leaves (optional)

     Hot cooked rice (optional)

     Steamed sugar snap or snow pea pods (optional)

① Preheat oven to 350°F. Cut chicken into bite-size chunks. Squeeze juice from 1 lime (2 tablespoons); cut remaining lime into wedges.

② In a large saucepan combine coconut milk, lime juice, crushed red pepper, and soy sauce. Add chicken and bring to boiling; reduce heat and cook, covered, for 12 to 15 minutes or until chicken is no longer pink, stirring occasionally.

③ Meanwhile, spread coconut in a shallow pan. Bake, uncovered, for 4 to 5 minutes or until toasted, stirring once.

④ Remove chicken and cooking liquid to a bowl. Add mangoes; toss to coat. Sprinkle with toasted coconut and serve with lime wedges. Serve with lettuce leaves, rice, and peas.

PER SERVING 302 calories; 10 g total fat (7 g sat. fat); 62 mg cholesterol; 381 mg sodium; 29 g carbohydrate; 4 g fiber; 27 g protein

Cajun Chicken Tortellini

Fettuccine with Chicken and Cherry Tomatoes ♨

For best flavor, use freshly grated Parmesan cheese.

MAKES 4 servings **START TO FINISH** 20 minutes

- 1 6- to 9-ounce package refrigerated or frozen cooked Italian or grilled chicken breast strips
- 1 9-ounce package refrigerated fettuccine
- ½ cup shredded Parmesan cheese (2 ounces)
- 2 tablespoons olive oil
- 2 cups cherry tomatoes, halved
- ½ cup pitted ripe olives, halved
   Salt and freshly ground black pepper

① Thaw chicken, if frozen. Using kitchen scissors, cut fettuccine into thirds. In a Dutch oven cook fettuccine according to package directions; drain. Return fettuccine to hot Dutch oven.

② Add chicken, cheese, and oil to cooked fettuccine; toss gently to combine. Cook over low heat until heated through. Remove from heat. Add tomatoes and olives; toss gently to combine. Season to taste with salt and pepper.

PER SERVING 371 calories; 15 g total fat (4 g sat. fat); 76 mg cholesterol; 866 mg sodium; 39 g carbohydrate; 3 g fiber; 22 g protein

quick tip If you prefer, substitute light Alfredo sauce for the richer version—the lighter version is still wonderfully creamy but contains 40 percent fewer calories and 60 percent less fat.

Cajun Chicken Tortellini

Cajun seasoning typically contains black pepper, white pepper, red pepper, garlic, and salt.

MAKES 6 servings **START TO FINISH** 20 minutes

- 1 20-ounce package refrigerated three-cheese tortellini
- 1 small red onion, cut into thin wedges
- 1 medium yellow sweet pepper, cut into bite-size strips
- 1 tablespoon olive oil
- 2 6-ounce packages refrigerated cooked chicken breast strips
- 1 10-ounce container refrigerated Alfredo pasta sauce
- 1 teaspoon Cajun seasoning

① Prepare tortellini according to package directions; drain and return to pan.

② Meanwhile, in a large skillet cook onion and sweet pepper in hot oil over medium heat for 5 to 7 minutes or until tender, stirring occasionally. Stir in chicken, pasta sauce, and Cajun seasoning. Heat through. Add to tortellini; toss to coat.

PER SERVING 574 calories; 22 g total fat (19 g sat. fat); 109 mg cholesterol; 1,417 mg sodium; 64 g carbohydrate; 4 g fiber; 43 g protein

❮ Refrigerated pastas make amazing meals manageable. ❯

One-Pot Chicken and Pasta Dinner 🍲

On the side serve sliced ripe tomatoes drizzled with balsamic vinegar and topped with sprigs of fresh basil and a sprinkling of pine nuts.

MAKES 4 servings **START TO FINISH** 30 minutes

8	ounces dried linguine or spaghetti, broken in half
3	cups packaged small broccoli florets
1	8-ounce tub cream cheese spread with roasted garlic, chive, and onion or cream cheese spread with garden vegetables
1	cup milk
¼	teaspoon black pepper
1	6-ounce package refrigerated chopped cooked chicken

① In a Dutch oven cook pasta according to package directions, adding broccoli the last 2 to 3 minutes of cooking. Drain.

② In the same Dutch oven combine cream cheese, milk, and pepper. Cook and stir over low heat until cream cheese is melted. Add pasta-broccoli mixture and chicken. Heat through. If necessary, stir in additional milk to make desired consistency.

PER SERVING 530 calories; 22 g total fat (14 g sat. fat); 90 mg cholesterol; 690 mg sodium; 54 g carbohydrate; 4 g fiber; 24 g protein

One-Pot Chicken and Pasta Dinner

Herbed Chicken Pasta Primavera ♥

Pine nuts' high oil content causes them to become rancid quickly. Once opened, be sure to store pine nuts tightly covered in the refrigerator.

MAKES 8 servings **START TO FINISH** 40 minutes

8	ounces dried mostaccioli pasta
	Nonstick cooking spray
8	ounces packaged peeled baby carrots, cut in half lengthwise
1½	cups fresh green beans bias-sliced into 2-inch pieces
2	green onions, sliced
1	clove garlic, minced
1	small zucchini, sliced
2	tablespoons water
2	cups chopped cooked chicken (about 10 ounces)
1	10.75-ounce can condensed cream of chicken soup
½	cup milk
1	teaspoon dried basil, crushed
1	teaspoon dried oregano, crushed
¼	cup pine nuts, toasted
	Cracked black pepper

① Cook mostaccioli according to package directions; drain and return pasta to saucepan.

② Meanwhile, lightly coat a large skillet with cooking spray. Heat skillet over medium-high heat. Add carrots; cook and stir for 5 minutes. Add green beans, green onions, and garlic. Cook and stir for 2 minutes more. Stir in zucchini and the water. Reduce heat. Cook, covered, for 4 to 5 minutes or until vegetables are crisp-tender.

③ Stir chicken, cream of chicken soup, milk, basil, oregano, and vegetables into pasta. Heat through. Sprinkle with pine nuts and cracked pepper. Serve immediately.

PER SERVING 269 calories; 9 g total fat (2 g sat. fat); 36 mg cholesterol; 333 mg sodium; 31 g carbohydrate; 3 g fiber; 17 g protein

Herbed Chicken Pasta Primavera

Chicken and Biscuit Pockets

Chicken and Biscuit Pockets

A hot handheld meal does not get any easier than this. Serve some sliced fresh fruit on the side and dinner is a done deal.

MAKES 4 servings **START TO FINISH** 30 minutes
OVEN 400°F

- 2   16.3-ounce packages (8 biscuits total) refrigerated large flaky biscuits
- 1   cup finely chopped cooked chicken or turkey (about 5 ounces)
- ⅔   cup coarsely shredded yellow summer squash
- ½   cup shredded Monterey Jack or cheddar cheese (2 ounces)
- ½   cup mayonnaise or salad dressing
- 1   tablespoon honey mustard

① Preheat oven to 400°F. Separate biscuits; use the palm of your hand to flatten each to a 4-inch circle. Divide chicken, squash, and cheese among dough circles, placing fillings on 1 side of each dough circle. Fold circles to cover filling; press edges with the tines of a fork to seal. Arrange filled biscuits about 2 inches apart on an ungreased baking sheet. Bake about 12 minutes or until golden on top and edges are set.

② Meanwhile, in a small bowl stir together mayonnaise and mustard. Serve as dipping sauce for warm biscuits.

PER SERVING 1062 calories; 61 g total fat (19 g sat. fat); 54 mg cholesterol; 2,668 mg sodium; 97 g carbohydrate; 3 g fiber; 30 g protein

quick tip Help kids become better eaters by allowing them to help create their own dinners. Little ones can complete Chicken Biscuit Pockets—a homemade version of a freezer case kids' favorite— before the window of their attention span closes.

Hawaiian Sweet-and-Sour Chicken ♥

When a trip to the tropics is not in the budget, put a taste of the Pacific islands on your plate.

MAKES 4 servings **START TO FINISH** 20 minutes
OVEN 350°F

- 2   tablespoons slivered almonds
- 1   tablespoon vegetable oil
- 1   medium carrot, thinly bias-sliced
- 1   medium green sweet pepper, cut into bite-size strips
- 4   green onions, bias-sliced
- 12   ounces chicken breast tenderloins, halved crosswise
- 1   8- to 10-ounce bottle sweet-and-sour sauce
- 1   8-ounce can pineapple chunks (juice pack), drained
- 1   8.8-ounce pouch cooked long grain rice

① Preheat oven to 350°F. Spread almonds in a single layer in a shallow baking pan. Bake for 5 to 10 minutes or until toasted, stirring once or twice; set aside.

② Meanwhile, heat oil in a wok or large skillet over medium-high heat. Add carrot; cook and stir 2 minutes. Add sweet pepper; cook and stir for 2 minutes. Add green onions; cook and stir for 1 minute more or until vegetables are crisp-tender. Remove vegetables from wok.

③ Add chicken to hot wok (add more oil if needed). Cook and stir for 3 to 4 minutes or until chicken is no longer pink. Return vegetables to wok. Add sweet-and-sour sauce and drained pineapple. Heat through.

④ Prepare rice according to package directions. Serve chicken mixture with rice; top with toasted almonds.

PER SERVING 390 calories; 8 g total fat (1 g sat. fat); 49 mg cholesterol; 263 mg sodium; 51 g carbohydrate; 3 g fiber; 23 g protein

Chicken and Sweet Pepper Linguine Alfredo ♥

Whole wheat pasta—such as the linguine in this recipe—sometimes takes longer to cook than white flour pasta, so be sure to check its package for the correct cooking time.

MAKES 4 servings **START TO FINISH** 25 minutes

- 1 9-ounce package refrigerated whole wheat linguine
  Nonstick cooking spray
- 1 cup red sweet pepper strips (1 medium)
- 2 medium zucchini and/or yellow summer squash, halved lengthwise and sliced (about 2½ cups)
- 8 ounces packaged chicken stir-fry strips
- 1 10-ounce container refrigerated light Alfredo pasta sauce
- ⅓ cup finely shredded Parmesan, Romano, or Asiago cheese (optional)
- 2 teaspoons snipped fresh thyme
- ⅛ teaspoon freshly ground black pepper

① Using kitchen scissors, cut linguine in half. In a Dutch oven cook linguine according to package directions; drain. Return linguine to hot Dutch oven; cover and keep warm.

② Meanwhile, coat a large skillet with cooking spray; heat skillet over medium-high heat. Add sweet pepper; cook and stir for 2 minutes. Add squash; cook and stir for 2 to 3 minutes more or until vegetables are crisp-tender. Remove from skillet.

③ Add chicken to skillet. Cook and stir for 3 to 4 minutes or until chicken is no longer pink. Return vegetables to skillet. Stir in pasta sauce; heat through.

④ Add chicken mixture, cheese (if desired), and thyme to cooked linguine; toss gently to combine. Sprinkle each serving with black pepper.

PER SERVING 371 calories; 11 g total fat (5 g sat. fat); 66 mg cholesterol; 461 mg sodium; 43 g carbohydrate; 7 g fiber; 26 g protein

Caribbean Chicken ♥

Add as much or little of the cayenne powder as you like.

MAKES 4 servings **START TO FINISH** 20 minutes

- 1½ cups quick-cooking brown rice
- 1 pound chicken breast tenderloins
- ¼ teaspoon salt
- ⅛ to ¼ teaspoon cayenne pepper
- 1 teaspoon roasted peanut oil or vegetable oil
- 1 medium sweet potato, peeled, halved lengthwise, and thinly sliced
- 1 small banana pepper, seeded and chopped
- ¾ cup unsweetened pineapple juice
- 1 teaspoon cornstarch
- 2 unripe bananas, quartered lengthwise and cut into ¾-inch pieces

① Prepare rice according to package directions.

② Meanwhile, season chicken with salt and cayenne pepper. In a large skillet cook chicken in hot oil over medium heat for 3 to 4 minutes or until browned, turning once. Add sweet potato slices and banana pepper. Cook for 5 to 6 minutes more or until chicken is no longer pink (170°F), stirring vegetables occasionally.

③ In a small bowl stir together unsweetened pineapple juice and cornstarch. Add to skillet. Cook, stirring gently, until bubbly. Add banana pieces. Cook and stir 2 minutes more. Serve over rice.

PER SERVING 335 calories; 4 g total fat (1 g sat. fat); 66 mg cholesterol; 244 mg sodium; 47 g carbohydrate; 5 g fiber; 30 g protein

Farfalle with Chicken and Tomato Pesto

Farfalle with Chicken and Tomato Pesto

Consider making a double batch of this delicious tomato pesto. It keeps, refrigerated, for a week, and makes a wonderful spread for chicken or turkey sandwiches.

MAKES 6 servings **START TO FINISH** 30 minutes

- 8   ounces dried farfalle (bow tie pasta)
- 2   cups frozen peas, chopped roasted red sweet peppers, and/or chopped marinated artichoke hearts
- ½   cup oil-pack dried tomatoes, drained
- ⅓   cup olive oil
- ½   cup slivered almonds, toasted (if desired)
- 2   cloves garlic
- ¼   teaspoon salt
- ¼   teaspoon black pepper
- ¼   cup freshly grated Parmesan cheese (1 ounce)
- 2   cups chopped or shredded purchased roasted chicken or cooked chicken
- ¼   cup snipped fresh basil
     Freshly grated Parmesan cheese (optional)

① Cook pasta according to package directions, adding peas (if using) for the last 2 minutes of cooking. Drain, reserving ½ cup of the cooking water. Return pasta and peas to hot pan.

② Meanwhile, for tomato pesto, in a food processor or blender combine dried tomatoes, oil, almonds, garlic, salt, and pepper. Cover and process or blend until almost smooth. Add the ¼ cup Parmesan cheese. Cover and process or blend just until combined.

③ Add the ½ cup reserved cooking water, tomato pesto, and roasted red peppers and/or artichoke hearts (if using) to pasta in pan. Add chicken and basil. Toss gently to mix well. If desired, serve with additional Parmesan cheese.

PER SERVING 484 calories; 27 g total fat (6 g sat. fat); 56 mg cholesterol; 605 mg sodium; 40 g carbohydrate; 5 g fiber; 23 g protein

Southwestern Cobb Salad

Feel free to compose these pretty salads ahead of time, but save the avocado slices for right before serving so they remain bright green.

MAKES 6 servings **START TO FINISH** 20 minutes

- 1   10-ounce package chopped hearts of romaine
- 1   6-ounce package refrigerated cooked Southwestern chicken breast strips
- 1   15-ounce can black beans, rinsed and drained
- 1   cup halved grape or cherry tomatoes
- 1   cup lime-flavor or plain tortilla chips, coarsely broken (about 1 ounce)
- 2   medium avocados, peeled, seeded, and sliced
- 1   11-ounce can whole kernel corn with sweet peppers, drained
- ½   cup shredded Mexican-style four-cheese blend
- ½   cup thinly sliced red onion
- ½   cup bottled spicy ranch salad dressing

① Spread romaine on a large serving platter. Arrange chicken, beans, tomatoes, tortilla chips, sliced avocados, corn, cheese, and onion in rows over the lettuce. Serve with dressing.

PER SERVING 363 calories; 22 g total fat (5 g sat. fat); 33 mg cholesterol; 880 mg sodium; 32 g carbohydrate; 9 g fiber; 17 g protein

quick tip If you can't find spicy ranch salad dressing, mix ½ cup ranch salad dressing with 2 tablespoons barbecue sauce.

Crunchy Chicken Strips

If you've been looking for a way to get your kids interested in cooking, let them help make these yummy chicken strips.

MAKES 8 servings **START TO FINISH** 30 minutes **OVEN** 425°F

Nonstick cooking spray

7   cups bite-size cheddar fish-shape crackers or 14 cups pretzels (14 ounces pretzels)

1½   cups bottled buttermilk ranch salad dressing

2   pounds chicken breast tenderloins

Bottled buttermilk ranch salad dressing (optional)

① Preheat oven to 425°F. Line two 15 x 10 x 1-inch baking pans with foil; lightly coat foil with cooking spray. Set aside.

② Crush crackers (should have 5 cups crumbs); transfer to a shallow dish. Pour the 1½ cups ranch dressing into another shallow dish. Dip chicken tenderloins into the dressing, allowing excess to drip off; dip into cracker crumbs, turning to coat. Arrange chicken in a single layer on prepared pans. Lightly coat chicken with cooking spray.

③ Bake, uncovered, for 10 to 15 minutes or until tender and no longer pink (170°F), rotating pans halfway through baking. If desired, serve with additional ranch dressing.

PER SERVING 582 calories; 35 g total fat (7 g sat. fat); 90 mg cholesterol; 765 mg sodium; 34 g carbohydrate; 1 g fiber; 33 g protein

Crunchy Chicken Strips

Garlic Parmesan Chicken and Noodles

Making homemade bread crumbs is quick and easy. If you have a few extra slices of bread when you prepare the crumbs for this recipe, make extra and store them, tightly covered, in the freezer.

MAKES 4 servings **START TO FINISH** 30 minutes **OVEN** 450°F

6   ounces extra-wide egg noodles

1   2- to 2¼-pound purchased roasted chicken

1   cup frozen peas

4   cloves garlic, minced or 2 teaspoons bottled minced garlic

1¾   cups whole milk or light cream

½   slice white or wheat bread

¾   cup shredded Parmesan cheese

2   tablespoons butter, melted

Snipped fresh thyme (optional)

① Preheat oven to 450°F. In a Dutch oven bring 6 cups salted water to boiling; add noodles. Cook for 10 minutes or until tender; drain.

② Meanwhile, remove chicken from bones. Discard skin and bones; shred chicken. In a saucepan combine chicken, peas, garlic, and whole milk; heat through. Cover and keep warm.

③ In a blender or food processor process bread until coarse crumbs form. Transfer to a small bowl; add ¼ cup of the Parmesan and the melted butter.

④ Stir noodles and remaining Parmesan into hot chicken mixture. Heat and stir until bubbly. Divide among four 16-ounce casseroles. Top each with some of the crumb mixture. Bake about 5 minutes or until top begins to brown. Top with fresh thyme, if desired.

PER SERVING 701 calories; 37 g total fat (16 g sat. fat); 222 mg cholesterol; 1,388 mg sodium; 45 g carbohydrate; 3 g fiber; 50 g protein

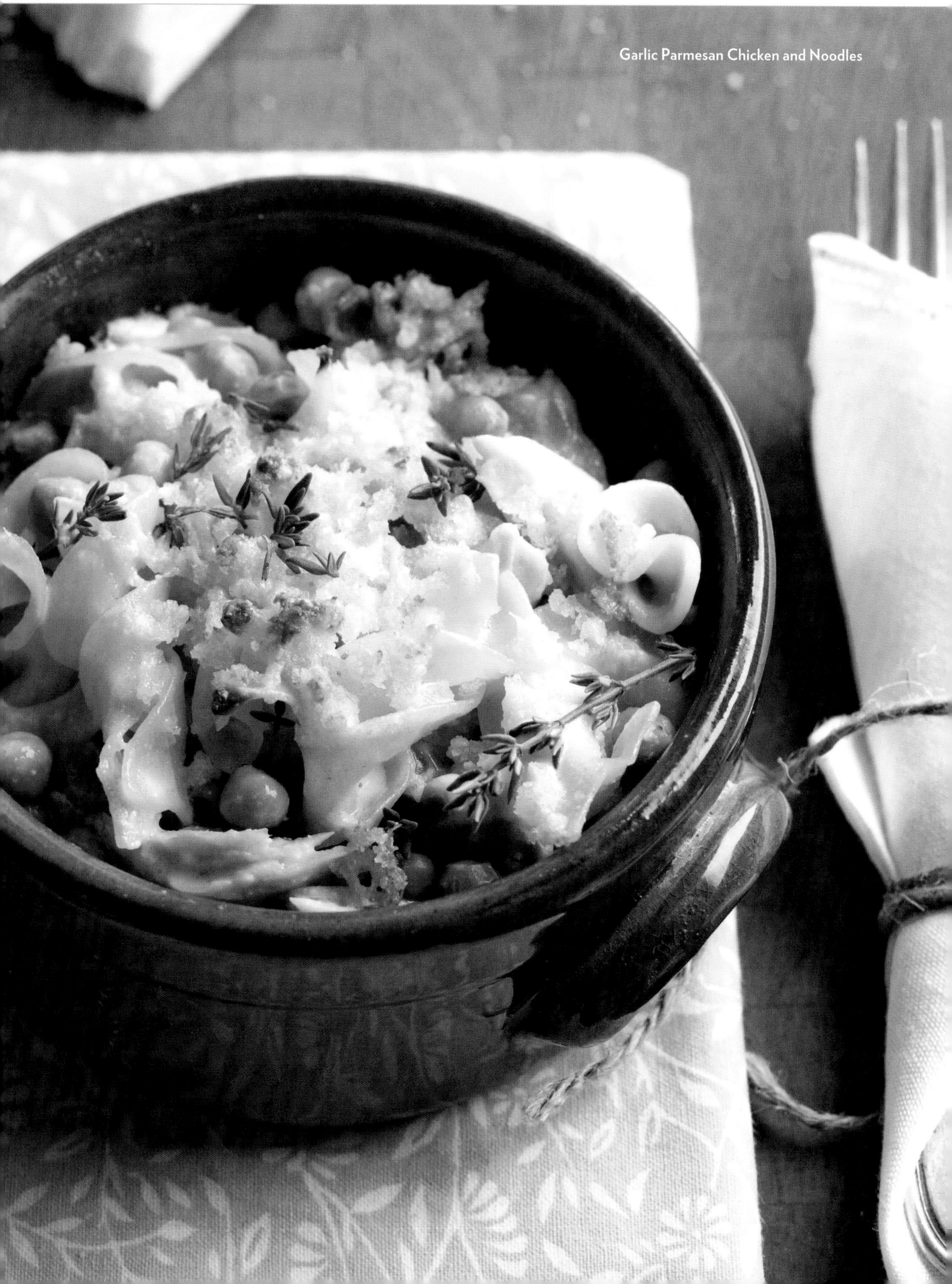
Garlic Parmesan Chicken and Noodles

Garden-Fresh Wagon Wheel Pasta

Garden-Fresh Wagon Wheel Pasta

Children are intrigued by the shape of wagon wheel pasta. Combined with chicken nuggets, this is a kids' meal made in heaven.

MAKES 4 servings **START TO FINISH** 25 minutes

1 12-ounce package frozen, cooked breaded chicken nuggets

8 ounces dried wagon wheel pasta

4 cups chopped or sliced assorted vegetables, such as broccoli, carrots, summer squash, cauliflower, and/or sweet peppers

½ of an 8-ounce tub cream cheese spread with chive and onion

¼ to ½ cup milk

Salt and black pepper

Shredded Parmesan cheese

① Heat chicken nuggets according to package directions.

② Meanwhile, in a Dutch oven cook pasta in a large amount of boiling, lightly salted water for 4 minutes. Add vegetables. Cook about 5 minutes more or until pasta is tender; drain. Return pasta mixture to hot Dutch oven.

③ Add cream cheese spread to pasta mixture; heat through. Thin with enough of the milk to reach desired consistency. Season to taste with salt and pepper.

④ Serve chicken nuggets with pasta mixture. Sprinkle each serving with cheese.

PER SERVING 643 calories; 27 g total fat (12 g sat. fat); 81 mg cholesterol; 811 mg sodium; 72 g carbohydrate; 4 g fiber; 25 g protein

Roasted Chicken, Focaccia, and Olive Salad

It's a shame to throw away day-old bread when you can bring it back to glory in this summertime salad.

MAKES 4 servings **START TO FINISH** 30 minutes

5 tablespoons olive oil

¼ cup white wine or cider vinegar

2 teaspoons Mediterranean seasoning blend or spaghetti seasoning

1 teaspoon sugar

3 cups torn day-old garlic focaccia or Italian bread (6 ounces)

2 cups shredded deli-roasted chicken (12 ounces)

¾ cup pitted olives

3 romaine hearts, cored and coarsely chopped

① For dressing, in a small bowl whisk together 4 tablespoons of the olive oil, the vinegar, seasoning blend, and sugar; set aside.

② In a very large skillet heat the remaining 1 tablespoon oil over medium-high heat. Add torn bread. Cook and stir for 5 minutes until lightly toasted. Remove from skillet. Add dressing, chicken, and olives to skillet; cook and stir for 2 to 3 minutes until chicken is heated through. Return bread to skillet; toss to coat.

③ Arrange lettuce on 4 plates; top with chicken mixture. Serve immediately.

PER SERVING 478 calories; 34 g total fat (8 g sat. fat); 83 mg cholesterol; 998 mg sodium; 22 g carbohydrate; 3 g fiber; 21 g protein

> Freeze leftover loaves until you have enough bread to make a wonderful Roasted Chicken, Focaccia, and Olive Salad.

Lemon-Ginger Chicken Thighs

Chicken thighs are an economical alternative to chicken breasts, and their tender, rich meat is especially delicious when paired with Asian ingredients, as they are here.

MAKES 4 servings **START TO FINISH** 30 minutes

- 1   lemon
- 1   tablespoon grated fresh ginger
- ½   teaspoon salt
- 2   tablespoons honey
- 1   tablespoon reduced-sodium soy sauce
- 2   tablespoons water
- 8   chicken thighs with bone
- 2   teaspoons vegetable oil
-   Sliced green onions (optional)

①   Finely shred peel from lemon; juice the lemon. In a bowl combine lemon peel, ginger, and salt. In another bowl combine lemon juice, honey, soy sauce, and the water.

②   Rub lemon peel mixture under the skin of the chicken thighs. In a very large skillet heat oil over medium-high heat. Cook chicken, skin sides down, in the oil about 7 minutes or until well browned; turn chicken and add lemon juice mixture. Reduce heat; cover and cook 14 to 18 minutes longer or until done (180°F).

③   Transfer chicken to plates. Skim fat from pan juices. Drizzle chicken with some of the pan juices. If desired, top with green onions.

PER SERVING 459 calories; 31 g total fat (8 g sat. fat); 158 mg cholesterol; 567 mg sodium; 12 g carbohydrate; 1 g fiber; 33 g protein

Lemon-Ginger Chicken Thighs

Pasta Stack-Ups with Chicken Sausage

Add a little architecture to your plates by building these clever pasta stacks.

MAKES 4 servings **START TO FINISH** 30 minutes

- 6   dried lasagna noodles
- 1   cup coarsely chopped dried tomatoes (not oil pack)
- 6   cloves garlic, minced
- 1   pound cooked chicken sausage links, halved lengthwise and cut into large pieces
- 2   tablespoons olive oil
- 1   5-ounce package baby spinach
- ½   teaspoon salt
- ½   teaspoon black pepper
-   Shaved Parmesan cheese (optional)

①   Cook lasagna noodles according to package directions; drain, reserving 1 cup of the cooking water. In a medium bowl combine dried tomatoes and garlic; pour the 1 cup reserved cooking water over. Set aside.

②   Meanwhile, in a very large skillet cook sausage in hot oil over medium-high heat until lightly browned and heated through, turning occasionally. Add tomato mixture. Cook, uncovered, for 2 minutes. Stir in spinach, salt, and pepper. Cover and remove from heat.

③   Cut each cooked lasagna noodle in half. To serve, layer noodles and sausage mixture on 4 serving plates. If desired, pass Parmesan cheese.

PER SERVING 430 calories; 19 g total fat (4 g sat. fat); 97 mg cholesterol; 1,074 mg sodium; 36 g carbohydrate; 4 g fiber; 30 g protein

quick tip   Even when the bag is marked "triple washed," it is smart to give prepackaged spinach and lettuces another bath before eating. To make it quick, drop greens in a colander, swish the colander around in a clean sink full of cool water, then drain.

Pasta Stack-Ups with Chicken Sausage

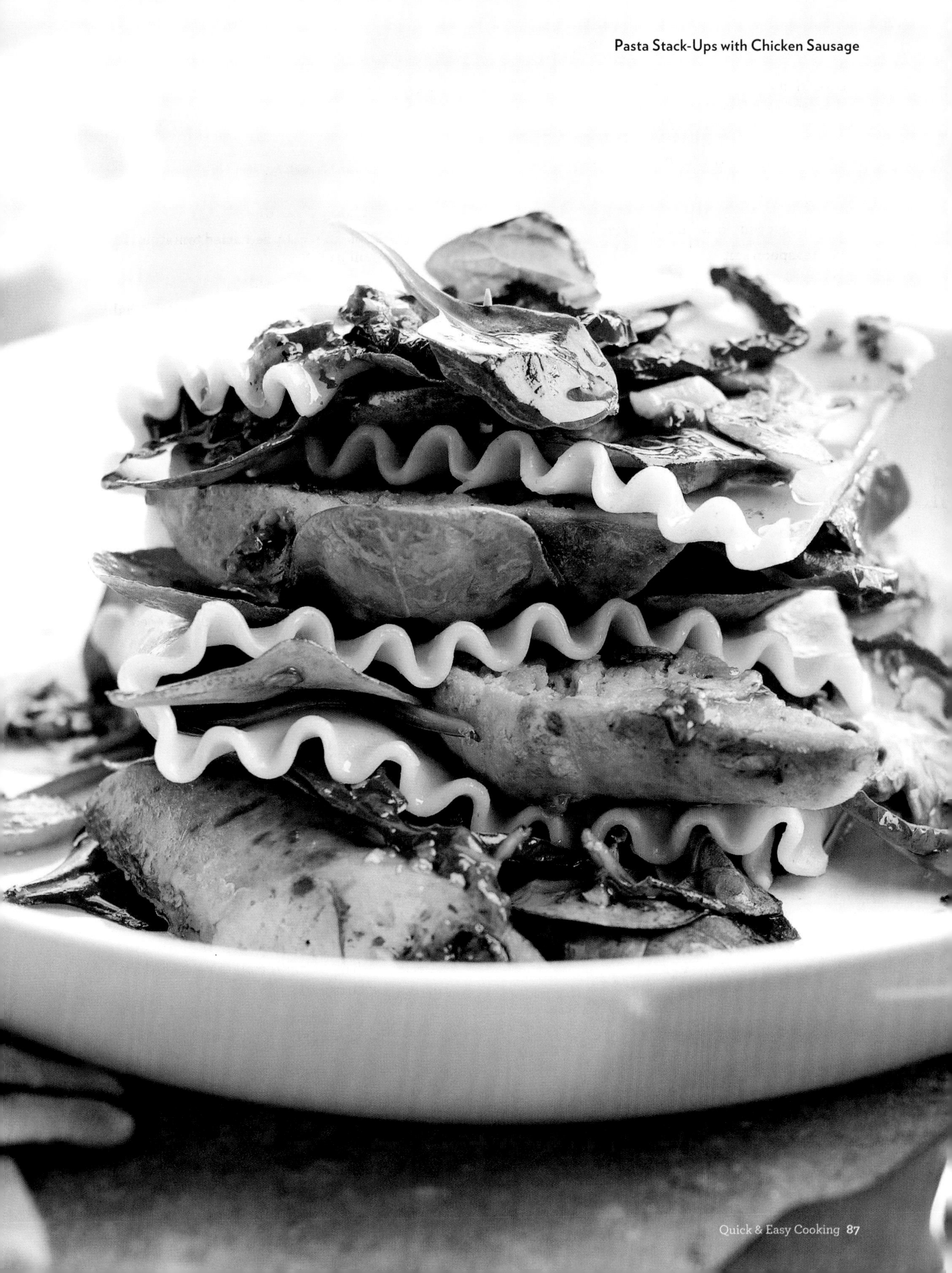

Saucy Barbecue Chicken

Saucy Barbecue Chicken

To round out this 30-minute meal, pick up some deli coleslaw and frozen sweet potato waffle fries.

MAKES 4 servings **START TO FINISH** 30 minutes

- 8 small chicken drumsticks
- 1 large onion, cut into 6 slices
- 1 tablespoon olive oil
- 1 cup ketchup
- ¼ cup molasses
- 3 to 4 tablespoons cider vinegar
- 2 tablespoons packed brown sugar
- 1 teaspoon smoked paprika
  - Several dashes bottled hot pepper sauce
  - Fresh parsley (optional)

① Preheat broiler. Arrange chicken on the unheated rack of the broiler pan. Broil chicken 4 to 5 inches from the heat for 10 minutes.

② Brush onion slices with olive oil. Remove pan from oven, turn chicken, and move to 1 side of the pan. Arrange onion slices in a single layer on the opposite side of the pan. Broil about 15 minutes or until meat is no longer pink and the juices run clear (180°F).

③ Meanwhile, for sauce, in a small saucepan combine ketchup, molasses, cider vinegar, brown sugar, paprika, and bottled hot pepper sauce. Bring to boiling over medium heat; keep warm. Remove onions from pan. Broil chicken 1 to 2 minutes more, brushing with some of the warm sauce for the last 1 minute of broiling.

④ Chop 2 of the onion slices and reserve 4 slices for serving. Stir chopped onion into the sauce.

⑤ Serve chicken with remaining onion slices and sauce. If desired, top with parsley. Cover and chill any remaining sauce; use within 3 days.

PER SERVING 426 calories; 16 g total fat (4 g sat. fat); 118 mg cholesterol; 802 mg sodium; 41 g carbohydrate; 1 g fiber; 30 g protein

Lime-Chicken Succotash Skillet

Edamame make a delicious stand-in for lima beans in this fresh-tasting succotash.

MAKES 4 to 6 servings **START TO FINISH** 25 minutes

- 1 lime
- 1 16-ounce package frozen corn
- 1 12-ounce package frozen shelled sweet soybeans (edamame) or one 16-ounce package frozen baby lima beans
- 1¾ cups water
- 1 2- to 2½-pound purchased roasted chicken, cut into serving-size pieces
- 1 16-ounce jar chipotle salsa

① Finely shred peel from lime; juice lime. Set aside. In a very large skillet combine corn and edamame; add the water. Bring to boiling; reduce heat. Simmer, uncovered, for 5 to 6 minutes or just until edamame is tender. Stir in lime peel and lime juice.

② Place chicken pieces on corn mixture; pour salsa over chicken and corn mixture. Cook, covered, over medium heat about 10 minutes or until heated through.

PER SERVING 621 calories; 28 g total fat (7 g sat. fat); 134 mg cholesterol; 823 mg sodium; 41 g carbohydrate; 8 g fiber; 58 g protein

Lime-Chicken Succotash Skillet

Turkey Cutlets with Provolone and Pears

Few fruits are as luscious as pears at their peak of ripeness. To determine when a pear is ready, press your finger into a spot close to the stem. When it yields slightly to pressure, it is perfect for this wonderful dish.

MAKES 4 servings **START TO FINISH** 25 minutes

- 1 pound turkey tenderloins
  Salt and black pepper
- 1 tablespoon honey mustard
- ¼ cup olive oil
- 2 pears, core if desired and sliced
- 4 slices provolone cheese, halved
- 5 ounces arugula (8 cups)
- 2 tablespoons cider vinegar
  Freshly ground pepper (optional)

① Bias-slice the turkey crosswise into 1-inch-thick slices. Flatten slightly with the palm of your hand and season with salt and pepper. Brush with about half of the honey mustard.

② In a very large skillet heat 2 tablespoons of the oil over medium-high heat. Add turkey in an even layer; cook 2 to 3 minutes on each side or until browned. Scatter pears over the turkey. Top each piece of turkey with a half slice of cheese. Reduce heat to medium-low. Cover and cook 3 to 4 minutes or until cheese is melted and pears are warm.

③ Place 2 cups of arugula on each of 4 serving plates; divide turkey and pears on top of arugula. Whisk remaining mustard, oil, and the vinegar into pan juices; cook about 30 seconds. Drizzle over each serving. If desired, sprinkle with freshly ground pepper.

PER SERVING 410 calories; 22 g total fat (7 g sat. fat); 90 mg cholesterol; 480 mg sodium; 16 g carbohydrate; 3 g fiber; 36 g protein

Turkey Steaks with Pear and Blue Cheese ♥

Unlike whole turkeys, turkey tenderloins thaw quickly. Keep a supply in your freezer for quick, easy meals like this.

MAKES 4 servings **START TO FINISH** 30 minutes

- 2 turkey breast tenderloins (1 to 1¼ pounds total)
- 1 teaspoon dried sage, crushed
- ¼ teaspoon salt
- ¼ teaspoon black pepper
- 1 tablespoon butter or margarine
- 1 tablespoon olive oil
- 1 large ripe pear, cored and thinly sliced
- 2 cups fresh baby spinach
- ¼ cup crumbled blue cheese (1 ounce)

① Horizontally split tenderloins to make four ½-inch steaks. Rub 1 side of each turkey steak with sage; sprinkle with salt and pepper. In an extra-large skillet combine butter and oil; heat over medium-high heat. Add turkey steaks; cook for 14 to 16 minutes or until tender and no longer pink (170°F), turning once halfway through cooking. (If turkey browns too quickly, reduce heat to medium.) Remove from skillet, reserving the butter and oil in the skillet. Cover turkey and keep warm.

② Add pear slices to hot skillet. Cook over medium heat about 2 minutes or until tender and lightly browned, stirring occasionally.

③ Serve turkey and pears over spinach; sprinkle with blue cheese.

PER SERVING 247 calories; 10 g total fat (4 g sat. fat); 84 mg cholesterol; 352 mg sodium; 9 g carbohydrate; 2 g fiber; 30 g protein

《 When pears meet blue cheese, it is love at first sight. 》

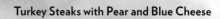

Moroccan Meat Loaf

Moroccan Meat Loaf

When purchasing ground turkey for this recipe, opt for ground whole turkey rather than ground turkey breast. Ground breast is so lean that it may make this meat loaf dry.

MAKES 4 servings **START TO FINISH** 30 minutes
OVEN 425°F

1½   cups golden raisins
1   small red onion, chopped
½   cup couscous
1   teaspoon salt
1   teaspoon curry powder
1   teaspoon ground cinnamon
¾   cup boiling water
1   pound ground turkey
1   egg, lightly beaten
1   pint grape tomatoes
¼   cup water

① Preheat oven to 425°F. Line an 8 x 8 x 2-inch baking pan with foil, extending foil over edges of pan. Grease foil; set aside.

② For meat loaf, in a large bowl combine 1 cup of the raisins, half of the red onion, the couscous, salt, curry powder, and ½ teaspoon of the cinnamon. Add the ¾ cup boiling water; cover and let stand for 2 minutes. Add ground turkey and egg; mix well. Pat turkey mixture into prepared pan. Bake in the top third of the oven about 20 minutes or until cooked through (165°F).

② Meanwhile, for chutney, in a medium saucepan combine remaining ½ cup raisins, remaining red onion, the remaining ½ teaspoon cinnamon, the tomatoes, and the ¼ cup water. Cook, covered, over medium-high heat, until tomatoes pop, stirring occasionally. Cover; reduce heat to low to keep warm.

③ Using the foil, lift meat loaf from pan with foil. Cut meat loaf into squares and serve with tomato chutney.

PER SERVING 487 calories; 11 g total fat (3 g sat. fat); 142 mg cholesterol; 721 mg sodium; 73 g carbohydrate; 5 g fiber; 27 g protein

Turkey Reuben Loaf

To bring out that classic Reuben taste, choose rye bread for this hot-from-the-oven treat.

MAKES 4 servings **PREP** 15 minutes **BAKE** 12 minutes
OVEN 400°F

½   cup mayonnaise or salad dressing
¼   cup sweet pickle relish
1   tablespoon ketchup
2   cups shredded cabbage
2   teaspoons vinegar
1   teaspoon caraway seeds
½   of an unsliced oblong loaf of bread
6   ounces Havarti cheese, sliced
8   ounces cooked turkey, sliced or chopped

① Preheat oven to 400°F. For sauce, in a bowl combine mayonnaise, pickle relish, and ketchup. In another bowl combine cabbage, vinegar, and caraway seeds.

② Slice bread lengthwise. Hollow out some of the bread, reserving it for another use. Spread some of the sauce on cut sides of bread; reserve the remaining sauce for serving. Arrange half of the cheese slices on the bottom half of the bread. Top with cabbage mixture, turkey, and the remaining cheese. Top with the top half of the bread.

③ Wrap filled bread loaf tightly in foil; place on baking sheet. Bake for 10 minutes. Carefully unwrap. Bake for 2 to 3 minutes more or until bread is crisp and cheese is melted.

④ To serve, use a sharp serrated knife to cut loaf into slices. Pass the remaining sauce.

PER SERVING 640 calories; 40 g total fat (13 g sat. fat); 85 mg cholesterol; 931 mg sodium; 37 g carbohydrate; 5 g fiber; 31 g protein

White Bean and Sausage Rigatoni

Rigatoni's ridges and holes make it perfect for capturing chunky sauces such as this one.

MAKES 4 servings **START TO FINISH** 20 minutes

- 2 cups packaged dried rigatoni (8 ounces)
- 1 15-ounce can white kidney (cannellini), Great Northern, or navy beans, rinsed and drained
- 1 14.5-ounce can Italian-style stewed tomatoes, undrained
- 8 ounces cooked smoked turkey sausage, halved lengthwise and cut into ½-inch slices
- ⅓ cup snipped fresh basil or 1 tablespoon dried basil, crushed
- ¼ cup shredded Asiago or Parmesan cheese (1 ounce)

① In a large saucepan cook pasta according to package directions. Drain; return pasta to saucepan.

② Meanwhile, in a large saucepan combine beans, undrained tomatoes, sausage, and dried basil (if using). Cook and stir until heated through. Add bean mixture and fresh basil (if using) to pasta; stir gently to combine. To serve, sprinkle each serving with cheese.

PER SERVING 419 calories; 9 g total fat (3 g sat. fat); 45 mg cholesterol; 992 mg sodium; 65 g carbohydrate; 8 g fiber; 24 g protein

White Bean and Sausage Rigatoni

Turkey Saltimbocca

In Italian "saltimbocca" means "jump in the mouth." While Italian Saltimbocca is made with veal, turkey is an equally delicious—and much more economical—substitution.

MAKES 4 servings **START TO FINISH** 30 minutes

- ¼ cup all-purpose flour
- ½ teaspoon salt
- ½ teaspoon dried sage, crushed
- ¼ teaspoon black pepper
- 4 turkey cutlets or slices (12 ounces total)
- 2 tablespoons vegetable oil
- 4 slices cooked ham (3 ounces)
- 4 slices fontina or Swiss cheese (2 ounces)
- ¼ cup dry white wine
- ¼ cup reduced-sodium chicken broth
- 2 tablespoons snipped fresh parsley (optional)

① In a shallow dish combine flour, salt, sage, and pepper. Set aside.

② Place each turkey cutlet between 2 pieces of plastic wrap. Using the flat side of a meat mallet, pound turkey lightly, working from the center to the edges, until about ¼ inch thick. Remove plastic wrap. Dip cutlets into flour mixture, turning to coat both sides; shake off excess.

③ In a very large nonstick skillet heat oil over medium-high heat. Add cutlets; cook about 2 minutes or until browned on bottom. Turn cutlets over; top each with 1 slice of the ham and 1 slice of the cheese. Add wine and broth; cook about 2 minutes more or until cheese melts and sauce thickens.

④ Transfer cutlets to a serving platter. Spoon sauce over cutlets. If desired, garnish with parsley.

PER SERVING 282 calories; 14 g total fat (4 g sat. fat); 66 mg cholesterol; 774 mg sodium; 7 g carbohydrate; 1 g fiber; 28 g protein

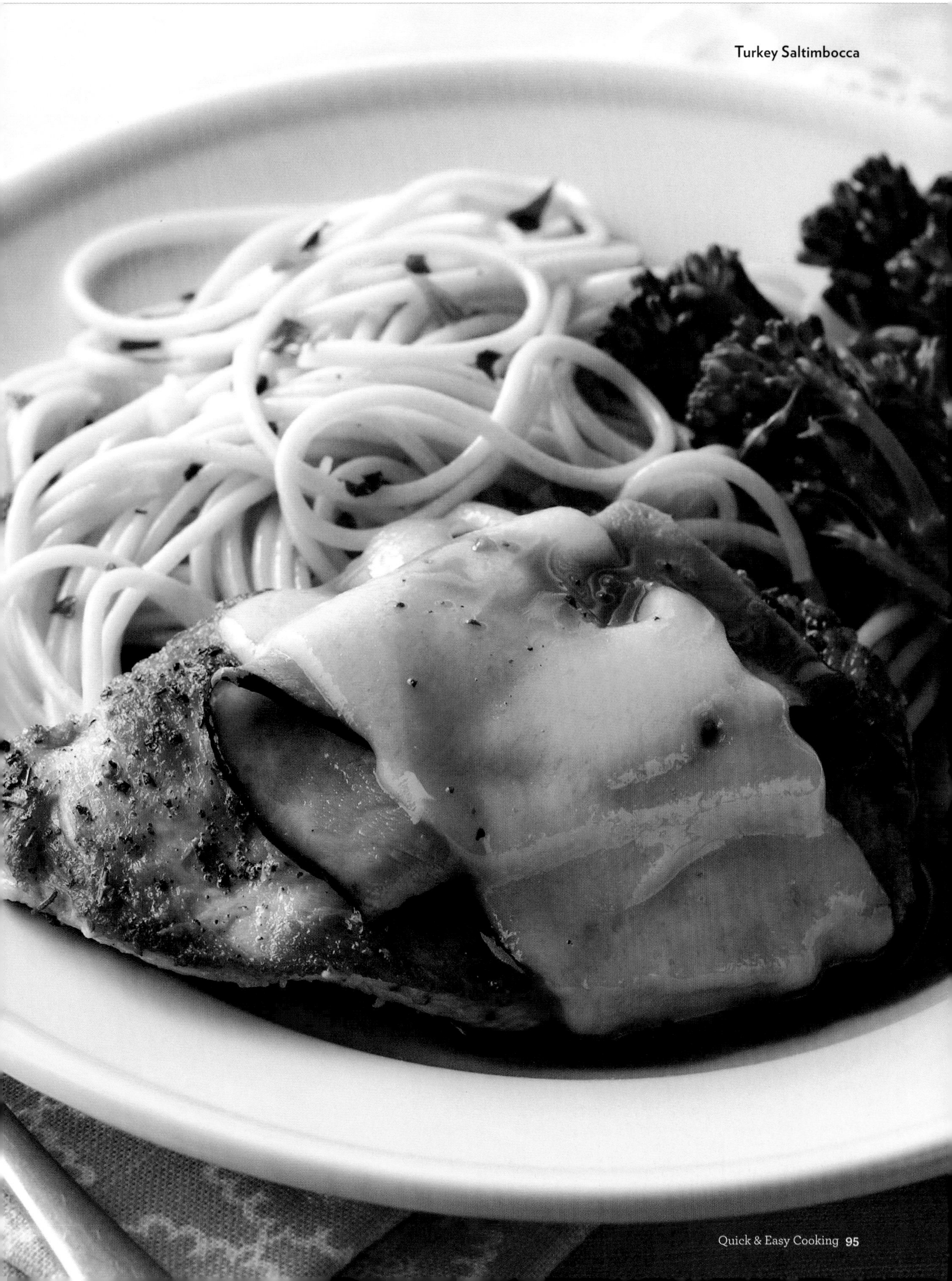
Turkey Saltimbocca

Drop your hook into these pages. You'll be sure to make a great catch—and net healthful, fuss-free meals that will make a big splash with your family.

106

118

129

SEAFOOD FAVORITES

102

Pan-Fried Fish with Peppers and Pecans

Instead of a traditional pecan crust, this richly flavored fish dish is topped with a candied pecan and sweet pepper relish. The relish would be delicious on pork as well.

MAKES 4 servings **START TO FINISH** 25 minutes

1	pound thin white fish fillets, such as trout, tilapia, or catfish (skinned if desired)
⅓	cup all-purpose flour
¼	teaspoon salt
6	tablespoons butter or margarine
1	tablespoon packed brown sugar
½	cup chopped pecans
½	of a red sweet pepper, seeded and cut into strips
⅛	teaspoon cayenne pepper
	Juice from 1 small lime
	Green onions, sliced

① If necessary, cut fish into serving-size pieces. Set aside. In a shallow dish combine flour and salt. Dip fish into flour mixture to coat.

② In a large skillet heat half of the butter over medium-high heat. Add fish in a single layer. Reduce heat to medium. Cook for 6 to 8 minutes or until golden and fish flakes easily when tested with a fork, turning once. Remove fish from skillet. Cover and keep warm.

③ Wipe out skillet. Add the remaining butter to skillet and melt over medium heat. Add brown sugar, stirring until dissolved. Stir in pecans, sweet pepper, and cayenne. Cook and stir over medium heat for 3 to 4 minutes or just until pecans are lightly toasted and pepper strips are tender. Remove from heat. Stir in lime juice. Spoon pecan mixture over fish. Top with green onions.

PER SERVING 364 calories; 24 g total fat (10 g sat. fat); 97 mg cholesterol; 268 mg sodium; 11 g carbohydrate; 1 g fiber; 26 g protein

Fish and Green Beans with Wasabi Mayonnaise

Cod—a traditional Japanese fish—is delicious in this Japanese-inspired dish of crispy panko-coated fillets served with a spicy wasabi mayonnaise.

MAKES 4 servings **START TO FINISH** 30 minutes
OVEN 450°F

	Nonstick cooking spray
1	lime
1	to 3 teaspoons wasabi paste
⅓	cup mayonnaise
1	to 1½ pounds firm white fish fillets ½ inch thick, rinsed and dried
	Salt
1	cup panko (Japanese-style bread crumbs)
1	tablespoon butter, melted
12	ounces tender young green beans, cooked

① Preheat oven to 450°F. Coat a shallow baking pan with cooking spray; set pan aside. Shred the peel and juice half the lime. Cut remaining lime half into wedges; set aside. For wasabi mayonnaise, in a small bowl combine peel, juice, wasabi paste, and mayonnaise.

② Sprinkle fish with salt. Place fish in prepared pan. Brush fish with 1 tablespoon of the wasabi mayonnaise; sprinkle with ¾ cup of the panko, pressing to adhere. Chill remaining wasabi mayonnaise until serving. Drizzle fish with melted butter. Bake about 20 minutes or until fish flakes easily with a fork.

③ Remove fish from pan. Toss beans with the panko that remains in baking pan. Sprinkle beans with the remaining ¼ cup panko. Serve fish and beans with remaining wasabi mayonnaise and lime wedges.

PER SERVING 349 calories; 19 g total fat (5 g sat. fat); 56 mg cholesterol; 384 mg sodium; 18 g carbohydrate; 4 g fiber; 26 g protein

quick tip Wasabi—a fleshy rhizome native to Japan—is so tongue-burningly potent that it is used in only miniscule quantities. Generally, however, wasabi pastes sold in mainstream markets are much milder. Once opened, wasabi paste may be stored in the refrigerator for as long as 18 months.

Fish and Green Beans with Wasabi Mayonnaise

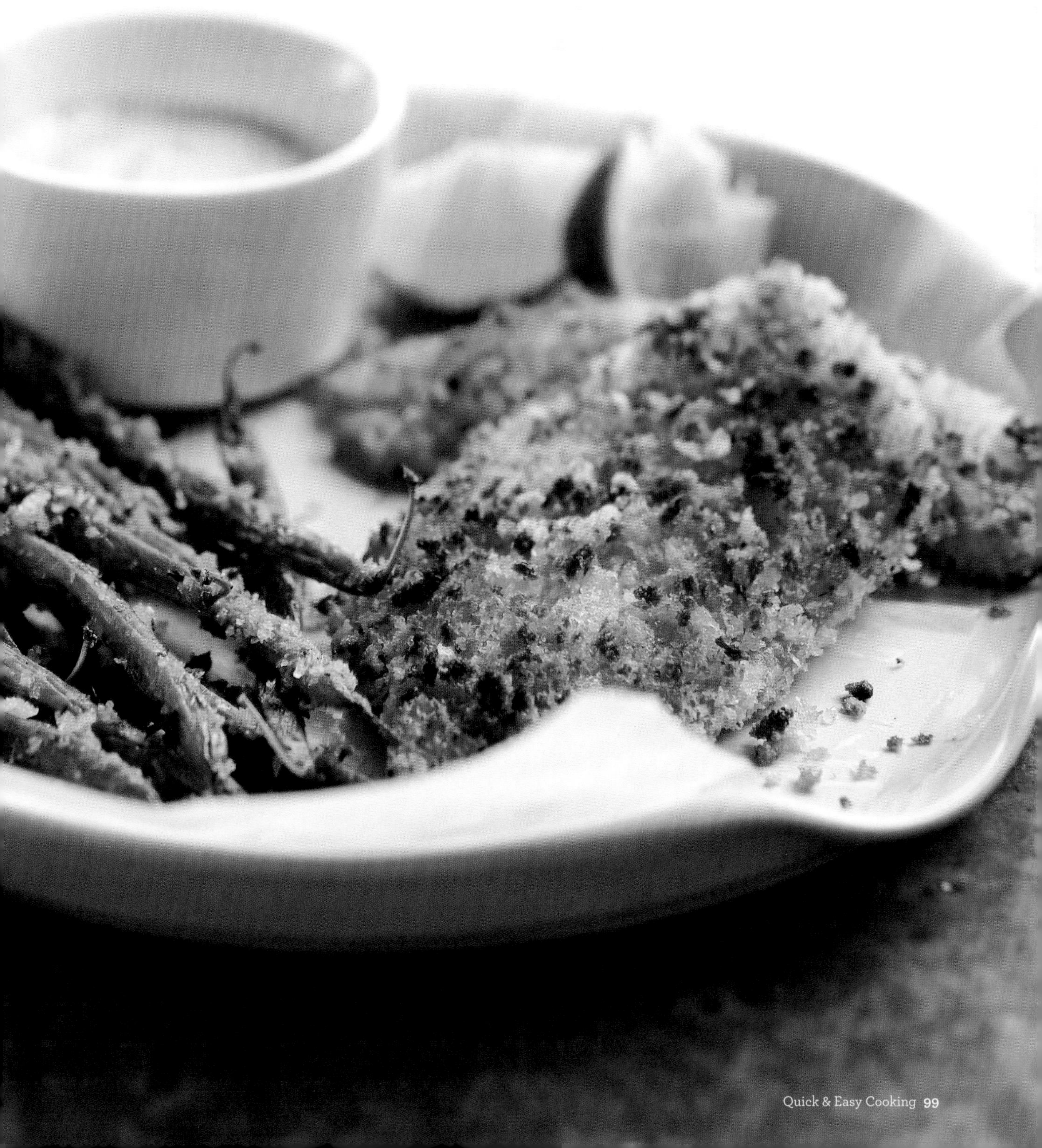

Tilapia Puttanesca

Tilapia Puttanesca 🍲 ♥

The best tilapia is farm-raised in the United States. Avoid farm-raised tilapia from China and Taiwan.

MAKES 4 servings **START TO FINISH** 25 minutes

- ½   of a medium red onion, cut into wedges
- 1   tablespoon olive oil
- 2   cloves garlic, minced
- 1   14.5-ounce can diced tomatoes, undrained
- 2   teaspoons dried oregano, crushed
- ¼   teaspoon crushed red pepper
- ¼   cup pitted kalamata olives
- 1   tablespoon capers, drained (optional)
- 1   pound skinless tilapia fillets
- ⅛   teaspoon salt
- 2   tablespoons coarsely chopped fresh parsley

① In a large skillet cook onion in oil on medium heat for 8 minutes or until tender; stirring occasionally. Stir in garlic, undrained tomatoes, oregano, and crushed red pepper. Bring to boiling; reduce heat. Simmer, uncovered, for 5 minutes.

② Add olives and, if desired, capers to sauce. Sprinkle tilapia with salt; add to sauce in skillet. Return sauce to boiling; reduce heat. Cook, covered, for 6 to 10 minutes or until fish flakes when tested with a fork. Using a slotted spatula, remove fish from sauce. Simmer sauce, uncovered, for 1 to 2 minutes more to thicken. To serve, spoon sauce over fish. Sprinkle with parsley.

PER SERVING 182 calories; 6 g total fat (1 g sat. fat); 56 mg cholesterol; 431 mg sodium; 8 g carbohydrate; 2 g fiber; 24 g protein

Thai-Style Tilapia and Vegetables

If you happen to have a can of regular coconut milk in your pantry, you can reduce the fat and calories in it: Let the can settle, skim some of the thick coconut cream off the top, and measure what remains in the can.

MAKES 4 servings **START TO FINISH** 30 minutes

- 1   red sweet pepper, seeded and cut into thin bite-size strips
- 1   cup thin asparagus spears or green beans trimmed and cut into 2-inch pieces
- 1   medium carrot, cut into thin bite-size strips
- 4   4- to 6-ounce skinless tilapia, cod, or other fish fillets, about ½ inch thick
- ¼   teaspoon salt
- ⅛   teaspoon black pepper
- ¾   cup canned unsweetened light coconut milk
- 2   teaspoons lime juice
- 2   teaspoons fish sauce or soy sauce
- 1   teaspoon grated fresh ginger or ½ teaspoon ground ginger
- ⅛   to ¼ teaspoon crushed red pepper
- 2   tablespoons chopped peanuts
- 1   tablespoon snipped fresh cilantro

① Fill a very large skillet with water to a depth of 1 inch. Bring water to boiling; reduce heat. Arrange sweet pepper, asparagus, and carrot in a steamer basket. Place fish on top of vegetables. Sprinkle fish and vegetables with salt and black pepper. Place steamer basket over the simmering water. Cover and simmer gently for 6 to 8 minutes or just until fish flakes easily when tested with a fork.

② Meanwhile, for sauce, in a small saucepan combine coconut milk, lime juice, fish sauce, ginger, and crushed red pepper. Bring to boiling; reduce heat. Boil gently, uncovered, for 2 to 3 minutes or until slightly thickened.

③ Remove fish and vegetables to serving plates. Drizzle with sauce and sprinkle with peanuts and cilantro.

PER SERVING 173 calories; 5 g total fat (2 g sat. fat); 48 mg cholesterol; 557 mg sodium; 8 g carbohydrate; 2 g fiber; 23 g protein

Lemony Cod with Asparagus ♥

Fillet of sole would make a lovely stand-in for the cod in this dish.

MAKES 4 servings **START TO FINISH** 25 minutes

- 4 soft breadsticks
- 2 tablespoons butter or margarine, melted
- ¼ teaspoon garlic salt
- 1 pound cod or flounder fillets, about ½ inch thick
- 12 ounces asparagus spears, trimmed
- 1 tablespoon lemon juice
- ½ teaspoon dried thyme, crushed
- ⅛ teaspoon black pepper
  Lemon wedges, halved crosswise (optional)

① Preheat broiler. Place breadsticks on the unheated rack of a broiler pan. Brush with 1 tablespoon of the melted butter and sprinkle with the garlic salt. Broil 4 inches from heat for 1 to 2 minutes or until golden brown, turning breadsticks once. Remove breadsticks from pan and keep warm.

② Arrange fish and asparagus in a single layer on the same broiler pan rack.

③ In a small bowl stir together the remaining 1 tablespoon butter and the lemon juice. Drizzle butter mixture over fish and brush over asparagus. Sprinkle fish and asparagus with thyme and pepper.

④ Broil 4 inches from heat for 4 to 6 minutes or just until fish begins to flake easily when tested with a fork and asparagus is crisp-tender, turning asparagus once. Serve fish and asparagus with breadsticks and, if desired, lemon wedges.

PER SERVING 293 calories; 8 g total fat (4 g sat. fat); 64 mg cholesterol; 454 mg sodium; 29 g carbohydrate; 3 g fiber; 27 g protein

Halibut with Angel Hair Pasta

Drizzle simple vinaigrette of olive oil and balsamic vinegar over the warm pasta, fish, and vegetables just before serving.

MAKES 4 servings **START TO FINISH** 30 minutes

- 4 coiled nests dried angel hair pasta (about 4 ounces)
- 5 cloves garlic
- 1 medium lemon
- 4 4- to 5-ounce fresh or frozen halibut fillets
- 2 medium tomatoes, sliced
- 2 tablespoons snipped fresh parsley (optional)
  Salt and black pepper
- 1 5- to 6-ounce package fresh baby spinach
- ¼ cup olive oil
- 2 tablespoons balsamic vinegar

① Fill a very large skillet or a Dutch oven with a steamer basket insert (see quick tip, below) half full with lightly salted water (steamer basket insert should not touch the water). Bring water to boiling. Add pasta to boiling water. Cook, covered, for 4 minutes. Using a slotted spoon, transfer pasta to a large bowl; cover and keep warm.

② Meanwhile, slice 4 cloves of the garlic; mince the remaining clove of garlic. Set aside. Cut lemon in half. Slice 1 lemon half; squeeze juice from the remaining lemon half; set aside.

③ In the steamer basket arrange fish, lemon slices, and tomato slices in single layers. Top with garlic slices and, if desired, parsley. Sprinkle with salt and pepper. Steam, covered, for 3 to 5 minutes or until fish flakes easily when tested with a fork. Top with spinach. Cook, covered, about 30 seconds more or just until spinach is wilted.

④ Divide pasta, fish, and spinach among dinner plates. Top fish with lemon and tomato slices.

⑤ For vinaigrette, in a screw-top jar combine minced garlic, lemon juice, oil, and vinegar. Cover and shake well. Drizzle each serving with vinaigrette.

PER SERVING 388 calories; 17 g total fat (2 g sat. fat); 36 mg cholesterol; 243 mg sodium; 31 g carbohydrate; 4 g fiber; 29 g protein

quick tip If you do not have a pan with a steamer insert that will leave room to cook the pasta, cook the pasta in a separate pot.

Lemon-Caper Tuna Noodles

Lemon-Caper Tuna and Noodles

Adding a squeeze of fresh lemon juice and piquant capers to a purchased Alfredo sauce makes this 20-minute entrée taste like your favorite restaurant fare.

MAKES 4 servings **START TO FINISH** 20 minutes

- 12 ounces extra-wide egg noodles
- 1 lemon
- 1 15-ounce jar light garlic Alfredo sauce or one 10-ounce container refrigerated light Alfredo pasta sauce
- 1 tablespoon capers, drained
- 1 12-ounce can solid white albacore tuna, drained

   Cracked black pepper and/or chives (optional)

① Cook noodles according to package directions; drain. Cover and keep warm. Finely shred lemon peel and squeeze juice from lemon; set aside.

② Meanwhile, in a medium saucepan combine Alfredo sauce, lemon juice, and capers. Heat through.

③ Add tuna and noodles to sauce; stir gently to combine. Return to heat just until heated through. Top with lemon peel, and if desired, cracked black pepper and/or chives.

PER SERVING 655 calories; 19 g total fat (11 g sat. fat); 154 mg cholesterol; 1,384 mg sodium; 78 g carbohydrate; 4 g fiber; 41 g protein

quick tip To encourage lemons to give up their juice more quickly and easily, let them stand in hot water for 15 to 20 minutes before squeezing.

Lemon-Pepper Tuna ♥

You can substitute instant brown rice for the couscous if you like. Just add it with the broccoli, carrots, chicken broth, water, and garlic. Cook and let stand as directed.

MAKES 4 servings **START TO FINISH** 20 minutes

- 2 tablespoons lemon juice
- 1 teaspoon reduced-sodium soy sauce
- 1 teaspoon snipped fresh thyme or ½ teaspoon dried thyme, crushed
- ½ teaspoon salt-free lemon-pepper seasoning
- 4 tuna steaks, cut 1 inch thick (about 1 pound)
   Nonstick cooking spray
- 2 cups chopped broccoli
- ½ cup packaged coarsely shredded fresh carrots
- 1 cup reduced-sodium chicken broth
- ¾ cup water
- 2 cloves garlic, minced
- 1 cup whole wheat couscous
- 1 tablespoon fresh thyme sprigs (optional)

① In a small bowl combine lemon juice, soy sauce, snipped thyme, and lemon pepper seasoning. Brush lemon juice mixture over 1 side of fish steaks.

② Lightly coat the unheated rack of a broiler pan with cooking spray. Place fish, brushed sides up, on broiler pan. Broil 4 inches from the heat for 8 to 12 minutes or until fish begins to flake when tested with a fork, turning once and brushing with lemon juice mixture halfway through cooking.

③ Meanwhile, in a medium saucepan bring broccoli, carrots, chicken broth, the water, and garlic just to boiling. Cook, covered, about 3 minutes or until broccoli is barely crisp-tender. Stir in couscous. Remove from heat; cover and let stand for 5 minutes. Fluff with a fork. Serve fish on couscous mixture. If desired, garnish with thyme sprigs.

PER SERVING 403 calories; 7 g total fat (1 g sat. fat); 43 mg cholesterol; 261 mg sodium; 51 g carbohydrate; 9 g fiber; 37 g protein

Salmon Pasta Toss

This creamy and aromatic pasta dish is simple to toss together, owing to a prepared pesto mix and jarred Alfredo sauce.

MAKES 6 servings **START TO FINISH** 25 minutes

- 1   0.5-ounce envelope pesto mix
- 3   tablespoons olive oil
- 12   ounces dried fettuccine
- 1   16-ounce jar dried tomato Alfredo sauce
- 1   14.5-ounce can diced tomatoes with basil, oregano, and garlic, undrained
- 1   7-ounce jar roasted red sweet peppers, drained and coarsely chopped (1 cup)
- ½   cup finely shredded Parmesan cheese (2 ounces)
- ⅓   cup milk
- 1   pound skinless salmon fillets, cooked (see quick tip, below) and flaked

① Combine pesto mix and olive oil; set aside.

② Meanwhile, in a large pot cook fettuccine according to package directions. Drain well; return to pot. Stir in pesto mixture, Alfredo sauce, undrained tomatoes, sweet peppers, ¼ cup of the Parmesan cheese, and the milk. Heat through.

③ Break salmon into large chunks; gently fold into pasta mixture. Heat through. Transfer to a serving bowl. Sprinkle with the ¼ cup remaining Parmesan cheese.

PER SERVING 561 calories; 24 g total fat (6 g sat. fat); 59 mg cholesterol; 1,166 mg sodium; 56 g carbohydrate; 3 g fiber; 29 g protein

quick tip   To cook salmon fillets, measure thickness. Pour 1½ cups water, chicken broth, or white wine into a large skillet; bring to boiling. Add fish. Return to boiling; reduce heat. Simmer, uncovered, for 4 to 6 minutes per ½-inch thickness or until fish begins to flake when tested with a fork.

Tuna Caponata

Caponata is a Sicilian eggplant relish that often contains some combination of tomatoes, onions, garlic, anchovies, olives, pine nuts, and vinegar. As it is here, it is most often served at room temperature as an accompaniment to fish.

MAKES 4 servings **START TO FINISH** 30 minutes

- 5   tablespoons olive oil
- 1   medium eggplant, cut into 1-inch pieces
- 1   medium onion, cut into thin wedges
- 3   cloves garlic, minced
- 1   19-ounce can cannellini beans (white kidney beans), rinsed and drained
- 1   8- or 9-ounce package frozen artichoke hearts, thawed and coarsely chopped
- 1   cup chopped tomatoes
- 2   tablespoons red wine vinegar
- 1   tablespoon capers, drained
- 2   teaspoons snipped fresh rosemary
- 1   teaspoon sugar
- ½   teaspoon salt
- ¼   teaspoon crushed red pepper
- ¼   cup pine nuts, toasted (see quick tip, page 272
- 12   ounces fresh tuna steaks, cut 1 inch thick

① In a very large skillet heat 4 tablespoons of the oil over medium-high heat. Add eggplant; cook about 5 minutes or until golden, stirring occasionally. Using a slotted spoon, remove eggplant from skillet; set aside. Add the remaining 1 tablespoon oil to skillet. Add onion and garlic; cook about 4 minutes or until onion is tender, stirring occasionally.

② Stir in drained beans, artichokes, tomatoes, vinegar, capers, the snipped rosemary, the sugar, the ½ teaspoon salt, and crushed red pepper. Bring to boiling; reduce heat. Simmer, uncovered, for 5 minutes, stirring occasionally. Remove from heat. Stir in eggplant and pine nuts. Cool to room temperature.

③ Meanwhile, sprinkle tuna lightly with salt and black pepper. Preheat a greased grill pan over medium-high heat. Place tuna in grill pan. Cook for 8 to 12 minutes or just until tuna flakes easily with a fork but is still slightly pink in center, turning once. Cut tuna into 4 serving-size pieces. Arrange eggplant mixture on a platter. Top with tuna. If desired, sprinkle with snipped *fresh parsley* and garnish with *fresh rosemary sprigs*.

PER SERVING 496 calories; 28 g total fat (4 g sat. fat); 32 mg cholesterol; 784 mg sodium; 38 g carbohydrate; 16 g fiber; 32 g protein

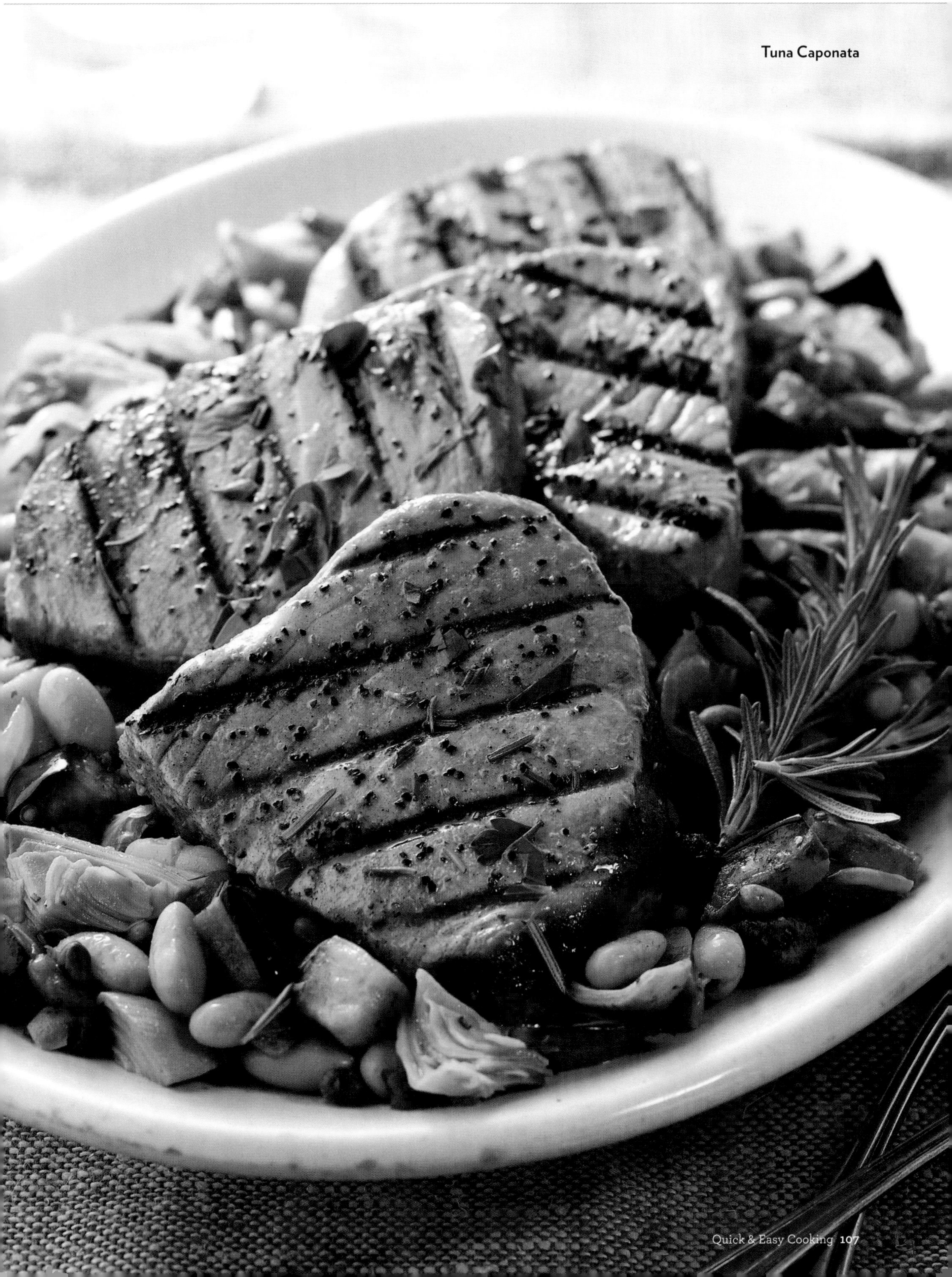
Tuna Caponata

Salmon with Tarragon Cream Sauce

Salmon with Tarragon Cream Sauce

Tarragon has an intense anise or licorice flavor. If you don't have tarragon or happen to have tarragon shunners in your family, use fresh basil instead.

MAKES 3 servings **START TO FINISH** 25 minutes

- 12 ounces salmon fillets or steaks
- 1 9-ounce package refrigerated fettuccine
- 1 cup sliced zucchini and/or yellow summer squash
- 1 cup red sweet pepper cut into bite-size strips
- 1 teaspoon cooking oil
- 1 cup milk
- 1 3-ounce package cream cheese, cut up
- 1 tablespoon snipped fresh tarragon or 1 teaspoon dried tarragon, crushed
- ¼ teaspoon salt
- ¼ teaspoon black pepper

① Skin fish, if necessary. Rinse fish; pat dry with paper towels. Cut fish into 1-inch pieces; set aside.

② Cook pasta according to package directions, adding squash and sweet pepper to pasta for the last minute of cooking. Drain and keep warm.

③ Meanwhile, in a large nonstick skillet heat oil over medium-high heat. Add fish; cook, stirring gently, for 3 to 5 minutes or until fish begins to flake when tested with a fork. Remove fish from skillet. Add milk, cream cheese, tarragon, salt, and pepper to skillet. Cook and whisk until cream cheese is melted and sauce is smooth. Stir in pasta mixture and fish. Heat through, tossing gently to mix.

PER SERVING 554 calories; 23 g total fat (8 g sat. fat); 142 mg cholesterol; 356 mg sodium; 51 g carbohydrate; 3 g fiber; 37 g protein

Salmon and Asparagus-Sauced Pasta

To snap the woody base off an asparagus spear, start at the base, working toward the tip, bending gently several times until you find a place where it breaks easily. Snap it in two and toss the bottom piece.

MAKES 4 servings **START TO FINISH** 25 minutes

- 1 pound asparagus spears
- 2⅔ cups packaged dried cavatappi or penne pasta (8 ounces)
- 1 small red or yellow sweet pepper, cut into bite-size strips
- ½ cup chopped onion (1 medium)
- 1 tablespoon butter or margarine
- 1 10-ounce container refrigerated Alfredo pasta sauce
- ¼ cup milk
- ⅛ teaspoon black pepper
- 3 ounces lox-style smoked salmon, coarsely chopped
- 2 teaspoons snipped fresh tarragon or ½ teaspoon dried tarragon, crushed

① Snap off and discard woody bases from asparagus. If desired, scrape off scales. Bias-slice asparagus into 2-inch pieces (you should have about 3 cups).

② In a large saucepan cook pasta according to package directions, adding asparagus the last 3 minutes of cooking. Drain; keep warm.

③ Meanwhile, for sauce, in a medium saucepan cook and stir sweet pepper and onion in hot butter over medium heat until tender. Stir in Alfredo sauce, milk, and black pepper; heat through. Gently stir in salmon and tarragon; heat through. Add to pasta mixture and gently stir to combine.

PER SERVING 446 calories; 18 g total fat (11 g sat. fat); 54 mg cholesterol; 910 mg sodium; 53 g carbohydrate; 4 g fiber; 18 g protein

Citrus Salmon with Broccoli

Just a spoonful of sugar tames the tartness in the simple lemon sauce for this fresh and bright salmon and broccoli dish.

MAKES 4 servings **START TO FINISH** 22 minutes

1	lemon
1	tablespoon sugar
2	tablespoons butter
4	4-ounce skinless salmon fillets
	Salt and black pepper
1	tablespoon snipped fresh dill
1	tablespoon olive oil
1	bunch broccoli, trimmed (1 pound)
4	cloves garlic, peeled and sliced
	Lemon slices and fresh dill (optional)

① Thinly slice half of the lemon; set aside. Juice remaining lemon half into a 1-cup measure; add water to equal ½ cup. Stir in sugar. Set aside.

② In a very large nonstick skillet heat butter over medium-high heat. Sprinkle salmon with salt and pepper; add to skillet. Cook salmon for 2 to 3 minutes or until bottom is golden; turn fillets. Add lemon juice mixture. Top with snipped dill and lemon slices. Reduce heat to medium; cover and cook for 5 to 6 minutes more or until fish flakes easily when tested with a fork.

③ Meanwhile, in another skillet heat olive oil. Quarter broccoli lengthwise into long spears; add to skillet along with garlic. Cook over medium heat for 8 to 10 minutes or until broccoli is crisp-tender, turning often. Serve salmon with broccoli; pour pan juices over salmon. If desired, serve with additional lemon slices and fresh dill.

PER SERVING 363 calories; 25 g total fat (8 g sat. fat); 78 mg cholesterol; 277 mg sodium; 12 g carbohydrate; 3 g fiber; 26 g protein

Maple-Bourbon Glazed Salmon

Serve this Southern-style glazed salmon with steamed broccoli and mashed or baked sweet potatoes.

MAKES 4 servings **START TO FINISH** 30 minutes

⅓	cup pure maple syrup or maple-flavor syrup
⅓	cup orange juice
3	tablespoons bourbon or orange juice
4	4- to 5-ounce fresh or frozen skinless salmon fillets
	Salt and black pepper
¼	cup coarsely chopped pecans or walnuts

① Preheat broiler. For glaze, in a small saucepan combine maple syrup, orange juice, and bourbon. Cook, uncovered, over medium heat for 5 minutes.

② Lightly sprinkle salmon with salt and pepper. Place on a lightly greased broiler pan. Broil 3 to 4 inches from heat for 5 minutes. Remove 2 tablespoons of the glaze and brush on all sides of salmon. Turn salmon; broil about 5 minutes more or just until salmon flakes easily when tested with a fork. Discard remainder of the glaze used as a brush-on.

③ Stir pecans into the remaining glaze; cook over high heat about 5 minutes or until glaze reaches the consistency of syrup. Serve salmon topped with pecan mixture.

PER SERVING 386 calories; 20 g total fat (4 g sat. fat); 62 mg cholesterol; 215 mg sodium; 21 g carbohydrate; 1 g fiber; 24 g protein

《 Whenever possible, purchase Alaskan wild-caught salmon—it is the most eco-friendly, sustainable choice. 》

Salmon and Couscous Casserole

Poached Salmon on Ciabatta

Poaching the salmon in a mixture of white wine and water infuses it with aroma and flavor.

MAKES 4 sandwiches **START TO FINISH** 30 minutes

- ½ cup dry white wine or water
- ½ cup water
- 12 ounces skinless salmon fillet, about 1 inch thick
- ¼ cup tub-style whipped cream cheese with garlic and herbs
- 2 tablespoons fat-free milk
- 1 tablespoon snipped fresh dill
- 1 teaspoon finely shredded lemon peel
- ⅛ teaspoon cracked black pepper
- 4 2-ounce ciabatta rolls, split and, if desired, toasted
- 1 cup fresh baby spinach

① In a large nonstick skillet combine wine and the water. Bring to boiling; add fish. Reduce heat. Cover and simmer for 8 to 12 minutes or just until fish flakes easily when tested with a fork. Remove fish from cooking liquid; discard liquid. Let fish cool to room temperature; break into large chunks.

② Meanwhile, in a small bowl combine cream cheese, milk, dill, lemon peel, and cracked pepper. Spread cream cheese mixture on cut sides of the ciabatta rolls. Arrange spinach and fish chunks on roll bottoms. Add roll tops, cream cheese sides down.

PER SANDWICH 395 calories; 16 g total fat (5 g sat. fat); 57 mg cholesterol; 458 mg sodium; 30 g carbohydrate; 2 g fiber; 23 g protein

quick tip For even more full-bodied flavor, substitute vegetable broth for the water called for in the couscous-making step.

Salmon and Couscous Casserole

If you cannot find toasted almonds at the supermarket, you can toast your own. Preheat oven to 350°F. Spread whole almonds in a single layer in a pie pan. Bake for 8 to 10 minutes or until lightly browned, stirring occasionally. Cool completely before using.

MAKES 4 servings **START TO FINISH** 25 minutes

- 1 cup water
- 2 cloves garlic, minced
- ⅔ cup whole wheat couscous
- 1 14.75-ounce can salmon, drained, flaked, and skin and bones removed
- 2 cups fresh baby spinach leaves
- ½ cup bottled roasted red sweet peppers, drained and chopped
- ⅓ cup bottled tomato bruschetta topper
- 2 tablespoons purchased toasted almonds

① In a 2-quart microwave-safe casserole combine the water and garlic. Microwave, uncovered, on high for 2½ to 3 minutes or until boiling. Remove from microwave and stir in couscous; spoon salmon on couscous mixture. Cover and let stand for 5 minutes.

② Add spinach, roasted peppers, and bruschetta topper to couscous mixture. Toss to combine. Divide mixture among 4 serving plates. Top with almonds.

PER SERVING 335 calories; 9 g total fat (2 g sat. fat); 41 mg cholesterol; 616 mg sodium; 34 g carbohydrate; 6 g fiber; 30 g protein

Poached Salmon on Ciabatta

Weeknight Salmon Cakes

Serve these crisp-broiled salmon cakes with a side of smoky mayonnaise. Add some buttered peas and boiled red potatoes to the plate and dinner's done.

MAKES 4 cakes **PREP** 20 minutes **BROIL** 14 minutes

- 1   pound skinless salmon fillet(s)
- ¾   cup soft bread crumbs (1 to 2 slices)
- 1   egg white
- ¼   cup thinly sliced green onions (2)
- 2   tablespoons chopped roasted red sweet pepper
- 1   tablespoon snipped fresh basil
- ¼   teaspoon salt
- ¼   cup mayonnaise
- ½   teaspoon smoked paprika or dash cayenne pepper
- ⅛   teaspoon freshly ground black pepper

① In a food processor or blender combine half of the salmon, all of the bread crumbs, egg white, green onions, roasted pepper, basil, and salt. Process or blend until combined. Chop the remaining salmon into ½-inch pieces. In a medium bowl combine salmon mixture and chopped salmon (mixture will be soft). Shape salmon mixture into four ¾-inch-thick cakes.

② Preheat broiler. Arrange cakes on a greased foil-lined baking sheet. Broil 4 to 5 inches from heat for 14 to 18 minutes or until done (160°F), turning once halfway through broiling time.

③ Meanwhile, in a small bowl combine mayonnaise, paprika, and black pepper. Serve salmon cakes with mayonnaise mixture.

PER CAKE 359 calories; 26 g total fat (5 g sat. fat); 67 mg cholesterol; 345 mg sodium; 4 g carbohydrate; 1 g fiber; 25 g protein

Simple Salmon, Greens, and Couscous

With heart-healthy, omega 3-rich salmon and vitamin-packed greens, this is one powerfully nutritious dish.

MAKES 4 servings **START TO FINISH** 30 minutes
OVEN 450°F

-     Nonstick cooking spray
- 4   skinless salmon fillets, about 1 inch thick (about 1 pound total)
- ¼   teaspoon salt
- ¼   teaspoon black pepper
- 2   teaspoons reduced-sodium soy sauce
- 1   tablespoon olive oil
- 3   cups trimmed and coarsely chopped mustard greens or collard greens
- 1   14.5-ounce can chicken broth
- 1   cup couscous
-     Lemon wedges (optional)

① Preheat oven to 450°F. Line a shallow baking pan with foil and lightly coat with cooking spray; set aside.

② Sprinkle fish fillets with salt and pepper. Arrange fillets in prepared pan. Drizzle with soy sauce. Bake, uncovered, for 15 to 18 minutes or just until fish flakes easily when tested with a fork.

③ Meanwhile, heat oil in a 2-quart saucepan over medium heat. Add greens and stir; cover and cook about 5 minutes or until greens are nearly tender, stirring once or twice. Add broth to the greens; bring to boiling.

④ Stir in couscous; remove from heat and let stand for 5 minutes.

⑤ Divide couscous mixture among 4 serving plates. Top with fish fillets. If desired, serve with lemon wedges.

PER SERVING 603 calories; 16 g total fat (3 g sat. fat); 67 mg cholesterol; 562 mg sodium; 74 g carbohydrate; 6 g fiber; 37 g protein

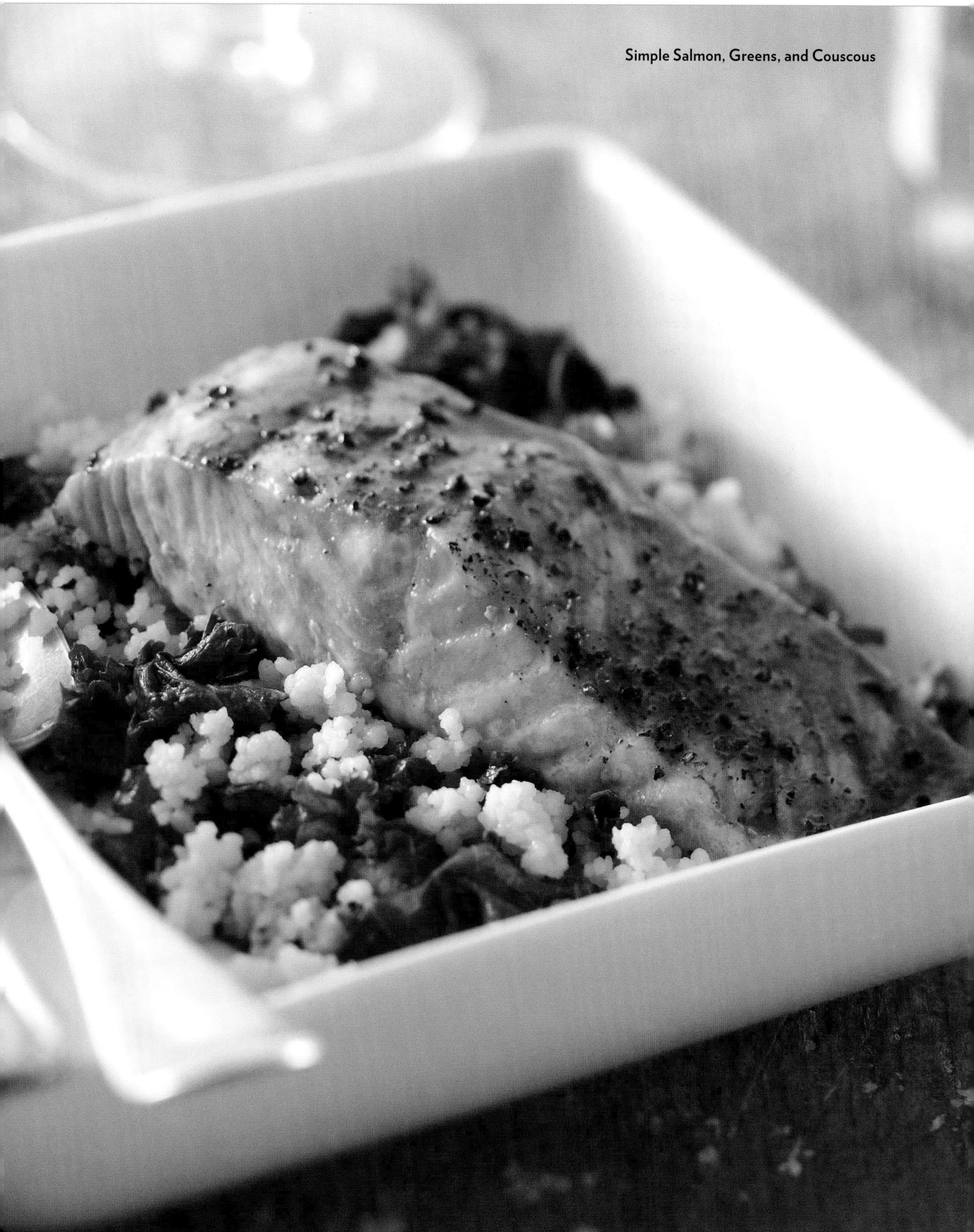

Simple Salmon, Greens, and Couscous

Catfish and Slaw Tacos

Catfish and Slaw Tacos

A quick lime slaw adds a cool and fresh crunch to these Cajun-spiced catfish tacos.

MAKES 4 servings **START TO FINISH** 30 minutes

- 1   pound catfish fillets
- 1   lime
- ¼   cup mayonnaise or salad dressing
- ½   teaspoon bottled hot pepper sauce
- ½   of a small head cabbage, shredded (about 2½ cups)
- 1   tablespoon Cajun seasoning
- ¼   cup cornmeal
- ¼   cup all-purpose flour
- ¼   cup vegetable oil
- 16   4-inch corn tortillas or eight 8-inch flour tortillas
       Lime wedges
       Bottled hot pepper sauce (optional)

① Cut fish into 1-inch strips. Set aside. Meanwhile, for slaw, squeeze about 3 tablespoons juice from the whole lime. In a medium bowl combine lime juice, mayonnaise, and the ½ teaspoon hot pepper sauce. Add cabbage; toss to coat. Set aside.

② Toss fish strips with Cajun seasoning. In a large bowl combine cornmeal and flour. Add fish strips; toss to coat.

③ In a large skillet heat oil over medium heat. Cook fish strips, half at a time, in hot oil for 4 to 6 minutes or until golden and fish flakes easily when tested with a fork, turning to brown evenly. Remove from skillet.

④ Wrap tortillas in paper towels. Heat in microwave oven on high for 1 minute (or toast in a dry skillet). If using corn tortillas, stack 2 for each taco, or use 1 flour tortilla for each taco. Divide fish and slaw among tortillas. Reserve any dressing left in bowl to serve with tacos. Serve tacos immediately with reserved dressing, lime wedges, and additional hot pepper sauce.

PER 2 TACOS 620 calories; 36 g total fat (5 g sat. fat); 59 mg cholesterol; 300 mg sodium; 53 g carbohydrate; 3 g fiber; 24 g protein

Ginger Shrimp and Rice 🍲 ♥

Starting with cooked shrimp makes this Asian-style dish a snap to prepare. Be sure to heat the cooked shrimp just until warm so they stay tender and don't get overcooked and rubbery.

MAKES 4 servings **START TO FINISH** 15 minutes

- 1   small bunch green onions
- 1   1-inch piece fresh ginger
- 1   tablespoon olive oil
- ¼   cup water
- 1   tablespoon soy sauce
- 2   8.8-ounce packages cooked long grain rice
- 1   pound peeled and deveined cooked medium shrimp
- ¼   cup mango chutney

① Slice green onions; reserve ¼ cup. Peel ginger and finely grate.

② In a very large skillet cook remaining green onions and grated ginger in hot oil for 1 to 2 minutes or until tender. Add the water and soy sauce. Cover and bring to boiling. Add rice and shrimp. Cook until most of the liquid is absorbed and shrimp are heated through. Divide among 4 shallow bowls. Top with chutney and reserved green onions.

PER SERVING 393 calories; 8 g total fat (1 g sat. fat); 172 mg cholesterol; 577 mg sodium; 53 g carbohydrate; 3 g fiber; 27 g protein

Ginger Shrimp and Rice

Linguine with Shrimp and Pine Nuts

Heat from the pasta and shrimp is just enough to barely wilt the baby spinach, keeping it fresh, flavorful—and at its most nutritious.

MAKES 4 servings **START TO FINISH** 30 minutes

8	ounces dried linguine
¾	cup chicken broth
⅓	cup dry sherry or chicken broth
2	tablespoons lemon juice
¼	teaspoon salt
¼	teaspoon crushed red pepper
9	ounces peeled and deveined medium shrimp
¼	cup pine nuts
2	cloves garlic, minced
1	tablespoon olive oil
1½	cups sliced assorted fresh mushrooms, such as button, cremini, and/or stemmed shiitake (4 ounces)
1	tablespoon butter
4	cups fresh baby spinach
¼	cup freshly grated Asiago cheese (1 ounce)
	Pine nuts, toasted (see quick tip, page 272) (optional)

① Cook linguine according to package directions; drain. Return linguine to hot pan; cover and keep warm.

② Meanwhile, in a small bowl combine broth, sherry, lemon juice, salt, and crushed red pepper; set aside.

③ In a large skillet cook shrimp, ¼ cup pine nuts, and garlic in hot oil over medium heat for 2 to 3 minutes or until shrimp are opaque, stirring frequently. Remove shrimp mixture from skillet.

④ Add mushrooms and butter to skillet. Cook about 3 minutes or until mushrooms are nearly tender, stirring occasionally. Carefully add broth mixture. Bring to boiling; reduce heat. Boil gently, uncovered, for 5 minutes. Return shrimp mixture to skillet; heat through.

⑤ Divide cooked linguine among shallow bowls. Top with shrimp mixture, spinach, cheese, and, if desired, additional pine nuts.

PER SERVING 492 calories; 17 g total fat (5 g sat. fat); 145 mg cholesterol; 577 mg sodium; 50 g carbohydrate; 2 g fiber; 31 g protein

Coconut Shrimp with Mango Sauce

Traditional deep-fried coconut shrimp is delicious but full of fat and calories. This oven-baked version delivers terrific flavor with far less fat.

MAKES 4 servings **START TO FINISH** 30 minutes
OVEN 425°F

	Nonstick cooking spray
1	lime
2	mangoes, halved, seeded, peeled, and chopped
¼	cup honey
⅛	teaspoon cayenne pepper
	Snipped fresh cilantro
12	ounces peeled and deveined large shrimp
	Salt
1	cup unsweetened flaked coconut (4 ounces)
	Lime wedges (optional)

① Preheat oven to 425°F. Line a baking sheet with foil and lightly coat with cooking spray. Finely shred 1 teaspoon peel from lime and squeeze juice from lime; add lime juice to blender with 1 cup of the chopped mangoes, the honey, and cayenne pepper; cover and process until smooth. Remove ¼ cup to a shallow dish. Transfer remaining to a bowl; top with lime peel and snipped fresh cilantro. Set aside for dipping sauce.

② Sprinkle shrimp with salt. Place coconut in a shallow dish. Dip shrimp in the ¼ cup mango sauce, then coconut, pressing to coat. Place on baking sheet.

③ Bake 8 to 10 minutes or until coconut is golden and shrimp are cooked through. Serve with dipping sauce, remaining chopped mangoes, cilantro, and lime wedges.

PER SERVING 414 calories; 20 g total fat (17 g sat. fat); 129 mg cholesterol; 285 mg sodium; 44 g carbohydrate; 7 g fiber; 20 g protein

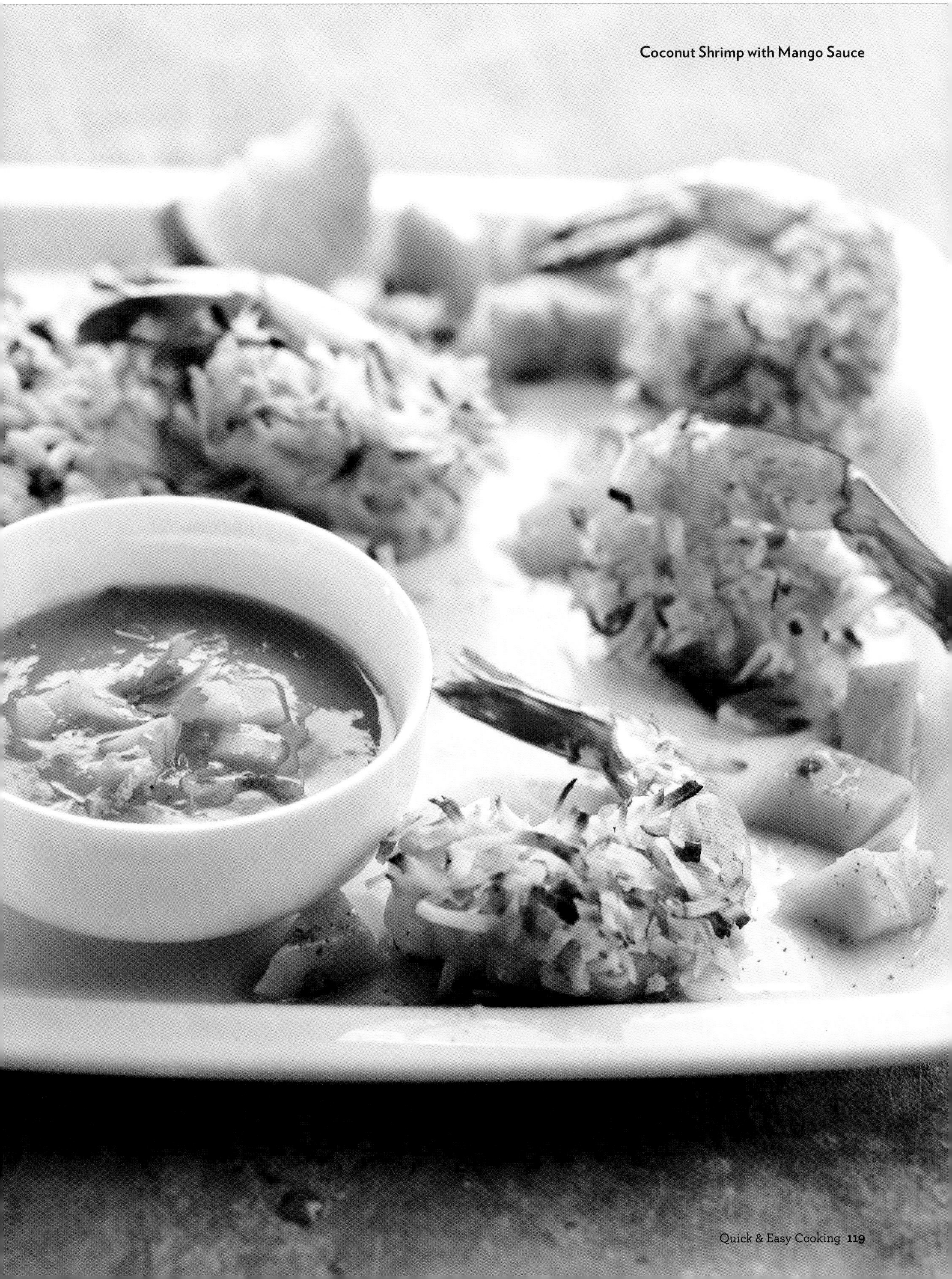

Coconut Shrimp with Mango Sauce

Garlicky Peppers and Shrimp

Garlicky Peppers and Shrimp

If you make this dish with spinach pasta, the pale pink of the shrimp and the pale green of the pasta make a pretty and colorful plate.

MAKES 4 servings **START TO FINISH** 20 minutes

- 1   9-ounce package refrigerated spinach or plain fettuccine
- 4   tablespoons olive oil
- 3   small red, green, yellow, and/or orange sweet peppers, seeded and cut into thin strips
- 2   medium onions, cut into thin wedges
- 4   cloves garlic, thinly sliced
- 1   pound peeled and deveined medium shrimp
- ⅛   teaspoon cayenne pepper
- 1   cup small fresh basil leaves (optional)

① Cook pasta according to package directions; drain and return to pan. Toss with 2 tablespoons of the olive oil. Keep warm.

② Meanwhile, in a very large skillet heat the remaining 2 tablespoons olive oil over medium-high heat. Stir in sweet peppers, onions, and garlic; stir-fry for 4 to 6 minutes or until crisp-tender. Add shrimp and cayenne pepper. Cook for 2 to 3 minutes or until shrimp are opaque, stirring occasionally.

③ Serve shrimp mixture over pasta. If desired, sprinkle with basil.

PER SERVING 477 calories; 18 g total fat (3 g sat. fat); 229 mg cholesterol; 256 mg sodium; 45 g carbohydrate; 4 g fiber; 33 g protein

quick tip   Reserve your expensive extra virgin olive oil for salads and cold dishes. In recipes like this—where the olive oil is used to cook already flavorful peppers, onions, and garlic—pure olive oil is just fine.

Mexican Shrimp Tostadas 🍲

It's just 20 minutes to tacos—from start to finish—with this recipe. Try a salsa verde, or green salsa, as the flavor agent. The bright lemony flavor of tomatillos is a nice match with shrimp.

MAKES 4 servings **START TO FINISH** 20 minutes

- 8   tostada shells
- 1   pound peeled and deveined cooked shrimp
- 1   8-ounce can no-salt-added tomato sauce
- 1   1.25-ounce envelope reduced-sodium taco seasoning mix
- 2   cups shredded lettuce
- 1   15-ounce can black beans, warmed
- ¼   cup sliced green onions (2)
- ½   cup shredded Monterey Jack cheese (2 ounces)
- ¼   cup sour cream
- ½   cup salsa
     Sliced green onions

① Heat tostada shells according to package directions.

② In a large nonstick skillet combine shrimp, tomato sauce, and taco seasoning. Bring to boiling; reduce heat. Simmer, uncovered, for 2 to 3 minutes or until shrimp are heated through, stirring occasionally.

③ To serve, arrange lettuce, black beans, and green onions on tostada shells; top with shrimp mixture. Serve with cheese, sour cream, salsa, and additional green onions.

PER SERVING 362 calories; 16 g total fat (6 g sat. fat); 190 mg cholesterol; 920 mg sodium; 27 g carbohydrate; 3 g fiber; 30 g protein

Shrimp Pasta Diavolo

Diavolo means devil in Italian. In this dish, it refers to the spiciness imparted by the crushed red pepper. Add more or less to your liking.

MAKES 4 servings **START TO FINISH** 20 minutes

1	9-ounce package refrigerated linguine
1	medium onion, cut into thin wedges
3	cloves garlic, minced
¼	teaspoon crushed red pepper
2	tablespoons olive oil
1	14.5-ounce can diced tomatoes, undrained
12	ounces peeled and deveined medium shrimp
½	cup torn fresh basil
2	cups fresh baby spinach
½	cup finely shredded Parmesan cheese

① Cook linguine according to package directions. Drain pasta and transfer to a very large bowl; set aside.

② Meanwhile, in a large skillet cook onion, garlic, and crushed red pepper in hot oil until tender. Stir in tomatoes. Bring to boiling; reduce heat. Simmer, uncovered, for 3 minutes. Add shrimp to skillet; cover and simmer for 3 minutes or until shrimp are opaque. Add shrimp mixture to pasta. Stir in basil and spinach. Top each serving with Parmesan cheese.

PER SERVING 412 calories; 13 g total fat (4 g sat. fat); 204 mg cholesterol; 528 mg sodium; 44 g carbohydrate; 4 g fiber; 30 g protein

Shrimp and Tomato Piccata ♥

The Italian term "piccata" means that a dish is flavored with lemon and briny capers. It is most often applied to thin scallops of chicken or veal. Here it pairs deliciously with shrimp.

MAKES 4 servings **START TO FINISH** 20 minutes

3	tablespoons olive oil
8	ounces small, thin green beans, trimmed (2 cups)
1	pound peeled and deveined medium shrimp
3	small tomatoes, cut into wedges
1	teaspoon finely shredded lemon peel
3	tablespoons lemon juice
1	tablespoon capers, drained
	Hot cooked pasta (optional)

① In a very large skillet heat 1 tablespoon of the oil over medium-high heat. Add green beans; cook for 3 minutes. Add shrimp; cook and stir about 3 minutes or until shrimp are opaque. Add tomato wedges; cook for 1 minute more. Divide shrimp mixture among 4 serving plates.

② For sauce, in a small bowl whisk together the remaining 2 tablespoons oil, the lemon peel, lemon juice, and drained capers. Drizzle sauce over shrimp mixture. If desired, serve with hot cooked pasta.

PER SERVING 244 calories; 12 g total fat (2 g sat. fat); 172 mg cholesterol; 239 mg sodium; 10 g carbohydrate; 4 g fiber; 25 g protein

❮ Shrimp are a dieter's dream— and at less than 30 calories each, that dream is sweet. ❯

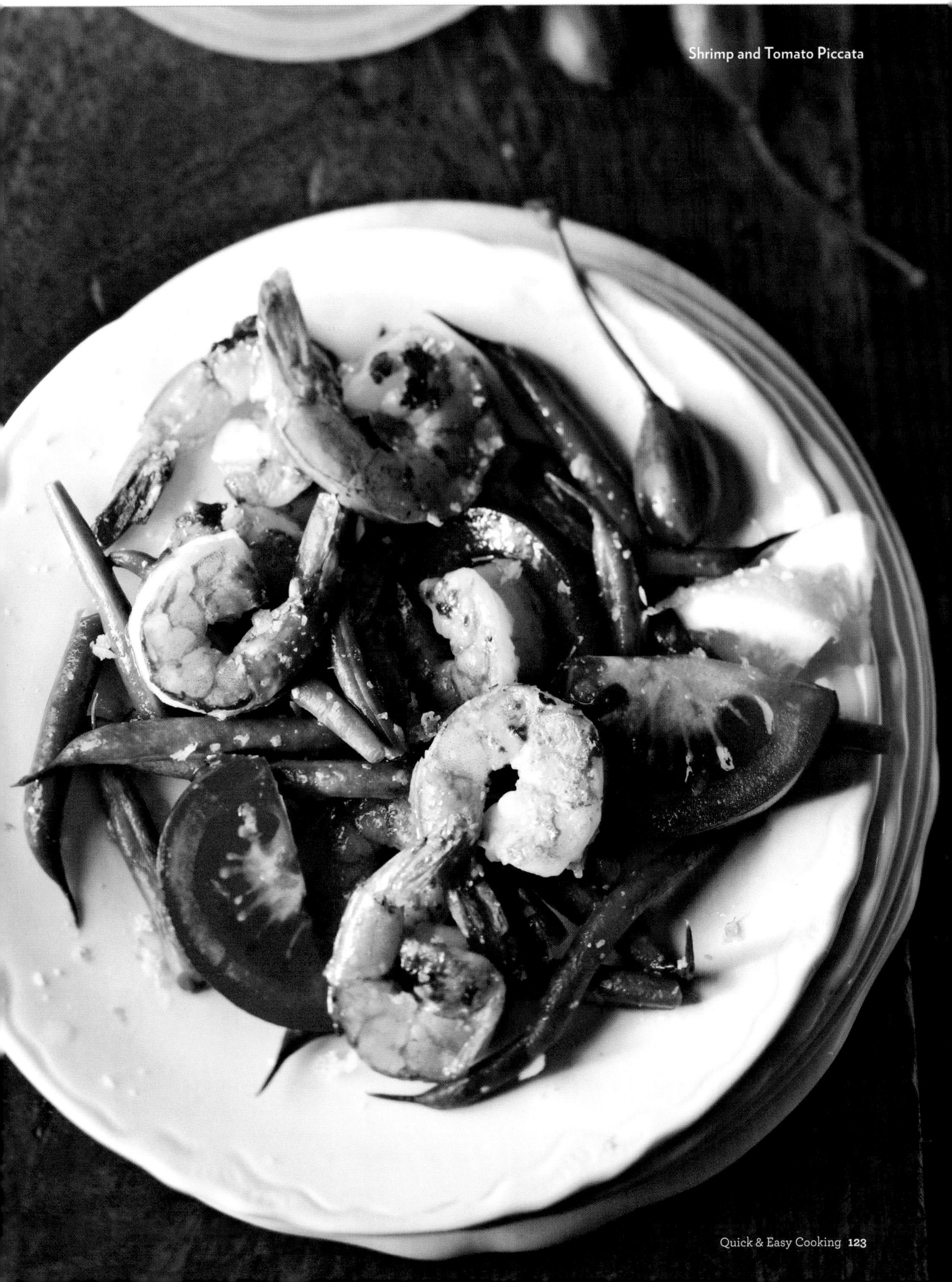
Shrimp and Tomato Piccata

Quick Cioppino with Basil Gremolata

Quick Cioppino with Basil Gremolata ▦

For a dramatic presentation, use shrimp with tails. Start with 8 ounces of unpeeled shrimp. Peel and devein the shrimp, leaving tails intact.

MAKES 4 servings **START TO FINISH** 25 minutes

6	ounces cod fillets
1	cup green sweet pepper strips (1 medium)
1	cup chopped onion (1 large)
2	cloves garlic, minced
1	tablespoon olive oil or vegetable oil
2	14.5-ounce cans Italian-style stewed tomatoes, undrained, cut up
½	cup water
¼	teaspoon salt
¼	teaspoon black pepper
6	ounces peeled and deveined shrimp
3	tablespoons snipped fresh basil
1	tablespoon finely shredded lemon peel
2	cloves garlic, minced

① Cut cod into 1-inch pieces; set aside. In a large pot cook and stir sweet pepper, onion, and 2 cloves minced garlic in hot oil until tender. Stir in tomatoes, the water, salt, and black pepper. Bring to boiling. Stir in cod and shrimp. Return to boiling; reduce heat. Simmer, covered, for 2 to 3 minutes or just until cod flakes easily when tested with a fork and shrimp are opaque.

② In a small bowl combine basil, lemon peel, and 2 cloves minced garlic. Sprinkle each serving with basil mixture.

PER SERVING 188 calories; 5 g total fat (1 g sat. fat); 83 mg cholesterol; 921 mg sodium; 20 g carbohydrate; 5 g fiber; 19 g protein

Iceberg Wedges with Shrimp and Blue Cheese Dressing ♥

Adding grilled shrimp to the popular iceberg-wedge salad found on restaurant menus makes it a knife-and-fork main dish.

MAKES 6 servings **START TO FINISH** 35 minutes

1½	pounds large shrimp in shells
3	tablespoons lemon juice
¼	teaspoon black pepper
½	cup light mayonnaise or salad dressing
¼	to ½ teaspoon bottled hot pepper sauce
2	tablespoons crumbled blue cheese
3	to 4 tablespoons fat-free milk
	Nonstick cooking spray
1	large head iceberg lettuce, cut into 12 wedges
1	large tomato, chopped
⅓	cup thinly sliced, quartered red onion
2	slices turkey bacon, cooked and crumbled

① Peel and devein shrimp, leaving tails intact if desired. Rinse shrimp; pat dry with paper towels. In a medium bowl combine shrimp, 2 tablespoons of the lemon juice, and ⅛ teaspoon of the black pepper. Toss to coat. Set shrimp aside.

② For dressing, in a small bowl combine the remaining 1 tablespoon lemon juice, the remaining ⅛ teaspoon black pepper, the mayonnaise, and hot pepper sauce. Stir in blue cheese. Stir in enough of the milk to make desired consistency.

③ Coat an unheated grill pan with cooking spray. Preheat grill pan over medium-high heat. Thread shrimp onto six 10- to 12-inch-long skewers (see quick tip, page 206). Place skewers on grill pan. Cook for 3 to 5 minutes or until shrimp are opaque, turning once halfway through cooking. (If necessary, cook shrimp skewers half at a time.)

④ Place 2 lettuce wedges on each of 6 serving plates. Top with shrimp, tomato, red onion, and bacon. Serve with dressing.

PER SERVING 190 calories; 10 g total fat (2 g sat. fat); 129 mg cholesterol; 360 mg sodium; 8 g carbohydrate; 1 g fiber; 18 g protein

Pasta with Broccoli Rabe and Clams

Broccoli rabe—or rapini, as Italians call it—is related to cabbage and turnips. The stalks have leafy greens and small broccoli-like florets. Buy it as fresh as you can and cook it as soon as you can. It has a naturally pleasant bitterness that can turn unpleasant when it sits in the refrigerator too long.

MAKES 6 to 8 servings **START TO FINISH** 25 minutes

- 12 to 16 ounces dried pasta
- 1 pound broccoli rabe, trimmed and cut into 2-inch pieces, or 3 cups broccoli florets
- 3 cloves garlic, sliced
- 2 tablespoons olive oil
- 2 6.5-ounce cans chopped clams, undrained
- ¼ cup butter
- ½ cup dry white wine
- ½ teaspoon crushed red pepper
- ¼ teaspoon black pepper
- ¼ cup grated Parmesan cheese

① Cook pasta according to package directions; drain. Return pasta to hot pan; cover and keep warm.

② Meanwhile, in a very large skillet cook broccoli and garlic in hot oil over medium-high heat for 5 minutes, stirring occasionally. Stir in clams and butter. Cook over medium heat until butter is melted.

③ Stir in wine, crushed red pepper, and black pepper. Bring just to boiling; reduce heat. Simmer, uncovered, about 2 minutes or until mixture is slightly reduced.

④ Serve broccoli mixture over cooked pasta. Sprinkle each serving with cheese.

PER SERVING 469 calories; 15 g total fat (6 g sat. fat); 64 mg cholesterol; 219 mg sodium; 49 g carbohydrate; 4 g fiber; 27 g protein

Pasta with White Clam Sauce

All you need to add to this Italian classic is a crisp green salad—and maybe a glass of chilled white wine.

MAKES 4 servings **START TO FINISH** 30 minutes

- 10 ounces packaged dried linguine or fettuccine
- 2 6.5-ounce cans chopped or minced clams
  About 2 cups half-and-half, light cream, or whole milk
- ½ cup chopped onion (1 medium)
- 2 cloves garlic, minced
- 2 tablespoons butter or margarine
- ¼ cup all-purpose flour
- 2 teaspoons snipped fresh oregano or ½ teaspoon dried oregano, crushed
- ¼ teaspoon salt
- ⅛ teaspoon black pepper
- ¼ cup snipped fresh parsley
- ¼ cup dry white wine, nonalcoholic dry white wine, or chicken broth
- ¼ cup finely shredded or grated Parmesan cheese (1 ounce)

① In a large saucepan cook pasta according to package directions. Drain; keep warm. Meanwhile, drain canned clams, reserving the juice from one of the cans (you should have about ½ cup). Add enough half-and-half to reserved clam juice to equal 2½ cups liquid. Set clams and clam juice mixture aside.

② In a medium saucepan cook onion and garlic in hot butter over medium heat until tender but not brown. Stir in flour, dried oregano (if using), salt, and pepper. Add clam juice mixture all at once. Cook and stir until thickened and bubbly. Cook and stir for 1 minute more. Stir in drained clams, fresh oregano (if using), parsley, and wine. Heat through. Serve over hot pasta. Sprinkle with Parmesan cheese.

PER SERVING 680 calories; 24 g total fat (14 g sat. fat); 125 mg cholesterol; 430 mg sodium; 72 g carbohydrate; 3 g fiber; 40 g protein

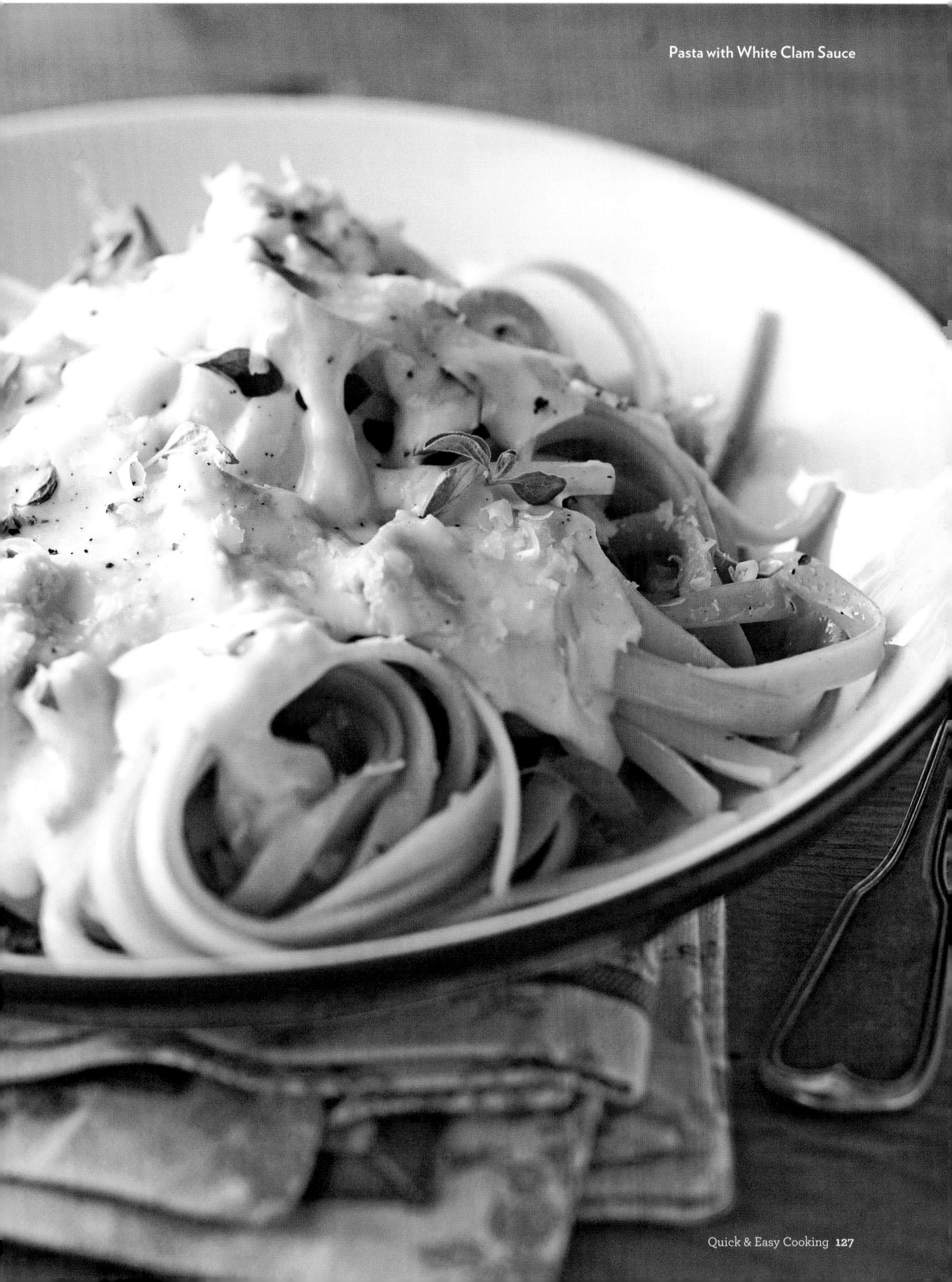
Pasta with White Clam Sauce

Scallops with Watercress and Fennel

Scallops with Watercress and Fennel ♥

Watercress has a delightfully peppery taste similar to arugula, which you could use in place of the watercress.

MAKES 4 servings **START TO FINISH** 30 minutes

1	medium fennel bulb
12	sea scallops (1 to 1½ pounds total)
⅛	teaspoon salt
⅛	teaspoon black pepper
⅓	cup plain low-fat yogurt
1	to 1½ teaspoons grated fresh ginger or ⅛ to ¼ teaspoon ground ginger
½	teaspoon finely shredded orange peel
1	teaspoon orange juice
1	teaspoon honey
2	medium oranges, peeled and thinly sliced crosswise
4	cups watercress, tough stems removed

① Preheat broiler. Cut off and discard upper stalks from fennel bulb. Remove any wilted outer layers and cut off and discard a thin slice from fennel base. Cut fennel bulb into very thin slices. Set aside.

② Meanwhile, sprinkle scallops with salt and pepper. Place scallops on the unheated rack of a broiler pan. Broil 4 inches from heat about 8 minutes or until scallops are opaque, turning once halfway through broiling.

③ Meanwhile, for dressing, in a small bowl whisk together yogurt, ginger, orange peel, orange juice, and honey. Set aside.

④ Cut orange slices in half. Divide sliced fennel and watercress among 4 serving plates. Top with scallops and orange slices. Drizzle with dressing.

PER SERVING 172 calories; 1 g total fat (0 g sat. fat); 39 mg cholesterol; 314 mg sodium; 18 g carbohydrate; 4 g fiber; 22 g protein

Mediterranean Scallops and Pasta

Using dried spinach fettuccine in this seafood and pasta dish gives it extra color and flavor—but plain pasta is just fine too.

MAKES 4 servings **START TO FINISH** 30 minutes

1	pound sea scallops
2	tablespoons olive oil
2	tablespoons lemon juice
2	teaspoons dried Mediterranean seasoning, crushed
8	ounces dried fettuccine
1	6-ounce jar quartered marinated artichoke hearts, drained
¼	cup oil-pack dried tomatoes, well drained and sliced
¼	cup purchased basil pesto

① Halve any large scallops. In a bowl combine oil, lemon juice, and Mediterranean seasoning; add scallops and toss to coat. Cover and chill for 15 minutes.

② Meanwhile, in a 4-quart Dutch oven or saucepan cook pasta according to package directions. Drain well; return to hot Dutch oven. Add artichokes, tomatoes, and pesto to cooked pasta. Toss to coat. Keep warm.

③ In a large skillet bring scallop mixture to boiling over medium-high heat. Boil gently, uncovered, for 3 to 4 minutes or until scallops are opaque, turning occasionally. Add scallop mixture to pasta mixture. Toss to coat. Heat through. Serve immediately.

PER SERVING 537 calories; 22 g total fat (1 g sat. fat); 40 mg cholesterol; 592 mg sodium; 54 g carbohydrate; 2 g fiber; 29 g protein

quick tip For large scallops, remove and discard the small piece of flesh attached to the scallop's edge. This is the muscle scallops use to open and close their shells—so it's a tough little muscle.

Mouthwatering meatless meals can be ready in a snap. These hearty vegetarian dinners will satisfy even diehard, steak-loving stalwarts.

139   140   147

MEATLESS MAIN DISHES

135

Fusilli with Greens and Romano Cheese

The broad, crisp leaves of escarole are milder than those of its sisters, Belgian endive and curly endive. If you're unable to find escarole, arugula leaves make a fine substitution.

MAKES 6 servings **START TO FINISH** 30 minutes

- 1 pound dried fusilli pasta
- 2 tablespoons olive oil
- 4 cups chopped onions (4 large)
- 1 large bunch escarole, coarsely chopped (about 14 ounces)
- 1 10-ounce package fresh spinach, coarsely chopped
- ½ teaspoon freshly ground black pepper
- ¼ teaspoon salt
- 2 cups shredded Romano cheese (8 ounces)

① Cook pasta according to package directions. Drain, reserving ⅓ cup of the cooking water. Return pasta and the reserved water to hot pan; cover and keep warm.

② Meanwhile, in a Dutch oven heat oil over medium-high heat. Add onions; cook about 10 minutes or until golden brown, stirring occasionally. Stir in escarole, spinach, pepper, and salt. Reduce heat to medium-low. Cook, covered, about 5 minutes or until greens are wilted and tender.

③ Stir cheese into cooked pasta. Add pasta mixture to greens mixture; stir to combine.

PER SERVING 489 calories; 13 g total fat (5 g sat. fat); 28 mg cholesterol; 473 mg sodium; 72 g carbohydrate; 6 g fiber; 21 g protein

quick tip Ignore instructions that tell you to clean mushrooms one by one with a soft brush rather than washing them in water. The idea that mushrooms will absorb water—and become soggy—when wet is a culinary myth. The flavorful fungi are already 92 percent water, and a thorough rinse won't hurt them at all.

Fettuccine Alfredo with Veggies

This recipe trims tons of fat and calories from the traditional cream-filled fettuccine Alfredo without sacrificing one bit of flavor.

MAKES 4 servings **START TO FINISH** 30 minutes

- 8 ounces dried fettuccine
- ½ cup dried tomatoes, snipped (not oil pack)
- 4 tablespoons butter
- 1 tablespoon olive oil
- 4 ounces asparagus spears, trimmed
- 4 ounces Brussels sprouts, trimmed and quartered
- 1½ cups broccoli florets
- 8 fresh mushrooms, sliced
- 2 tablespoons all-purpose flour
- 1¼ cups milk
- ½ cup finely shredded Parmesan cheese
  Milk (optional)
- 2 teaspoons finely shredded lemon peel
  Finely shredded Parmesan cheese

① Cook pasta according to package directions, adding dried tomatoes for the last 2 minutes of cooking. Drain and return to saucepan; keep warm.

② Meanwhile, in a large skillet heat 1 tablespoon of the butter and the olive oil over medium heat. Add asparagus, Brussels sprouts, broccoli, and mushrooms. Cook about 8 minutes or until vegetables are tender, stirring frequently. Remove vegetables from skillet; set aside.

③ In the same skillet melt the remaining 3 tablespoons butter over medium heat. Stir in flour. Cook and stir for 1 minute. Stir in the 1¼ cups milk. Cook and stir until thickened and bubbly. Stir in the ½ cup Parmesan cheese. Gently stir in cooked pasta and vegetables. If necessary, stir in additional milk to reach desired consistency. Sprinkle with lemon peel and additional Parmesan cheese.

PER SERVING 500 calories; 21 g total fat (11 g sat. fat); 46 mg cholesterol; 491 mg sodium; 60 g carbohydrate; 5 g fiber; 20 g protein

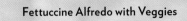

Noodle Bowls with Spinach and Tofu

Noodle Bowls with Spinach and Tofu

Thick and spicy hoisin sauce is made from a combination of soybeans, garlic, chile peppers, and spices.

MAKES 6 servings **START TO FINISH** 20 minutes

   Nonstick cooking spray
1 16-ounce package extra-firm or firm tofu (fresh bean curd), drained
⅔ cup hoisin sauce (7.25-ounce jar)
4 14.5-ounce cans chicken broth
1 tablespoon bottled minced roasted garlic
12 ounces dried udon noodles or linguine, broken
2 6-ounce packages fresh baby spinach
¼ cup chopped green onions (2)

① Preheat broiler. Lightly coat the unheated rack of a broiler pan with cooking spray. Cut tofu crosswise into 6 slices; pat dry with paper towels. Arrange tofu in a single layer on the prepared rack of the broiler pan; brush with 3 tablespoons of the hoisin sauce. Broil 4 to 6 inches from heat for 8 to 10 minutes or until hoisin is bubbly (do not turn slices).

② Meanwhile, in a 4- to 6-quart Dutch oven combine broth, roasted garlic, and the remaining hoisin sauce. Bring to boiling. Add noodles and cook according to package directions. Spoon noodle mixture over spinach. Divide mixture spinach among 4 large soup bowls.

③ Cut tofu into slices and place on noodle mixture. Sprinkle with green onions.

PER SERVING 340 calories; 6 g total fat (1 g sat. fat); 3 mg cholesterol; 1,573 mg sodium; 55 g carbohydrate; 4 g fiber; 16 g protein

Ravioli and Zucchini Skillet

Turn to this warm bowl of yumminess when you crave comfort food.

MAKES 4 servings **START TO FINISH** 20 minutes

1 14.5-ounce can Italian-style stewed tomatoes, undrained
½ cup water
2 medium zucchini and/or yellow summer squash, halved lengthwise and cut into ½-inch pieces (about 2½ cups)
1 9-ounce package refrigerated whole wheat four-cheese ravioli
1 15-ounce can cannellini beans (white kidney beans) or navy beans, rinsed and drained
2 tablespoons finely shredded or grated Parmesan cheese
2 tablespoons sliced fresh basil or parsley

① In an extra-large skillet combine tomatoes and the water. Bring to boiling. Stir in zucchini and ravioli. Return to boiling; reduce heat. Boil gently, covered, for 6 to 7 minutes or until ravioli are tender, stirring gently once or twice.

② Stir beans into ravioli mixture; heat through. Sprinkle with cheese and basil.

PER SERVING 305 calories; 8 g total fat (4 g sat. fat); 44 mg cholesterol; 986 mg sodium; 49 g carbohydrate; 11 g fiber; 18 g protein

Ravioli and Zucchini Skillet

Summer Pasta Your Way ♥

Not only does feta cheese boast a tangy-fresh taste, but it contains about 30 percent less calories and fat than other cheeses.

MAKES 4 servings **START TO FINISH** 25 minutes

- 10 ounces dried spinach or whole grain spaghetti
- 2 tablespoons sliced green onion (1)
- 1 tablespoon olive oil
- 1½ cups assorted summer vegetables, such as halved sugar snap peas, chopped eggplant, quartered and sliced zucchini or yellow summer squash, sliced mushrooms, chopped sweet pepper, cooked lima beans, sliced asparagus, and/or sliced carrot
- ¼ cup snipped oil-packed dried tomato
- 2 cups assorted cherry tomatoes, halved, or seeded and chopped tomatoes
- ½ cup dry white wine, chicken broth, or vegetable broth
- ¼ cup pitted kalamata olives, sliced (optional)
  Salt and black pepper
- ½ cup crumbled garlic-and-herb or plain feta cheese, crumbled goat cheese (chèvre), or chopped smoked Gouda cheese (2 ounces) or ¼ cup shredded Parmigiano-Reggiano cheese (1 ounce)
- 2 tablespoons snipped fresh basil

① In a Dutch oven cook spaghetti according to package directions; drain. Return spaghetti to hot Dutch oven; cover and keep warm.

② Meanwhile, in a large skillet cook green onion in hot oil over medium heat for 30 seconds. Stir in assorted vegetables and dried tomato. Cook, covered, for 5 minutes, stirring once. Stir in fresh tomatoes, wine, and, if desired, olives; cook for 30 seconds more.

③ Add tomato mixture to cooked spaghetti; toss gently to combine. Season to taste with salt and pepper. Sprinkle each serving with cheese and basil.

PER SERVING 399 calories; 9 g total fat (3 g sat. fat); 13 mg cholesterol; 356 mg sodium; 62 g carbohydrate; 10 g fiber; 14 g protein

Pasta Puttanesca ♥

Another way to infuse the rustic pasta with anchovies' intense salty taste is to opt for about a tablespoon of anchovy paste instead of chopping fillets. This product comes in a tube like toothpaste and is usually shelved near tins of anchovies in supermarkets.

MAKES 4 servings **START TO FINISH** 30 minutes

- 1 clove garlic, thinly sliced
- 2 tablespoons olive oil
- 2 cups peeled and chopped roma tomatoes (about 1 pound)
- ½ cup coarsely chopped pitted kalamata or ripe olives
- 4 to 5 anchovy fillets, chopped
- 1 teaspoon capers, drained and chopped
- ½ teaspoon black pepper
- ¼ to ½ teaspoon crushed red pepper
- 6 ounces dried thin spaghetti
- ¼ cup snipped fresh parsley

① For sauce, in a large skillet cook and stir garlic in hot oil over medium heat for 30 seconds. Stir in tomatoes, olives, anchovies, capers, black pepper, and crushed red pepper. Bring just to boiling; reduce heat. Simmer, uncovered, for 5 to 7 minutes or until slightly thickened, stirring occasionally.

② Meanwhile, cook spaghetti according to package directions; drain. Return spaghetti to hot pan; cover and keep warm. Transfer sauce to a serving bowl. Sprinkle with parsley. Serve with warm spaghetti.

PER SERVING 265 calories; 10 g total fat (1 g sat. fat); 3 mg cholesterol; 323 mg sodium; 37 g carbohydrate; 3 g fiber; 8 g protein

quick tip Feel free to omit the anchovies when preparing Pasta Puttanesca. Simply add ¼ to ½ teaspoon of salt to the sauce to make up for anchovies' natural salinity.

Greek Spinach-Pasta with Beans

Greek Spinach-Pasta with Beans ☕ ♥

If you are lucky enough to have any of this savory mixture left over, rejoice—you have tomorrow's appetizer in the bag. Simply spread a layer of the mixture on slices of toasted Italian bread, sprinkle with Parmesan, and broil until bubbly.

MAKES 6 servings **START TO FINISH** 30 minutes

- 12 ounces dried cavatappi or farfalle pasta (bow ties)
- 1 15-ounce can Great Northern beans, rinsed and drained
- 1 5- to 6-ounce package fresh baby spinach
- 1 cup crumbled feta cheese (4 ounces)
- ¼ cup dried tomatoes (not oil pack), snipped
- 2 green onions, chopped
- 2 cloves garlic, minced
- 1 teaspoon finely shredded lemon peel
- 2 tablespoons lemon juice
- 2 tablespoons olive oil
- 1 tablespoon snipped fresh oregano
- 1 tablespoon snipped fresh lemon thyme or regular thyme
- ½ teaspoon kosher salt or sea salt
- ½ teaspoon freshly ground black pepper
  Shaved Parmesan or Pecorino Romano cheese

① Cook pasta according to package directions. Meanwhile, in a large serving bowl combine beans, spinach, cheese, tomatoes, green onions, garlic, lemon peel, lemon juice, oil, oregano, thyme, salt, and pepper.

② Drain cooked pasta, reserving ¼ cup of the cooking water. Toss pasta and the reserved cooking water with the spinach mixture. Serve warm or at room temperature. Top with shaved Parmesan cheese.

PER SERVING 408 calories; 10 g total fat (4 g sat. fat); 19 mg cholesterol; 487 mg sodium; 62 g carbohydrate; 6 g fiber; 17 g protein

Ravioli with Garden Vegetables

To shred spinach easily, stack 10 or more leaves together, then slice across the stacked leaves at ¼-inch intervals.

MAKES 4 servings **START TO FINISH** 25 minutes

- 1 9-ounce package refrigerated cheese-filled ravioli or tortellini
- 2 cloves garlic, minced
- 2 teaspoons olive oil or vegetable oil
- 1¼ cups thinly sliced yellow summer squash (1 medium)
- 1 15-ounce can garbanzo beans (chickpeas), rinsed and drained
- 4 plum tomatoes, quartered
- 2 teaspoons snipped fresh thyme or ½ teaspoon dried thyme, crushed
- ¼ teaspoon black pepper
- 4 cups shredded fresh spinach
  Olive oil (optional)
  Grated Parmesan cheese (optional)

① Cook ravioli according to package directions.

② Meanwhile, in a large skillet cook and stir garlic in the 2 teaspoons hot oil for 30 seconds. Add squash, garbanzo beans, tomatoes, thyme, and pepper. Cook and stir over medium-high heat for 4 to 5 minutes or until squash is crisp-tender and mixture is heated through.

③ Drain ravioli; add to vegetable mixture. Toss lightly. Arrange spinach on 4 serving plates; top with ravioli mixture. If desired, drizzle with a little additional olive oil and sprinkle with Parmesan cheese.

PER SERVING 304 calories; 7 g total fat (2 g sat. fat); 25 mg cholesterol; 688 mg sodium; 48 g carbohydrate; 7 g fiber; 15 g protein

Rice and Bean Tostadas

This Mexican-style recipe provides a great way to introduce whole grain brown rice into your family's diet.

MAKES 4 servings **START TO FINISH** 30 minutes
OVEN 350°F

- 1 cup water
- 1 cup quick-cooking brown rice
- ½ cup chopped onion (1 medium)
- 1 15-ounce can chili beans with chili gravy, undrained
- 1 8.75-ounce can whole kernel corn, drained
- 8 tostada shells
- 3 cups shredded lettuce
- ½ cup shredded cheddar cheese (2 ounces)
- 1 cup quartered cherry tomatoes
  Salsa

① Preheat oven to 350°F. In a large saucepan bring the water to boiling. Stir in rice and onion. Return to boiling; reduce heat. Simmer, covered, for 5 minutes. Remove from heat. Stir. Cover and let stand for 5 minutes. Stir chili beans and corn into rice mixture. Heat through.

② Meanwhile, place tostada shells on a baking sheet. Bake about 5 minutes or until warm.

③ To assemble, place 2 of the tostada shells on each dinner plate. Top tostadas with shredded lettuce and the rice-bean mixture. Sprinkle with cheese; top with tomatoes and salsa.

PER SERVING 417 calories; 14 g total fat (4 g sat. fat); 15 mg cholesterol; 816 mg sodium; 63 g carbohydrate; 12 g fiber; 15 g protein

Rice and Sweet Pepper Bowl

Good recipes always instruct cooks to cut away peppers' inner, fleshy white membranes because that part of the vegetable is a bit bitter.

MAKES 4 servings **START TO FINISH** 30 minutes

- 4 medium green and/or red sweet peppers
- 2 tablespoons water
- 1 8.8-ounce pouch cooked Spanish-style rice
- 1 14.5-ounce can stewed tomatoes
- 4 1-ounce slices Monterey Jack cheese with jalapeño peppers
- 1 ounce Parmesan cheese, shaved
  Fresh oregano sprigs (optional)
- 1 tablespoon olive oil

① Quarter peppers; remove stems, seeds, and membranes. Place in a 2-quart square baking dish. Add the water. Cover with parchment paper. Microwave on high for 4 to 6 minutes or until crisp-tender, turning dish once halfway through cooking. Using tongs, remove peppers from dish; discard water. Set peppers aside.

② Microwave rice according to package directions. Drain tomatoes, reserving 2 tablespoons of the liquid. In the 2-quart square baking dish layer half of the peppers, cut sides up; the rice; drained tomatoes; Monterey Jack cheese; and the remaining peppers, cut sides down. Drizzle with reserved tomato liquid.

③ Cover with parchment paper. Microwave on high for 5 to 6 minutes or until heated through, turning dish once halfway through cooking. Let stand for 5 minutes.

④ To serve, spoon peppers into shallow bowls. Top with Parmesan cheese and, if desired, oregano. Drizzle with olive oil.

PER SERVING 319 calories; 16 g total fat (8 g sat. fat); 36 mg cholesterol; 733 mg sodium; 31 g carbohydrate; 3 g fiber; 14 g protein

 Latin flavors—even in small quantities—jazz up weeknight dinners in a big way.

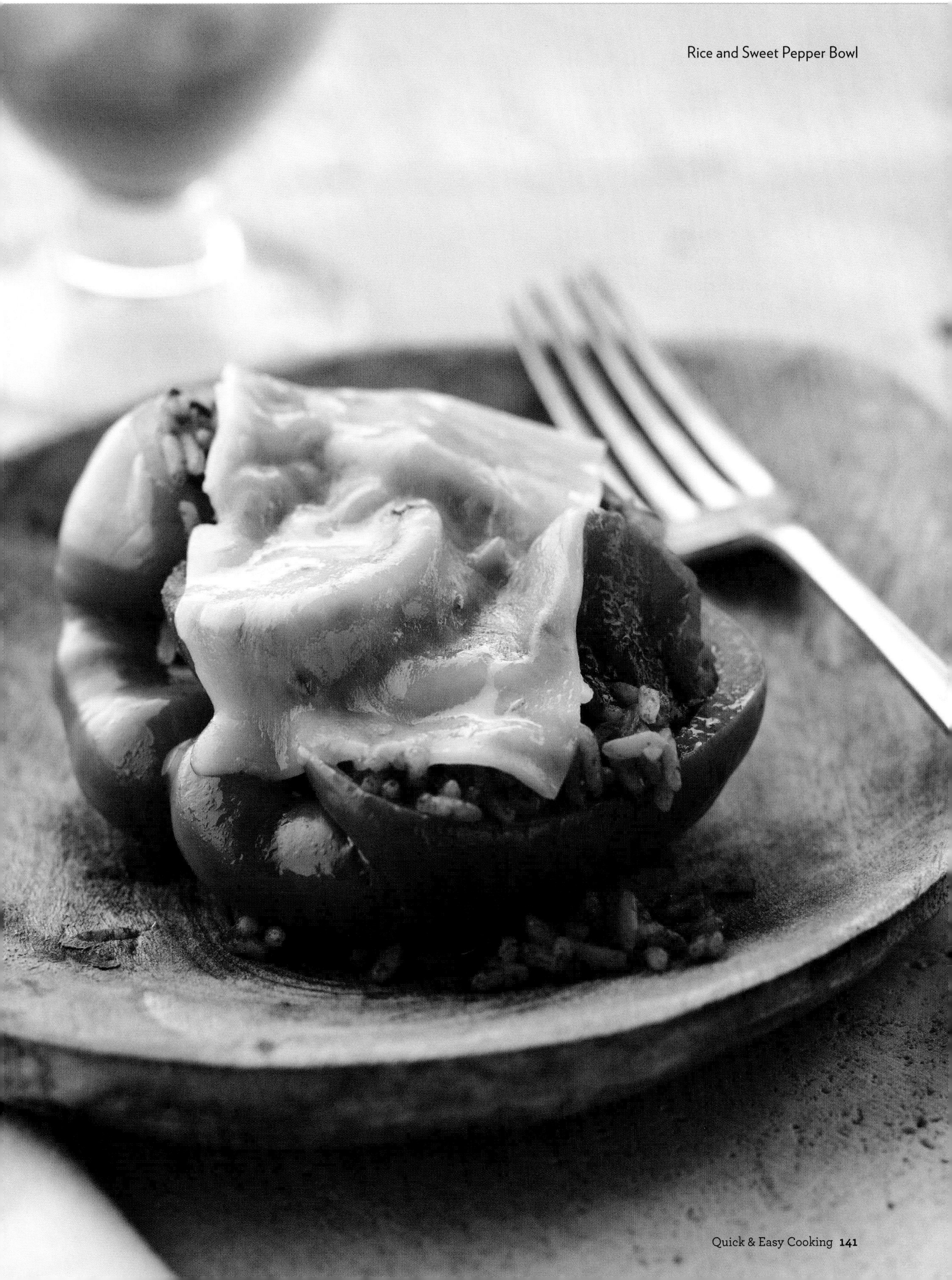

Rice and Sweet Pepper Bowl

Herbed Garden Couscous

Herbed Garden Couscous ♥

To toast walnuts quickly and easily, place nuts in a skillet over medium heat. Shake skillet back and forth just until nuts become fragrant. Remove from heat at once and cool before adding to couscous.

MAKES 6 servings **START TO FINISH** 30 minutes

- 1 cup whole wheat couscous
- 2 cups cherry tomatoes, halved
- 1½ cups coarsely chopped cucumber (1 medium)
- ¾ cup chopped green sweet pepper (1 medium)
- ½ cup snipped fresh chives
- ¼ cup snipped fresh parsley
- ¼ cup snipped fresh mint
- ¼ cup snipped fresh oregano
- ⅓ cup balsamic vinegar
- ⅓ cup olive oil
- 2 teaspoons sugar
- ½ teaspoon salt
- ¼ teaspoon black pepper
- ½ cup crumbled feta cheese (2 ounces)
- ½ cup coarsely chopped walnuts, toasted

① Cook couscous according to package directions. Fluff with a fork.

② Meanwhile, in a large bowl combine tomatoes, cucumber, sweet pepper, chives, parsley, mint, and oregano. Fold in couscous.

③ In a small bowl whisk together vinegar, oil, sugar, salt, and black pepper. Pour over couscous mixture; toss to combine. To serve, top with feta cheese and walnuts.

PER SERVING 392 calories; 12 g total fat (4 g sat. fat); 12 mg cholesterol; 344 mg sodium; 42 g carbohydrate; 6 g fiber; 10 g protein

quick tip If you like, skip the bowl and whisk method of mixing vinaigrette dressings. Opt instead for the shaker technique—just combine dressing ingredients in a jar with a tight-fitting lid, shake, and pour.

Quinoa Toss with Chickpeas and Herbs

Quinoa has more protein than any other grain. Delicate and as bland as couscous, it is a highly nutritious grain that readily absorbs the flavors of the ingredients it is cooked with.

MAKES 6 servings **START TO FINISH** 30 minutes

- 1 cup quinoa
- 2 cups chicken broth or vegetable broth
- ¼ cup olive oil
- 2 tablespoons lemon juice
- ½ teaspoon salt
- ½ teaspoon black pepper
- 1 15-ounce can garbanzo beans (chickpeas), rinsed and drained
- 1 cup frozen corn, thawed
- ½ cup crumbled feta cheese (2 ounces)
- ¼ cup finely chopped sweet onion, such as Vidalia or Maui Maui
- 3 tablespoons snipped fresh basil
- 2 tablespoons snipped fresh parsley
- 1 cup canned diced beets, drained
  Romaine leaves

① Rinse quinoa in a fine-mesh sieve under cold running water; drain. In a medium saucepan bring broth to boiling. Add quinoa. Return to boiling; reduce heat. Simmer, covered, about 15 minutes or until broth is absorbed. Remove from heat; set aside to cool.

② Meanwhile, for dressing, in a small bowl whisk together oil, lemon juice, salt, and pepper. In a large bowl combine cooked quinoa, garbanzo beans, corn, cheese, onion, basil, and parsley. Add dressing to quinoa mixture; toss to coat.

③ Stir in beets. Serve warm in romaine-lined bowls.

PER SERVING 349 calories; 14 g total fat (3 g sat. fat); 9 mg cholesterol; 918 mg sodium; 46 g carbohydrate; 8 g fiber; 12 g protein

Sweet Potato and Chickpea Coconut Curry

Because coconut milk naturally separates, be sure to give the can a vigorous shaking before adding its liquid to your curry.

MAKES 4 servings **START TO FINISH** 30 minutes

½	cup chopped onion
½	cup chopped red sweet pepper
1	tablespoon olive oil
2	cups peeled and cubed sweet potatoes
1	16-ounce can garbanzo beans (chickpeas), drained
1	tablespoon curry powder
1	teaspoon ground cumin
½	teaspoon salt
¼	teaspoon ground cinnamon
1	14.5-ounce can vegetable broth or chicken broth
⅓	cup canned coconut milk
2	cups hot cooked rice or couscous
	Snipped fresh cilantro
	Lime wedges

① In a large saucepan cook onion and sweet pepper in hot oil over medium heat for 5 to 7 minutes or until tender and lightly browned, stirring occasionally. Add sweet potato pieces, beans, curry powder, cumin, salt, and cinnamon. Cook 5 minutes more, stirring occasionally.

② Add broth and coconut milk. Bring to boiling; reduce heat. Simmer, uncovered, for 8 to 10 minutes or until potato pieces are tender. Serve over rice. Garnish with cilantro and serve with lime wedges.

PER SERVING 337 calories; 10 g total fat (1 g sat. fat); 1 mg cholesterol; 1,134 mg sodium; 59 g carbohydrate; 7 g fiber; 11 g protein

Sweet Potato Hash ♥

To determine when an avocado is perfectly ripe, try this test. Press on your forehead. If the avocado is as hard as your forehead, it is not ripe enough. Press on your cheek. If your avocado feels like your cheek, it is too soft. Press on your nose. A perfect avocado will feel just like your nose.

MAKES 4 servings **START TO FINISH** 25 minutes

1	large or 2 small sweet potatoes, peeled and quartered (about 1 pound)
	Salt
1	tablespoon vegetable oil
1	11-ounce can Southwestern-style corn with black beans and peppers, rinsed and drained
½	cup sour cream
2	tablespoons chipotle salsa
3	medium avocados, peeled, seeded, and sliced
	Fresh cilantro leaves and chili powder (optional)

① Place sweet potatoes in a microwave-safe dish; cover and cook on high for 5 to 8 minutes or just until tender enough to chop. Cool slightly; cut into chunks. Sprinkle lightly with salt.

② In a large skillet heat oil over medium heat. Add potatoes; cook until browned and crisp-tender, about 3 minutes. Add drained corn to skillet. Cook 3 minutes or until potatoes are tender.

③ Meanwhile, stir together sour cream and chipotle salsa.

④ To serve, divide sweet potato mixture among 4 shallow bowls. Top with avocado slices and serve with chipotle sour cream sauce. If desired, sprinkle with cilantro and chili powder.

PER SERVING 246 calories; 13 g total fat (4 g sat. fat); 12 mg cholesterol; 463 mg sodium; 29 g carbohydrate; 5 g fiber; 4 g protein

❮ Enticing flavor, uplifting color, and over-the-top nutrition—sweet potatoes deliver it all. ❯

Chickpea Salad with Grilled Pita

Chickpea Salad with Grilled Pita

If packaged pita loaves feel a bit dry or brittle, brush them lightly with water before grilling—the bit of steam created will make the bread taste fresh again.

MAKES 4 servings **START TO FINISH** 15 minutes

- 2 15-ounce cans no-salt-added garbanzo beans (chickpeas) or regular garbanzo beans, rinsed and drained
- 6 plum tomatoes, sliced
- 4 ounces crumbled feta cheese with tomato and basil
- ¼ cup lightly packed small fresh mint leaves
- ⅓ cup white vinegar
- ¼ cup olive oil
- 1 tablespoon sugar
- ½ teaspoon black pepper
- 1 to 2 pita bread rounds

① For salad, in a large bowl combine beans, tomatoes, feta, and mint. In a screw-top jar combine vinegar, oil, sugar, and pepper; shake to combine. Pour over salad mixture; set aside.

② Grill pita rounds on an indoor or outdoor grill over medium heat until warm and toasted. Cut into wedges. Serve pita wedges with salad.

PER SERVING 454 calories; 22 g total fat 21 mg cholesterol; 878 mg sodium; 49 g carbohydrate; 10 g fiber; 17 g protein

Beets and Greens with Cheesy Baguette Bites

Beets and Greens with Cheesy Baguette Bites

Always wear an apron when working with ruby-color beets—this root vegetable's juices really do stain clothing.

MAKES 4 servings **START TO FINISH** 30 minutes

- 6 small golden and/or red beets
- ½ cup cider vinegar
- 2 tablespoons sugar
- 2 tablespoons water
- 1 small baguette, diagonally sliced
- 4 ounces semisoft cheese with garlic and herb
- ¼ cup olive oil
- ½ teaspoon salt
- ½ teaspoon black pepper
- 8 cups mixed salad greens
- ⅓ cup dried cranberries
  Shelled roasted pumpkin seeds (optional)

① Place whole beets (greens trimmed) in a 1-quart microwave-safe casserole dish; add vinegar, sugar, and the water. Microwave, covered, on high for 9 to 12 minutes or until tender, stirring once. Trim stems and slip off skins. Slice beets; reserve cooking liquid.

② While beets are in microwave, preheat broiler. Spread baguette slices with cheese. Broil 4 inches from heat about 3 minutes or until cheese is melted and bread edges are toasted; set aside.

③ For dressing, add oil, salt, and pepper to reserved beet cooking liquid; whisk to combine. In a serving bowl combine beets, salad greens, and cranberries. Add dressing; toss to coat. Sprinkle with pumpkin seeds, if desired. Serve with toast.

PER SERVING 581 calories; 24 g total fat (8 g sat. fat); 22 mg cholesterol; 1,070 mg sodium; 74 g carbohydrate; 6 g fiber; 19 g protein

Portobello Fajitas

Grill-cooked mushrooms and sweet peppers give fajitas a remarkably authentic taste.

MAKES 4 servings **START TO FINISH** 30 minutes

- 2 tablespoons olive oil
- ¼ teaspoon salt
- ¼ teaspoon black pepper
- 3 medium portobello mushrooms
- 1 red or yellow sweet pepper, seeded and quartered
- 8 6- to 7-inch flour tortillas
- 2 medium avocados, halved, seeded, and peeled
- ¼ cup light mayonnaise or salad dressing
- 1 teaspoon chili powder
  Salt
  Black pepper
  Salsa verde (optional)
  Fresh cilantro sprigs (optional)
  Lime wedges (optional)

① In a small bowl combine oil, the ¼ teaspoon salt, and the ¼ teaspoon black pepper. Brush mushrooms and sweet pepper with the oil mixture. Stack tortillas and wrap in foil.

② For a charcoal grill, place mushrooms, pepper quarters, and foil packet on the rack of an uncovered grill directly over medium coals. Grill for 8 to 10 minutes or until mushrooms and pepper quarters are tender, turning once halfway through grilling. (For a gas grill, preheat grill. Reduce heat to medium. Place mushrooms, pepper quarters, and foil packet on grill rack over heat. Cover and grill as above.)

③ Slice mushrooms and sweet pepper into strips. In a medium bowl use a fork to mash 1 of the avocados; stir in mayonnaise and chili powder. Season to taste with salt and black pepper. Slice the remaining avocado. Serve mushrooms, sweet pepper, and sliced avocado on tortillas. Top with mayonnaise mixture. If desired, serve with salsa verde, cilantro, and lime wedges.

PER SERVING 479 calories; 30 g total fat (3 g sat. fat); 5 mg cholesterol; 401 mg sodium; 40 g carbohydrate; 7 g fiber; 10 g protein

Herbed Frittata with Edamame

Pretty protein-packed pearls of edamame dot this open-face omelet with vibrant green color.

MAKES 4 servings **START TO FINISH** 20 minutes

- 8 eggs
- ⅓ cup water
- 2 finely chopped green onions (¼ cup)
- ¼ cup snipped fresh cilantro
- ¼ teaspoon salt
- ¼ teaspoon black pepper
- 1 tablespoon olive oil
- 1 cup shredded Italian cheese blend (4 ounces)
- 1 medium carrot, cut into ribbons or coarsely shredded
- 1 cup frozen shelled sweet soybeans (edamame), thawed
  Shaved Parmesan cheese (optional)
  Fresh cilantro sprigs (optional)

① Preheat broiler. In a medium bowl whisk together eggs, the water, green onions, the snipped cilantro, salt, and pepper; set aside.

② In an extra-large broiler-proof skillet with flared sides heat oil over medium heat. Add egg mixture. Lift edges of egg mixture as it sets, allowing uncooked mixture to flow underneath. When edges begin to set (top is soft but not runny), place eggs under broiler 3 to 4 inches from heat. Broil about 1 minute or just until set. Top with cheese blend; broil just until cheese is melted.

③ Cut frittata into 12 wedges. Stack 3 wedges on each of 4 plates; top each with some of the carrot and soybeans. If desired, garnish with Parmesan cheese and cilantro sprigs.

PER SERVING 306 calories; 22 g total fat (8 g sat. fat); 443 mg cholesterol; 482 mg sodium; 6 g carbohydrate; 2 g fiber; 23 g protein

Farmer's Market Grilled Cheese

Farmer's Market Grilled Cheese

Take a clue from this sandwich's name and make it the first meal you prepare with the fresh vegetables you toted home from the farmer's market.

MAKES 4 servings **START TO FINISH** 30 minutes

- ¼ cup mayonnaise
- 2 cups baby spinach
- 1 teaspoon minced garlic
- ¼ teaspoon salt
- ¼ teaspoon black pepper
- 8 ½-inch-thick slices sourdough bread
- 2 tablespoons olive oil
- ½ of a 3.5 to 4-ounce package garlic-and-herb goat cheese, softened
- 1 small zucchini, thinly sliced lengthwise
- 1 tomato, sliced

① In blender or food processor combine mayonnaise, 1 cup of the spinach, the garlic, salt, and black pepper. Set aside.

② Brush 1 side of each bread slice with oil; place, oiled sides down, on waxed paper. Spread goat cheese on half the slices; layer zucchini, tomato, and remaining spinach. Spread some of the spinach mayonnaise on remaining slices; place on the vegetables, spread sides down.

③ Cook sandwiches in a very large skillet over medium-high heat for 6 to 8 minutes or until bread is golden brown, turning once. Pass any remaining spinach mayonnaise.

PER SERVING 369 calories; 22 g total fat (6 g sat. fat); 15 mg cholesterol; 636 mg sodium; 32 g carbohydrate; 3 g fiber; 10 g protein

quick tip Opt for baby spinach any time a recipe calls for the healthful green. Unlike grown-up spinach, whose fibrous stems often need to be removed, the stems of baby spinach are young, tender to the bite, and ready to toss into any recipe.

Veggie Frittata

Frittatas—or open-face-omelets—provide a fabulously filling supper at a bargain price.

MAKES 4 servings **START TO FINISH** 30 minutes

- ⅓ cup dried orzo pasta (rosamarina)
- 2 medium red, yellow, and/or orange sweet peppers, seeded and chopped
- 2 tablespoons olive oil
- 8 eggs
- ¼ cup milk
- ½ cup chopped pitted ripe olives
- ¼ cup snipped fresh basil
- ¼ teaspoon salt
- ¼ teaspoon black pepper
- 2 tablespoons shredded Parmesan cheese

① Preheat broiler. In a large saucepan cook pasta in boiling lightly salted water according to package directions; drain. Meanwhile, in a large oven-going skillet cook chopped sweet peppers in hot oil over medium-high heat until tender. Stir in cooked pasta.

② In a large bowl beat together eggs and milk. Stir in olives, basil, salt, and black pepper. Pour over vegetable mixture in skillet. Cook over medium heat. As mixture sets, run a spatula around the skillet edge, lifting egg mixture so uncooked portion flows underneath. Continue cooking and lifting edges until egg mixture is almost set. Reduce heat as necessary to prevent overcooking.

③ Place skillet under the broiler 4 to 5 inches from heat. Broil about 3 minutes or until top is set. Sprinkle with cheese. Cover and let stand for 5 minutes. Cut into wedges to serve.

PER SERVING 319 calories; 20 g total fat (5 g sat. fat); 426 mg cholesterol; 525 mg sodium; 17 g carbohydrate; 3 g fiber; 17 g protein

Leave those fussy, simmered-all-day soups and stews to your grandmother. This time-trimming collection of beautiful bowl-foods will fit perfectly into your busy life.

157

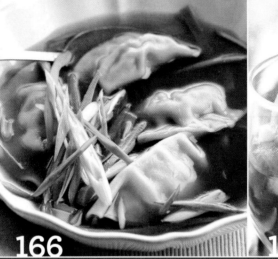

166

169

SOUPS & STEWS

157

Beef Stew and Garlic Mash

If you'd prefer, add 2 teaspoons of dried oregano to the cooking vegetables and garnish the dish with freshly chopped parsley instead.

MAKES 4 servings **START TO FINISH** 25 minutes

- 1 1-pound bag frozen assorted vegetable blend (carrots, peas, and onions)
- ½ cup water
- 1 17-ounce package refrigerated cooked beef tips in gravy
- 2 teaspoons Worcestershire sauce
- 6 cloves garlic
- 2 tablespoons garlic
- 1 pound Yukon gold or red potatoes, halved
- 2 tablespoons olive oil
- ¼ teaspoon salt
- ¼ teaspoon freshly ground black pepper
- 2 tablespoons fresh oregano leaves

① In 4-quart Dutch oven combine vegetables and the ½ cup water. Bring to boiling over medium heat. Meanwhile, microwave beef tips according to package directions. Add beef and Worcestershire to vegetables. Reduce heat to low. Cook, covered, for 5 minutes or until vegetables are tender.

② In small microwave-safe bowl cover garlic and the 2 tablespoons water with vented plastic wrap. Microwave on high 1 minute; set aside. In large microwave-safe bowl microwave potatoes on high 8 to 10 minutes; stirring once halfway through.

③ Peel and mash garlic. Add garlic, olive oil, salt, and pepper to potatoes; mash. Divide among 4 dishes. Ladle stew over potatoes; sprinkle with oregano.

PER SERVING 368 calories; 14 g total fat (3 g sat. fat); 47 mg cholesterol; 888 mg sodium; 42 g carbohydrate; 8 g fiber; 24 g protein

Basil, Beef, and Barley Soup

Barley has a stick-to-the-ribs quality that makes this savory soup a great winter warmup.

MAKES 4 servings **START TO FINISH** 30 minutes

- 1 pound boneless sirloin steak
- ¼ cup all-purpose flour
- 1 tablespoon dried basil, crushed
- ½ teaspoon salt
- 1 teaspoon black pepper
- 1 tablespoon vegetable oil
- 1 cup quick-cooking barley
- 1 14.5-ounce can diced tomatoes with basil, garlic, and oregano, undrained
- 1 cup packaged peeled fresh baby carrots, bias-sliced
- 1 cup lower-sodium beef broth
- 3 cups water
  Small fresh basil leaves (optional)

① Cut steak into ½-inch pieces. In a shallow dish combine flour, dried basil, salt, and pepper Add meat; toss to coat.

② In a 4- to 5-quart Dutch oven heat oil over medium-high heat. Add meat; cook until browned on all sides. Stir in any remaining flour mixture. Stir in barley, undrained tomatoes, carrots, beef broth, and the water. Bring to boiling; reduce heat. Cover and simmer 10 minutes.

③ Ladle into bowls and top with fresh basil, if desired.

PER SERVING 506 calories; 19 g total fat (6 g sat. fat); 53 mg cholesterol; 1,014 mg sodium; 55 g carbohydrate; 7 g fiber; 31 g protein

❰ Grab a bigger pot and prepare a double batch—soups and stews freeze beautifully. ❱

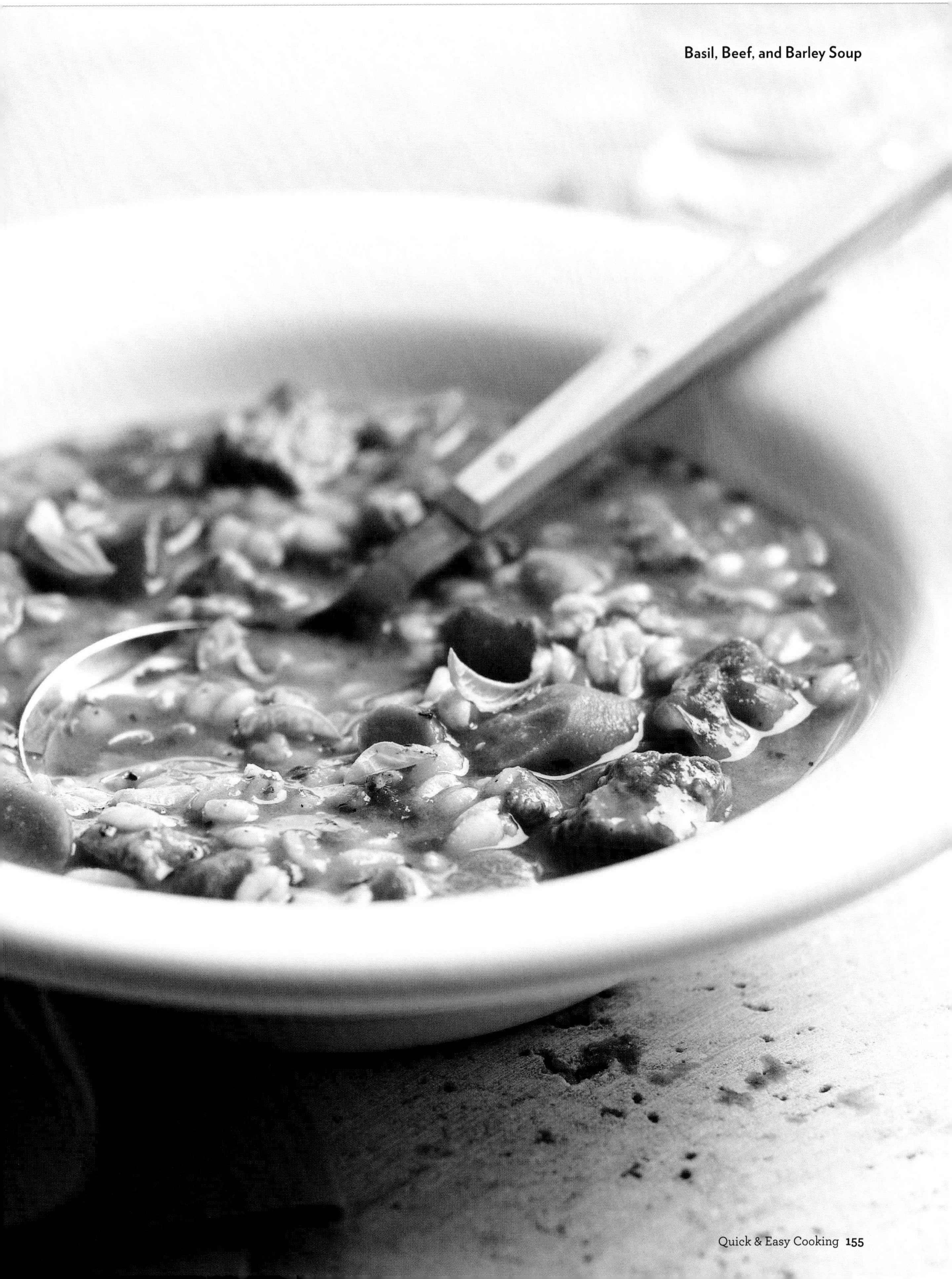
Basil, Beef, and Barley Soup

Meatball Soup with Tiny Pasta

Meatball Soup with Tiny Pasta

Frozen cooked meatballs are one of the best convenience products to hit the market in recent years. They put seemingly labor-intensive soups—like this one—on the table in less than 30 minutes.

MAKES 4 servings   **START TO FINISH** 25 minutes

- 1   14.5-ounce can diced tomatoes with onion and garlic, undrained
- 1   14.5-ounce can beef broth
- 1½   cups water
- ½   teaspoon dried Italian seasoning, crushed
- ½   of a 16-ounce package frozen cooked Italian-style meatballs
- 1   cup loose-pack frozen Italian blend vegetables (zucchini, carrots, cauliflower, lima beans, and Italian beans) or desired frozen mixed vegetables
- ½   cup small dried pasta (such as tripolini, farfallini, ditalini, stellini, or orzo)
- 2   tablespoons finely shredded or grated Parmesan cheese

① In a large saucepan stir together undrained tomatoes, beef broth, the water, and Italian seasoning; bring to boiling.

② Add meatballs, frozen vegetables, and uncooked pasta. Return to boiling; reduce heat. Simmer, covered, about 10 minutes or until pasta and vegetables are tender. Sprinkle with Parmesan cheese.

PER SERVING 280 calories; 14 g total fat (6 g sat. fat); 38 mg cholesterol; 1,335 mg sodium; 23 g carbohydrate; 4 g fiber; 15 g protein

quick tip   During the week pop odds and ends of uneaten veggies in your freezer—they'll make a tasty, no-cost addition to vegetable soups.

Beefy Vegetable Soup

Consider making a double batch of this family favorite on some rainy weekend day—it freezes wonderfully, and you'll love having a stash of this good stuff at your fingertips.

MAKES 6 servings   **START TO FINISH** 30 minutes

- 1½   pounds ground beef sirloin
- 1   cup chopped onion (1 large)
- 1   cup sliced celery (2 stalks)
- 2   14.5-ounce cans lower-sodium beef broth
- 1   28-ounce can diced tomatoes, undrained
- 1   10-ounce package frozen mixed vegetables
- 2   tablespoons steak sauce
- 2   teaspoons Worcestershire sauce
- ¼   teaspoon salt
- ¼   teaspoon black pepper
- ¼   cup all-purpose flour
     Snipped fresh parsley

① In a 4-quart Dutch oven cook ground beef, onion, and celery over medium heat until meat is brown. Drain off fat.

② Stir in 1 can of the broth, the tomatoes, frozen vegetables, steak sauce, Worcestershire sauce, salt, and pepper. Bring to boiling; reduce heat. Simmer, covered, for 15 to 20 minutes or until vegetables are tender.

③ In a medium bowl whisk together the remaining can of broth and flour; stir into meat mixture. Cook and stir until thickened and bubbly. Sprinkle with snipped fresh parsley.

PER SERVING 306 calories; 12 g total fat (5 g sat. fat); 74 mg cholesterol; 747 mg sodium; 21 g carbohydrate; 4 g fiber; 27 g protein

Beefy Vegetable Soup

Tortellini Meatball Soup

Refrigerated pasta products are a boon to busy cooks. Unlike dry pasta, which takes at least 10 minutes to cook, these tender bites are ready in just a few minutes.

MAKES 4 to 6 servings **START TO FINISH** 30 minutes

- 1 cup chopped sweet onion (1 large)
- 1 cup coarsely chopped carrots (2 medium)
- 3 cloves garlic, minced
- 1 tablespoon olive oil or vegetable oil
- 1 32-ounce carton reduced-sodium or regular chicken or beef broth
- ½ cup water
- 1 9-ounce package refrigerated 4-cheese tortellini
- ½ of a 16-ounce package frozen cooked Italian-style meatballs (16)
- 1 teaspoon dried Italian seasoning, crushed
- 3 cups chopped fresh spinach or half of a 10-ounce package frozen chopped spinach, thawed and drained
- 3 tablespoons chopped roasted red sweet pepper
- 1 tablespoon lemon juice (optional)
  Salt and black pepper
- 1 tablespoon snipped fresh basil

① In a Dutch oven cook onion, carrots, and garlic in hot oil over medium heat for 3 minutes, stirring occasionally. Add broth and the water. Bring to boiling. Stir in tortellini, meatballs, and Italian seasoning. Return to boiling; reduce heat. Simmer, uncovered, for 4 minutes.

② Stir in spinach, roasted pepper, and, if desired, lemon juice. Simmer, uncovered, about 3 minutes more or until tortellini are tender. Season to taste with salt and black pepper. Before serving, stir in basil.

PER SERVING 461 calories; 23 g total fat (9 g sat. fat); 68 mg cholesterol; 1,443 mg sodium; 44 g carbohydrate; 5 g fiber; 22 g protein

Green Chile Pork Stew

Although optional, wedges of fresh lime really add spark and zest to this soup.

MAKES 4 servings **START TO FINISH** 30 minutes

- 1 pound pork tenderloin
  Salt and black pepper
- 1 tablespoon olive oil
- 3 7-ounce packages frozen yellow carrots, spinach. and white bean medley in garlic herb sauce, thawed
- 1 4.5-ounce can diced green chiles
- 1 teaspoon ground cumin
- 1 cup water
  Fresh cilantro
  Lime wedges

① Cut pork into ¾-inch pieces; sprinkle lightly with salt and pepper. In a Dutch oven heat olive oil over medium-high heat. Add pork; cook 4 to 5 minutes or until browned. Stir in 2 packages of the thawed vegetables, the chiles, and the cumin.

② In a blender combine remaining thawed vegetables and the water. Process until smooth. Add pureed vegetables to Dutch oven. Bring to a simmer. Cook, covered, over medium heat about 15 minutes or until pork is cooked through, stirring occasionally. Ladle into soup bowls. Top with cilantro and a squeeze of lime juice.

PER SERVING 297 calories; 11 g total fat (2 g sat. fat); 74 mg cholesterol; 823 mg sodium; 21 g carbohydrate; 7 g fiber; 30 g protein

《 A squeeze of zesty fresh lime brightens this simple version of chile verde. 》

Mexican-Style Chicken Soup

Mexican-Style Chicken Soup

You may obtain the chopped cooked chicken for this recipe in one of three ways. Buying ready-to-go packaged chopped chicken and chopping chicken pulled from a deli-roasted bird is quicker—but you may also grill or broil chicken breasts while the soup simmers.

MAKES 6 servings **START TO FINISH** 30 minutes

- 1   32-ounce carton reduced-sodium chicken broth
- 1   15.5-ounce can golden hominy, rinsed and drained
- 1   15-ounce can black beans, rinsed and drained
- 1   green sweet pepper, seeded and cut into strips
- 1   cup salsa
- 1   4-ounce can diced green chile peppers, undrained
- 1   tablespoon chili powder
- 1   teaspoon ground cumin
- 2½ cups chopped cooked chicken (12 ounces)
     Snipped fresh herbs (optional)

① In a 4-quart Dutch oven combine broth, hominy, black beans, green pepper, salsa, chile peppers, chili powder, and cumin. Bring to boiling; reduce heat. Simmer, covered, for 20 minutes.

② Add chicken and heat through. If desired, sprinkle with fresh herbs.

PER SERVING 240 calories; 6 g total fat (1 g sat. fat); 52 mg cholesterol; 1,060 mg sodium; 25 g carbohydrate; 7 g fiber; 25 g protein

quick tip Although rinsing and draining canned beans seems like an unnecessary step, it is a good idea to do so— the process removes excess salt and carbohydrate that might make your soup or stew cook cloudy.

Southwestern White Chili

White chili is a delicious alternative to traditional, tomato-base chili.

MAKES 8 servings **START TO FINISH** 30 minutes

- 1   cup chopped onion (1 large)
- 4   cloves garlic, minced
- 1   tablespoon olive oil
- 2   teaspoons ground cumin
- 1   teaspoon dried oregano, crushed
- ¼   teaspoon cayenne pepper
- 3   15-ounce cans Great Northern beans, rinsed and drained
- 4   cups chicken broth or reduced-sodium chicken broth
- 2   4-ounce cans diced green chile peppers or jalapeños, undrained
- 3   cups chopped cooked chicken (about 1 pound)
- 2   cups shredded Monterey Jack cheese (8 ounces)
     Sour cream (optional)
     Canned diced green chile peppers or jalapeños (optional)

① In a large Dutch cook onion and garlic in hot oil over medium heat until onion is tender, stirring occasionally. Stir in cumin, oregano, and cayenne pepper. Cook and stir for 2 minutes more.

② Add 1 can of the beans; mash with a potato masher or fork. Stir in the remaining beans, broth, and the 2 cans chile peppers. Bring to boiling; reduce heat. Simmer, uncovered, for 5 minutes. Stir in chicken; heat through.

③ Top each serving with ¼ cup of the cheese. If desired, top with sour cream and additional chile peppers.

PER SERVING 471 calories; 16 g total fat (7 g sat. fat); 76 mg cholesterol; 468 mg sodium; 43 g carbohydrate; 9 g fiber; 38 g protein

Tortellini Florentine Soup

Recipes with the word "Florentine" in their titles may be fashioned according to the cooking style of Italy's beautiful city of Florence—or they may contain spinach, which is a favored ingredient in Florentine cooking.

MAKES 6 servings **START TO FINISH** 30 minutes

1   9-ounce package refrigerated 3-cheese tortellini

2   14.5-ounce cans reduced-sodium chicken broth

1   10-ounce container refrigerated light Alfredo pasta sauce

2   cups shredded purchased roasted chicken

½   cup oil-pack dried tomato strips, drained

½   of a 5-ounce package (about 3 cups) fresh baby spinach

Shaved or shredded Parmesan cheese (optional)

① In a 4-quart Dutch oven cook tortellini according to package directions; drain in a colander. Set aside.

② In the same Dutch oven combine broth and pasta sauce. Stir in chicken and dried tomatoes. Bring just to boiling; reduce heat. Simmer, uncovered, for 5 minutes.

③ Stir in cooked tortellini and spinach. Cook for 1 to 2 minutes or just until tortellini is heated through and spinach is wilted. If desired, top each serving with cheese.

PER SERVING 286 calories; 15 g total fat (6 g sat. fat); 77 mg cholesterol; 1,094 mg sodium; 21 g carbohydrate; 1 g fiber; 20 g protein

Tortellini Florentine Soup

Soba Noodle Bowl

Freeze chicken breasts for about 20 minutes before slicing—when frozen, they will slice super thinly.

MAKES 4 servings **START TO FINISH** 25 minutes

2   14.5-ounce cans reduced-sodium chicken broth

1   cup water

12 ounces skinless, boneless chicken breast halves, cut into very thin slices

6   ounces soba (buckwheat noodles)

1   cup thinly sliced carrots (2 medium)

2   tablespoons reduced-sodium soy sauce

1   fresh red or green jalapeño, thinly sliced and seeded (see quick tip, page 28)

8   ounces fresh sugar snap pea pods, halved if desired

Crushed red pepper (optional)

Snipped fresh parsley (optional)

① In a large saucepan combine broth and the water. Bring to boiling. Stir in chicken, soba, carrots, soy sauce, and jalapeño pepper. Return to boiling; reduce heat to medium. Cook, covered, about 7 minutes or until chicken is no longer pink and soba is tender.

② Stir in sugar snap peas. Cook, covered, about 3 minutes more or just until snap peas are tender.

③ If desired, sprinkle each serving with crushed red pepper and parsley.

PER SERVING 295 calories; 1 g total fat (0 g sat. fat); 49 mg cholesterol; 1,172 mg sodium; 41 g carbohydrate; 4 g fiber; 30 g protein

Pumpkin, Barley, and Sage Soup

Pumpkin, Barley, and Sage Soup

When purchasing pumpkin, check labels carefully, making sure that you buy pure pumpkin puree—and not pumpkin pie filling.

MAKES 4 servings **START TO FINISH** 30 minutes

- 8 ounces cooked andouille or smoked sausage links, chopped
- 1 small onion, chopped
- 1 tablespoon snipped fresh sage
- 1 tablespoon vegetable oil
- 1 cup quick-cooking barley
- 4 cups water
- 1 teaspoon instant chicken bouillon granules
- 1 15-ounce can pumpkin
- 2 tablespoons maple syrup
- 1 tablespoon cider vinegar
  Salt and black pepper

① In a 4-quart pot or Dutch oven cook sausage, onion, and sage in hot oil over medium heat for 3 minutes, stirring often. Add barley, the water, and bouillon granules. Bring to boiling. Reduce heat; simmer, covered, for 12 minutes, stirring occasionally.

② Stir in pumpkin, maple syrup, and vinegar; heat through. Season to taste with salt and pepper.

PER SERVING 439 calories; 21 g total fat (6 g sat. fat); 35 mg cholesterol; 832 mg sodium; 51 g carbohydrate; 11 g fiber; 14 g protein

quick tip If you like, garnish this sumptuous soup with a sprinkling of roasted and salted, pumpkin seeds, also known as pepitas.

Fast Paella

Whether guests love poultry, seafood, rice, or vegetables, they'll all find their favorites in this classic Spanish dish.

MAKES 6 servings **START TO FINISH** 30 minutes

- 1 14.5-ounce can Mexican-style or Cajun-style stewed tomatoes, undrained and cut up
- 1 14.5-ounce can reduced-sodium chicken broth
- 1 cup chopped onion (1 large)
- 2 teaspoons dried oregano, crushed
- 1 teaspoon garlic salt
- 1 teaspoon ground turmeric
- 1 teaspoon paprika
- ¼ teaspoon crushed red pepper or ⅛ teaspoon bottled hot pepper sauce
- ¼ teaspoon black pepper
- 1 14- to 16-ounce package cooked smoked turkey or chicken sausage, halved lengthwise and cut into 1-inch pieces
- 12 ounces frozen peeled and deveined cooked shrimp
- 1 10-ounce package frozen peas
- 1 8.8-ounce pouch cooked long grain rice
  Lemon slices or wedges
  Snipped fresh cilantro or parsley

① In a very large skillet combine tomatoes, broth, onion, oregano, garlic salt, turmeric, paprika, crushed red pepper, and black pepper. Bring to boiling; reduce heat. Simmer, covered, for 10 minutes.

② Stir in sausage, shrimp, peas, and cooked rice; heat through. Serve in shallow soup bowls. Garnish with lemon slices and sprinkle with cilantro.

PER SERVING 303 calories; 9 g total fat (2 g sat. fat); 154 mg cholesterol; 1,269 mg sodium; 29 g carbohydrate; 5 g fiber; 27 g protein

Soups and stews celebrate the bounty of each and every season.

Crab and Poblano Soup

When choosing poblano chiles for this soup, go for the ones with the darkest color—they will be sweetest.

MAKES 4 servings **START TO FINISH** 30 minutes

- ¼ **cup butter**
- 2 **fresh poblano chile peppers, seeded and chopped (see quick tip, page 28)**
- ¾ **cup chopped red sweet pepper (1 medium)**
- ½ **cup chopped onion (1 medium)**
- 2 **cloves garlic, minced**
- ¼ **cup all-purpose flour**
- ¼ **teaspoon salt**
- ¼ **teaspoon black pepper**
- 1 **14.5-ounce can chicken broth**
- 2 **cups milk**
- 1½ **cups shredded asadero cheese or Monterey Jack cheese (6 ounces)**
- 1 **6-ounce can crabmeat, drained, cut into bite-size pieces, and cartilage removed, or 1 cup cooked crabmeat, cut into bite-size pieces and cartilage removed**
- 1 **recipe Fresh Tomato Salsa**

① In a large saucepan melt butter over medium heat. Add poblano peppers, sweet pepper, onion, and garlic; cook until tender, stirring occasionally. Stir in flour, salt, and black pepper. Add broth all at once. Cook and stir until thickened and bubbly. Cook and stir 1 minute more.

② Reduce heat to medium-low. Stir in milk and cheese. Cook and stir for 3 to 5 minutes or until cheese is melted. Stir in crabmeat; heat through.

③ Top each serving with Fresh Tomato Salsa.

Fresh Tomato Salsa: In a small bowl combine 1 cup seeded and chopped roma tomatoes (3 medium), 1 tablespoon thinly sliced green onion (1), 1 tablespoon snipped fresh cilantro, 2 teaspoons lime juice, and 1 teaspoon finely chopped fresh jalapeño (see Quick Tip, page 28). Season to taste with salt and black pepper.

PER SERVING 406 calories; 24 g total fat (16 g sat. fat); 120 mg cholesterol; 1,328 mg sodium; 22 g carbohydrate; 2 g fiber; 28 g protein

Pork Potsticker Soup

Doll up a carton of ready-to-go broth with Asian flavors for a soup every bit as enticing as those at your favorite Chinese restaurant.

MAKES 4 servings **START TO FINISH** 25 minutes

- 1 **32-ounce carton mushroom broth or vegetable broth**
- 1 **cup water**
- 2 **teaspoons grated fresh ginger**
- 2 **10-ounce packages frozen pork potstickers or dumplings with sauce**
- 2 **medium carrots, cut into thin 2-inch strips, or 1 cup shredded carrots**
- 1 **small bunch green onions, trimmed and sliced diagonally**

① In a Dutch oven combine broth, the water, and ginger. Add contents of the seasoning packet from 1 package of potstickers (see quick tip, below). Bring to boiling.

② Add potstickers, carrots, and most of the green onions. Bring to simmering. Simmer, covered, for 8 to 10 minutes or until potstickers are heated through.

③ Sprinkle each serving with the remaining green onions.

PER SERVING 369 calories; 16 g total fat (6 g sat. fat); 18 mg cholesterol; 1,207 mg sodium; 42 g carbohydrate; 4 g fiber; 14 g protein

quick tip If no seasoning packet is provided, add 2 teaspoons soy sauce and 1 teaspoon toasted sesame oil.

Shrimp Cocktail Soup

Shrimp Cocktail Soup

Serve cold soups like this one in chilled bowls. To chill, simply place bowls in your freezer for about an hour before serving time.

MAKES 6 servings **START TO FINISH** 30 minutes

3	cups seeded and chopped ripe tomatoes
1¾	cups peeled, seeded, and chopped cucumber (1 medium)
½	cup finely chopped green sweet pepper (1 small)
⅓	cup finely chopped red onion (1 small)
2	cloves garlic, minced
2	cups tomato juice
1	14.5-ounce can reduced-sodium chicken broth
¼	cup red wine vinegar
2	tablespoons snipped fresh basil or 2 teaspoons dried basil, crushed
½	teaspoon salt
¼	to ½ teaspoon bottled hot pepper sauce
¼	teaspoon black pepper
12	ounces chopped, peeled, and deveined cooked shrimp
	Lime wedges (optional)

① In an extra-large bowl combine tomatoes, cucumber, sweet pepper, red onion, and garlic. Stir in tomato juice, broth, vinegar, basil, salt, hot pepper sauce, and black pepper (see quick tip, below). Stir in shrimp.

② If desired, serve with lime wedges.

PER SERVING 109 calories; 1 g total fat (0 g sat. fat); 111 mg cholesterol; 734 mg sodium; 11 g carbohydrate; 2 g fiber; 16 g protein

quick tip If time permits, cover and chill soup up to 24 hours to allow flavors to blend. Before serving, stir in shrimp.

Italian Bean and Pasta Soup

If you'd like, brighten this soup even more by using yellow sweet peppers in place of green ones.

MAKES 6 servings **START TO FINISH** 30 minutes

1	large onion, chopped (1 cup)
1	teaspoon bottled minced garlic
1	tablespoon olive oil
2	14-ounce cans vegetable broth
1	medium green sweet pepper, seeded and chopped
½	cup dried orzo
2	14.5-ounce cans diced tomatoes with basil, garlic, and oregano, undrained
1	19-ounce can fava beans, rinsed and drained
1	15-ounce can navy beans, rinsed and drained
¼	cup snipped fresh parsley

① In a 4-to 5-quart Dutch oven cook onion and garlic in hot oil over medium heat for 5 minutes or until tender, stirring occasionally. Add broth; bring to boiling.

② Add sweet pepper and orzo. Return to boiling; reduce heat. Simmer, uncovered, for 8 to 10 minutes or until orzo is tender. Stir in undrained tomatoes, fava beans, and navy beans. Cover; simmer for 5 minutes. Serve with parsley.

PER SERVING 295 calories; 3 g total fat (0 g sat. fat); 0 mg cholesterol; 1,953 mg sodium; 54 g carbohydrate; 9 g fiber; 15 g protein

Italian Bean and Pasta Soup

Beer and Cheese Soup

As the beer's foamy head deflates in the blender, it wraps its hoppy flavor all around the potatoes and peppers.

MAKES 4 servings **START TO FINISH** 30 minutes

- 1   bunch green onions
- 3   tablespoons olive oil
- ¾   cup bottled roasted red sweet peppers, drained
- ¾   cup pale lager or nonalcoholic beer
- 2   cups refrigerated shredded hash brown potatoes
- 2   cups milk
- 2   cups shredded American cheese (8 ounces)
- ¼   teaspoon paprika, plus additional for sprinkling

① Slice green onions, separating white and green pieces; reserve green pieces. In a Dutch oven cook white portions in 1 tablespoon hot oil until tender. Set aside.

② In a blender or food processor combine red peppers, cooked onions, beer, and 1 cup of the potatoes; blend or process until smooth. Return to Dutch oven; bring to boiling. Reduce heat and simmer, uncovered, 5 minutes.

③ Add milk and cheese to potato mixture. Cook and stir over medium heat until cheese is melted and soup is hot (do not boil).

④ In a medium skillet cook remaining 1 cup potatoes in remaining hot oil over medium-high heat for 8 minutes or until golden, stirring occasionally. Drain on paper towels; sprinkle with paprika. Ladle soup into serving bowls; top with potatoes, reserved green onions, and additional paprika.

PER SERVING 467 calories; 30 g total fat (14 g sat. fat); 63 mg cholesterol; 1,096 mg sodium; 28 g carbohydrate; 2 g fiber; 19 g protein

Minestrone

If you follow this recipe word by word, the minestrone will be magnificent. But keep in mind that this soup is a divine destination for any leftover vegetables or meats you happen to have in the fridge—just throw them in with abandon.

MAKES 6 servings **START TO FINISH** 30 minutes

- ½   cup chopped onion (1 medium)
- 2   cloves garlic, minced
- 1   tablespoon olive oil
- 2   14.5-ounce cans vegetable or beef broth
- 2   cups water
- 1¼   cups coarsely chopped zucchini (1 medium)
- 1¼   cups coarsely chopped yellow sweet pepper (1 large)
- 1   15-ounce can cannellini beans (white kidney beans), rinsed and drained
- 8   ounces fresh green beans, trimmed and cut into 1½-inch pieces (1½ cups)
- 1   cup dried mostaccioli
- ¼   cup coarsely snipped fresh basil or 2 teaspoons dried basil, crushed
- 2   cups fresh baby spinach
- 1½   cups coarsely chopped tomatoes or halved cherry tomatoes
       Salt and black pepper
       Shaved Parmesan cheese (optional)

① In a 5- to 6-quart Dutch oven cook onion, and garlic in hot oil over medium heat until tender, stirring occasionally. Add broth, the water, zucchini, and sweet pepper. Stir in cannellini beans, green beans, pasta, and dried basil (if using). Bring to boiling; reduce heat. Simmer, covered, 10 to 12 minutes or until pasta is tender, stirring occasionally.

② Stir in spinach, tomatoes, and fresh basil (if using). Remove from heat. Season to taste with salt and black pepper. If desired, top each serving with cheese.

PER SERVING 186 calories; 3 g total fat (0 g sat. fat); 0 mg cholesterol; 621 mg sodium; 34 g carbohydrate; 7 g fiber; 10 g protein

Spring Greens Soup

Spring Greens Soup

Spinach and arugula—most often enjoyed fresh—make wonderful, highly nutritious additions to hot soups.

MAKES 3 servings **START TO FINISH** 30 minutes

- 1 medium onion, halved and sliced
- 1 tablespoon vegetable oil
- 3 cups reduced-sodium chicken broth or vegetable broth
- ¼ to ½ teaspoon freshly ground black pepper
- 12 ounces Yukon gold potatoes, cut into 1-inch pieces
- 3 cups sliced fresh mushrooms (8 ounces)
- 2 tablespoons butter
- 3 cups fresh spinach leaves
- 3 cups arugula leaves
- 2 cups fresh parsley leaves and tender stems
   Salt
   Snipped fresh parsley (optional)

① In a large saucepan cook onion in hot oil over medium heat about 5 minutes or until tender, stirring occasionally. Add broth and pepper. Bring to boiling. Add potatoes. Return to boiling; reduce heat. Simmer, covered, for 10 minutes. Remove from heat.

② Meanwhile, in a large skillet cook mushrooms in hot butter over medium heat for 6 to 8 minutes until tender and liquid has evaporated. Set aside.

③ Using an immersion blender, blend potato mixture in saucepan until nearly smooth. Stir in spinach, arugula, and parsley. Bring to boiling; remove from heat. Using immersion blender, blend mixture again until nearly smooth and flecks of green remain. (Or place half the potato mixture and half the spinach and arugula in a food processor or blender; process until nearly smooth. Remove soup to a serving bowl. Repeat with remaining potatoes, spinach, and arugula.) Season to taste with salt.

④ Top each serving with cooked mushrooms and, if desired, snipped fresh parsley.

PER SERVING 184 calories; 6 g total fat (0 g sat. fat); 0 mg cholesterol; 824 mg sodium; 28 g carbohydrate; 6 g fiber; 8 g protein

Tomato-Barley Soup with Garden Vegetables

You'll almost always find the ingredients for this quick-as-a-wink soup on your pantry shelves, which makes it a simple throw-together supper.

MAKES 4 servings **PREP** 10 minutes **COOK** 18 minutes

- 1 14-ounce can vegetable broth
- 1¾ cups water
- ¾ cup quick-cooking barley
- ¾ cup thinly sliced carrots
- 1 teaspoon dried thyme, crushed
- ⅛ teaspoon black pepper
- 1 19-ounce can ready-to-serve tomato-basil soup
- 2 cups coarsely chopped zucchini and/or yellow summer squash
- 1 cup loose-pack frozen cut green beans

① In a large saucepan combine vegetable broth, the water, uncooked barley, carrots, thyme, and pepper. Bring to boiling; reduce heat. Simmer, covered, for 10 minutes, stirring occasionally.

② Stir in tomato-basil soup, zucchini, and green beans. Return to boiling; reduce heat. Simmer, covered, for 8 to 10 minutes more or until vegetables and barley are tender, stirring occasionally.

PER SERVING 243 calories; 3 g total fat (0 g sat. fat); 0 mg cholesterol; 988 mg sodium; 49 g carbohydrate; 9 g fiber; 7 g protein

Tomato-Barley Soup with Garden Vegetables

Creamy Tortellini Tomato Soup

Bake some quick and easy refrigerated breadsticks to make this the fastest—yet most satisfying—supper ever.

MAKES 4 servings **START TO FINISH** 20 minutes

  2   14.5-ounce cans reduced-sodium chicken broth or vegetable broth
  1   9-ounce package refrigerated tortellini
  ½   of an 8-ounce tub cream cheese spread with chive and onion
  1   10.75- or 11-ounce can condensed tomato or tomato bisque soup
       Snipped fresh chives (optional)

① In a medium saucepan bring broth to boiling. Stir in tortellini; reduce heat. Simmer, uncovered, for 5 minutes.

② In a small bowl whisk ⅓ cup of the hot broth into cream cheese spread until smooth. Return cream cheese mixture to saucepan. Stir in tomato soup; heat through. If desired, sprinkle each serving with chives.

PER SERVING 363 calories; 14 g total fat (8 g sat. fat); 57 mg cholesterol; 1,264 mg sodium; 44 g carbohydrate; 1 g fiber; 14 g protein

Creamy Tortellini Tomato Soup

O'Brien Potato Soup

There is nothing like a bowl of potato soup to warm up a cold day. And this hepped-up version goes together with no trouble at all.

MAKES 4 servings **START TO FINISH** 30 minutes

  1   28-ounce package frozen diced hash brown potatoes with onions and peppers
  3   cups fat-free half-and-half
  1   cup chopped miniature sweet peppers
  1   cup water
  ½   teaspoon salt
  ½   teaspoon curry powder
  ⅛   to ¼ teaspoon cayenne pepper or black pepper
  1½   cups shredded cheddar cheese (6 ounces)
       Sliced miniature sweet peppers (optional)
       Snipped fresh parsley (optional)

① In a 4-quart Dutch oven combine potatoes, half-and-half, 1 cup sweet peppers, ½ cup of the water, the salt, curry powder, and cayenne pepper. Bring just to boiling; reduce heat to medium. Cook, covered, for 10 minutes, stirring occasionally. Cool slightly.

② Transfer 3 cups of the potato mixture to a blender; add the remaining ½ cup water. Cover and blend until nearly smooth. Return to Dutch oven. Cook and stir until mixture is heated through and potatoes are tender. Stir in cheese. Cook and stir over low heat until cheese is melted.

③ If desired, top each serving with sliced sweet peppers and parsley.

PER SERVING 438 calories; 17 g total fat (11 g sat. fat); 54 mg cholesterol; 883 mg sodium; 53 g carbohydrate; 5 g fiber; 19 g protein

quick tip Shredding your own cheese used to be a real budget saver. Today, however, the costs of bulk and preshredded cheeses are almost equal, making bagged and ready-to-go cheeses a better buy.

Grilling can be as fast as it is fun. When thoughts of sunny skies, green grass, and sizzling suppers beckon, head outdoors with these superlative, ready-in-a cinch suppers.

182

190

210

FROM THE GRILL

206

Flat-Iron Steak with Avocado Butter

This relatively unknown cut of meat was discovered recently and has taken the beef industry by storm. As all shoulder cuts are, it is exceedingly tender, robust in flavor, and quite affordable.

MAKES 6 servings **PREP** 20 minutes **GRILL** 7 minutes

- 6 beef shoulder top blade (flat-iron) steaks or boneless ribeye steaks, cut ¾ inch thick
- 1 tablespoon olive oil
- 1 tablespoon herbes de Provence, crushed
- ½ teaspoon salt
- ½ teaspoon freshly ground black pepper
- 1 recipe Avocado Butter

① Trim fat from steaks. Brush steaks with the olive oil. For rub, in a small bowl combine herbes de Provence, salt, and pepper. Sprinkle evenly over both sides of each steak; rub in with your fingers. If desired, cover and chill steaks up to 24 hours.

② For a charcoal grill, grill steaks on the rack of an uncovered grill directly over medium coals to desired doneness, turning once halfway through grilling. Allow 7 to 9 minutes for medium rare (145°F) and 10 to 12 minutes for medium (160°F). (For a gas grill, preheat grill. Reduce heat to medium. Place steaks on the grill rack over heat. Cover and grill as directed) Serve steaks with Avocado Butter.

Avocado Butter: Halve, seed, peel, and chop 1 ripe avocado. In a medium bowl combine the chopped avocado, ¼ cup softened butter, 3 tablespoons lime juice, 2 tablespoons snipped fresh chervil or parsley, 1 tablespoon snipped fresh tarragon, ¼ teaspoon salt, and, if desired, ⅛ teaspoon cayenne pepper. Using a fork, gently mash the ingredients together until thoroughly combined (if desired, leave mixture somewhat chunky). Spoon mixture into a small bowl; chill until almost firm.

PER SERVING 369 calories; 25 g total fat (10 g sat. fat); 109 mg cholesterol; 463 mg sodium; 3 g carbohydrate; 2 g fiber; 33 g protein

Grilled Steak with Cheddar Crisps

If you have them, add a few juicy blackberries to the kaleidoscope of color that makes this dish as gorgeous as it is delicious.

MAKES 4 servings **START TO FINISH** 30 minutes

- 1 cup fresh raspberries
- 1 tablespoon Dijon mustard
- ¼ cup cider vinegar
- 2 teaspoons sugar
- ¼ cup olive oil
- 12 ounces flank steak
  Salt and black pepper
- 2 cups refrigerated shredded hash brown potatoes
- 4 ounces smoked cheddar cheese, shredded
- 1 head romaine lettuce

① Heat broiler. For dressing, in a small bowl mash 8 berries. Stir in mustard, vinegar, and sugar. Whisk in the olive oil; set aside.

② Lightly sprinkle the steak with salt and pepper. For a charcoal grill, grill steak on the rack of an uncovered grill directly over medium coals for 17 to 21 minutes for medium (160°F), turning once halfway through grilling. (For a gas grill, preheat grill. Reduce heat to medium. Place steak on grill rack over heat. Cover and grill as directed.) Slice steak into strips.

③ Meanwhile, generously grease a 13 x 9 x 2-inch baking pan. Toss together potatoes and cheese; spread in pan. Broil 3 to 4 inches from heat for 6 to 8 minutes or until golden brown and crisp. Remove from pan; cut into pieces.

④ Remove core from lettuce; cut into quarters. Serve with steak, potatoes, and berries. Pass dressing.

PER SERVING 479 calories; 29 g total fat (10 g sat. fat); 60 mg cholesterol; 514 mg sodium; 25 g carbohydrate; 5 g fiber; 28 g protein

quick tip To bring limp and lifeless heads of packaged romaine back to crisp and crunchy glory, trim ½ inch from the romaine cores, then stand the heads upright in 2 inches of cold water. Refrigerate. The leaves will quickly draw up water—just like cut flowers do—and within a few hours the romaine will seem garden fresh again.

Hanger Steak with Asian Dipping Sauce

Hanger Steak with Asian Dipping Sauce

Hanger steak is prized for its robust beefy flavor. Sometimes the cut is called butcher's steak because it is so good that butchers often saved the cut for themselves.

MAKES 4 servings **PREP** 15 minutes **GRILL** 10 minutes

½	cup beef broth
¼	cup water
¼	cup reduced-sodium soy sauce
1	tablespoon oyster sauce
1	tablespoon rice vinegar
2	teaspoons cornstarch
1	teaspoon sugar
1	1½-pound beef hanger steak
¼	teaspoon salt
2	tablespoons cream sherry
⅓	cup chopped green onions (3)
1	tablespoon minced fresh ginger
2	cloves garlic, minced
3	cups hot cooked ramen noodles or rice
	Radish strips (optional)
	Sliced green onions (optional)

① In a small bowl stir together broth, the water, soy sauce, oyster sauce, vinegar, cornstarch, and sugar; set aside. Trim fat from steak. Sprinkle steak with salt.

② For a charcoal grill, grill steak on the rack of an uncovered grill directly over medium coals for 10 to 12 minutes for medium (160°F), turning once halfway through grilling. (For a gas grill, preheat grill. Reduce heat to medium. Place steak on grill rack over heat. Cover; grill as directed.)

③ Meanwhile, for sauce, in a small saucepan bring sherry to simmering over medium heat; simmer for 1 minute. Stir in the ⅓ cup green onions, ginger, and garlic; simmer for 1 minute. Stir in the broth mixture; simmer about 2 minutes more or until slightly thickened. Cool slightly.

④ Thinly slice steak diagonally across the grain. Arrange meat slices on hot cooked noodles; drizzle with a few tablespoons of the sauce. If desired, garnish with radish strips and additional green onions. Serve with the remaining sauce.

PER SERVING 438 calories; 10 g total fat (4 g sat. fat); 56 mg cholesterol; 1,442 mg sodium; 40 g carbohydrate; 1 g fiber; 42 g protein

Strip Steaks with Lime and Sweet Onion Salsa

Onions that have earned a place in the sweet category include the Vidalia and Walla Walla varieties.

MAKES 4 servings **PREP** 20 minutes **GRILL** 10 minutes

4	boneless beef top loin (strip) steaks, cut 1 inch thick
1	fresh habanero chile pepper, seeded and finely chopped (see quick tip, page 28)
2	tablespoons snipped fresh sage
½	teaspoon salt
1	recipe Lime and Sweet Onion Salsa

① Trim fat from steaks. In a small bowl combine habanero pepper, sage, and salt. Wearing plastic or rubber gloves, sprinkle mixture evenly over both sides of each steak; rub in with your fingers. If desired, cover and marinate in the refrigerator for up to 24 hours.

② Prepare Lime and Sweet Onion Salsa. Cover and chill until ready to serve.

③ For a charcoal grill, grill steaks on the rack of an uncovered grill directly over medium coals to desired doneness, turning once halfway through grilling. Allow 10 to 12 minutes for medium rare (145°F) or 12 to 15 minutes for medium (160°F). (For a gas grill, preheat grill. Reduce heat to medium. Place steaks on grill rack over heat. Cover; grill as directed.) Serve steaks with salsa.

Lime and Sweet Onion Salsa: Peel and section 2 large limes; chop lime segments. In a medium bowl stir together chopped lime, ½ cup finely chopped sweet onion (1 medium), 3 tablespoons snipped fresh cilantro, ½ teaspoon sugar, and ¼ teaspoon salt.

PER SERVING 431 calories; 17 g total fat (6 g sat. fat); 166 mg cholesterol; 581 mg sodium; 4 g carbohydrate; 1 g fiber; 62 g protein

Grilled Steak, Mango, and Pear Salad

Fresh mangoes can be challenging to seed, peel, and slice. Refrigerated jarred mangoes solve the problems beautifully.

MAKES 4 servings **PREP** 15 minutes **GRILL** 14 minutes

- 12   ounces boneless beef top loin steak (1 inch thick)
- ½   teaspoon salt
- ¼   teaspoon black pepper
- 1   10-ounce package torn mixed salad greens (about 8 cups)
- 1   24-ounce jar refrigerated sliced mango, drained
- 1   medium pear, peeled, cored, and chopped
- ¾   cup refrigerated fat-free blue cheese salad dressing
     Cracked black pepper (optional)

① Sprinkle both sides of steak with salt and the ¼ teaspoon black pepper.

② For a charcoal grill, grill steak on the rack of an uncovered grill directly over medium coals until desired doneness, turning once halfway through grilling. Allow 14 to 18 minutes for medium rare (145°F) or 18 to 22 minutes for medium (160°F). (For a gas grill, preheat grill. Reduce heat to medium. Place steak on grill rack over heat. Cover and grill as directed.)

③ To serve, thinly slice steak across the grain. Arrange greens on a serving platter; top with steak, mango, and pear. Drizzle with salad dressing. If desired, sprinkle with cracked black pepper.

PER SERVING 307 calories; 5 g total fat (2 g sat. fat); 50 mg cholesterol; 900 mg sodium; 49 g carbohydrate; 4 g fiber; 19 g protein

Pepper-Punched T-Bones

Green peppercorns are pepper berries that are harvested before they ripen and then packed in brine. Their flavor is fresh-tasting and not as pungent as the flavor of dried peppercorns.

MAKES 4 servings **PREP** 15 minutes **GRILL** 7 minutes

- ½   cup steak sauce
- 2   tablespoons snipped fresh thyme
- 2   tablespoons whole green peppercorns in brine, drained and chopped
- 2   teaspoons cracked black pepper
- ½   teaspoon cayenne pepper
- 4   beef T-bone steaks, cut ¾ inch thick

① In a small bowl stir together steak sauce, thyme, green peppercorns, black pepper, and cayenne pepper. Trim fat from steaks. Spread half of the pepper mixture on one side of each steak.

② For a charcoal grill, place steaks, pepper sides down, on the rack of an uncovered grill directly over medium coals. Spread the remaining pepper mixture on tops of steaks. Grill for 7 to 10 minutes for medium rare (145°F) or 10 to 13 minutes for medium (160°F), turning once halfway through grilling. (For a gas grill, preheat grill. Reduce heat to medium. Place steaks on grill rack over heat. Cover; grill as directed.)

PER SERVING 583 calories; 38 g total fat (15 g sat. fat); 146 mg cholesterol; 567 mg sodium; 5 g carbohydrate; 1 g fiber; 52 g protein

《 It takes very little to bring a steak from simple to sensational. 》

Jerk Burgers with Mango Salsa

Jerk Burgers with Mango Salsa

To keep a knob of gingerroot fresh, store it tightly wrapped in the freezer for up to 6 months. You'll find that grating frozen ginger is a snap too!

MAKES 4 burgers **PREP** 20 minutes **GRILL** 10 minutes

1	cup finely chopped green sweet pepper (1 large)
¼	cup finely chopped red sweet pepper
¼	cup finely chopped onion
1	teaspoon grated fresh ginger
1	tablespoon vegetable oil
1	mango, seeded, peeled, and chopped (1 cup)
¼	cup apple jelly
1	tablespoon lime juice
	Dash salt
1	egg, lightly beaten
⅓	cup bottled jerk sauce
¼	cup fine dry bread crumbs
1	pound lean ground beef
4	ciabatta rolls or hamburger buns, split and toasted
1	cup shredded Monterey Jack cheese (4 ounces)

① For salsa, in a medium saucepan cook sweet peppers, onion, and ginger in hot oil over medium heat for 3 minutes. Add mango, jelly, lime juice, and salt; cook and stir until jelly melts. Set aside.

② In a large bowl combine egg, ¼ cup of the jerk sauce, and the bread crumbs. Add beef; mix well. Shape meat mixture into four ½-inch-thick patties.

③ For a charcoal grill, grill patties on the rack of an uncovered grill directly over medium coals for 10 to 13 minutes or until done (160°F), turning and brushing once with the remaining jerk sauce halfway through grilling. (For a gas grill, preheat grill. Reduce heat to medium. Place patties on grill rack over heat. Cover; grill as directed.)

④ Divide cheese among bottoms of rolls. Serve burgers on rolls with some of the salsa. Pass the remaining salsa.

PER BURGER 808 calories; 50 g total fat (20 g sat. fat); 167 mg cholesterol; 740 mg sodium; 60 g carbohydrate; 3 g fiber; 31 g protein

Summertime Stuffed Burgers

Everybody loves a surprise, especially when it is wrapped in a burger.

MAKES 4 burgers **START TO FINISH** 20 minutes

8	½-inch-thick prepared beef burger patties
4	1-ounce slices Colby cheese or Monterey Jack cheese with peppers
4	kaiser rolls, split and toasted
½	cup sour cream horseradish-flavor dip or bottled chutney
4	to 5 miniature sweet peppers, sliced

① Place 4 patties on a piece of waxed paper. Top each with a slice of cheese and another patty. Press to flatten slightly and pinch edges to seal.

② For a charcoal grill, grill patties on the rack of an uncovered grill directly over medium coals for 14 to 16 minutes or until done (160°F), turning once halfway through grilling. (For a gas grill, preheat grill. Reduce heat to medium. Place patties on grill rack over heat. Cover; grill as directed.)

③ Spread cut sides of buns with horseradish dip. Add a burger to bottom halves of buns. Top with sweet peppers and bun tops.

PER BURGER 875 calories; 57 g total fat (23 g sat. fat); 192 mg cholesterol; 822 mg sodium; 35 g carbohydrate; 2 g fiber; 56 g protein

quick tip To toast kaiser rolls, hamburger buns, and ciabatta on the grill, simply split the rolls, brush both sides lightly with olive oil, and place them—split sides down—on the grill grate over medium heat for 10 to 15 seconds. Remove with tongs.

Sesame-Ginger Barbecued Breasts ♥

For fun, serve this Asian-inspired grilled meal in big bowls and eat it with chopsticks!

MAKES 6 servings **PREP** 15 minutes **GRILL** 12 minutes

- ⅓ cup plum sauce or sweet-and-sour sauce
- ¼ cup water
- 3 tablespoons hoisin sauce
- 1½ teaspoons sesame seeds, toasted, if desired
- 1 teaspoon grated fresh ginger or ¼ teaspoon ground ginger
- 1 clove garlic, minced
- ¼ to ½ teaspoon Asian chili sauce or several dashes bottled hot pepper sauce
- 6 skinless, boneless chicken breast halves and/or thighs
  Hot cooked rice noodles
  Sugar snap peas, bias-sliced in half
  Slivered green onions
  Sesame seeds, toasted

① For sauce, in a small saucepan combine plum sauce, the water, hoisin sauce, 1½ teaspoons sesame seeds, the ginger, garlic, and Asian chili sauce. Bring to boiling over medium heat, stirring frequently; reduce heat. Cover and simmer for 3 minutes. Remove from heat.

② For a charcoal grill, grill chicken on the rack of an uncovered grill directly over medium coals for 12 to 15 minutes or until chicken is no longer pink (170°F for breast halves, 180°F for thighs), turning once halfway through grilling and brushing once or twice with some of the sauce during the last 5 minutes of grilling. (For a gas grill, preheat grill. Reduce heat to medium. Place chicken on grill rack over heat. Cover and grill as directed.)

③ To serve, slice chicken and serve on rice noodles. Sprinkle with green onions and additional sesame seeds. Reheat and pass the remaining sauce.

PER SERVING 166 calories; 4 g total fat (1 g sat. fat); 59 mg cholesterol; 216 mg sodium; 9 g carbohydrate; 0 g fiber; 22 g protein

Lamb Chops with Blackberry-Pear Chutney ♥

The light, spicy acidity of this fruity chutney makes a wonderful counterpoint for the richness of lamb.

MAKES 4 servings **PREP** 20 minutes **GRILL** 12 minutes

- 1 large pear, peeled, cored, and coarsely chopped (about 1⅓ cups)
- ¼ cup sliced green onions (2)
- ⅛ teaspoon ground cloves
- 2 teaspoons vegetable oil
- 1 cup fresh blackberries or frozen blackberries, thawed
- 1 tablespoon red wine vinegar
- ½ teaspoon ground allspice
- ¼ teaspoon salt
- ¼ teaspoon coarsely ground black pepper
- 8 lamb loin chops, cut 1 inch thick

① For chutney, in a large skillet cook pear, green onions, and cloves in hot oil over medium heat about 3 minutes or just until pear is tender, stirring occasionally. Add blackberries; reduce heat to medium-low. Cook and stir for 3 minutes; remove from heat. Stir in vinegar. Set aside to cool.

② In a small bowl stir together allspice, salt, and pepper. Sprinkle evenly over both sides of chops; rub in with your fingers.

③ For a charcoal grill, grill chops on the rack of an uncovered grill directly over medium coals until desired doneness, turning once halfway through grilling. Allow 12 to 14 minutes for medium rare (145°F) or 15 to 17 minutes for medium (160°F). (For a gas grill, preheat grill. Reduce heat to medium. Place chops on grill rack over heat. Cover; grill as directed.)

④ Serve lamb with chutney.

PER SERVING 161 calories; 8 g total fat (3 g sat. fat); 40 mg cholesterol; 197 mg sodium; 11 g carbohydrate; 3 g fiber; 13 g protein

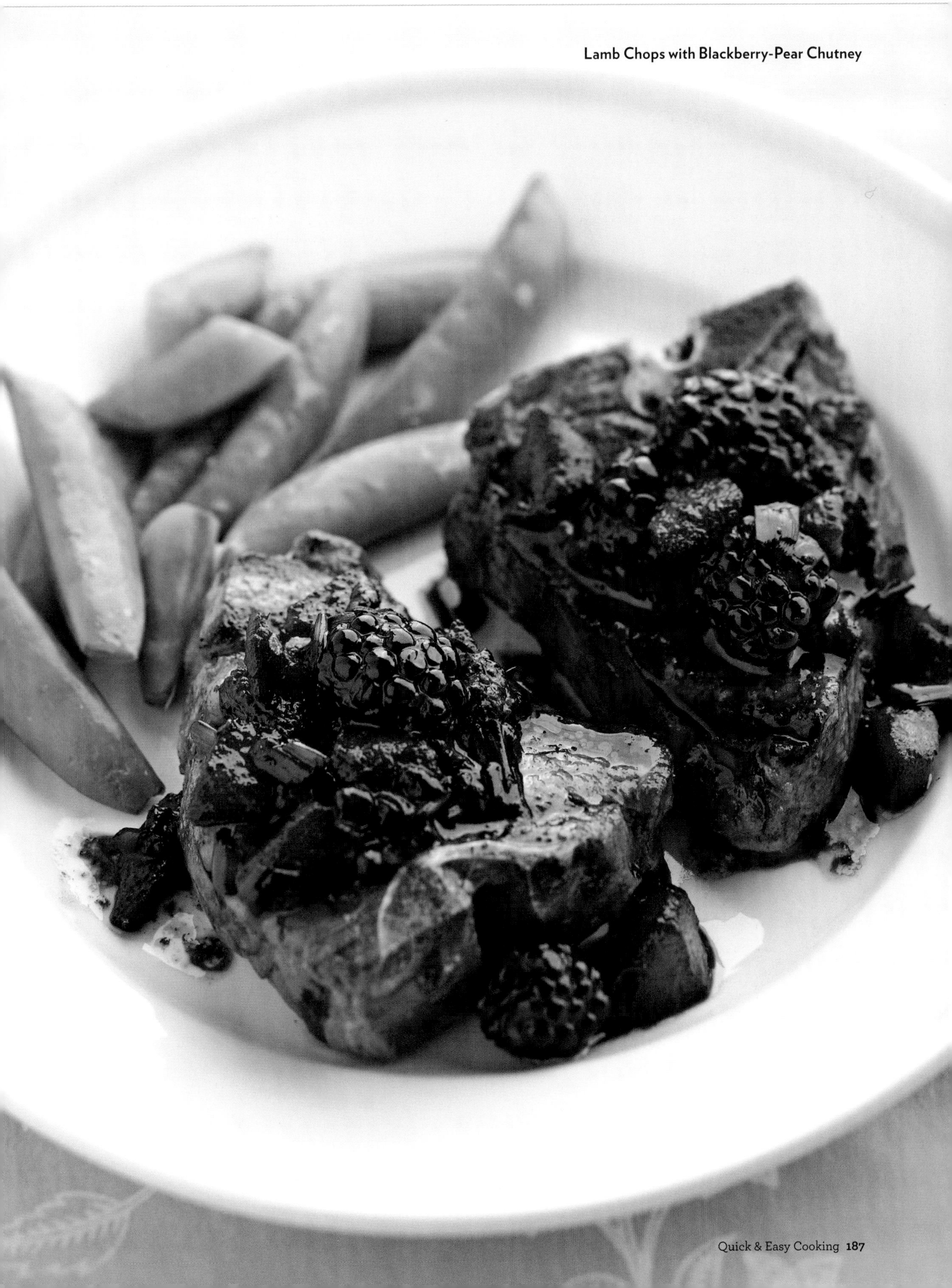

Lamb Chops with Blackberry-Pear Chutney

Grilled Chicken-Mole Sandwiches

Grilled Chicken-Mole Sandwiches

The intoxicating flavor of Mexico's famous mole sauce comes from its combination of garlic, onion, herbs, seeds, spices, chiles, and sometimes a bit of chocolate.

MAKES 4 sandwiches **START TO FINISH** 30 minutes

1   small avocado, seeded, peeled, and mashed

2   tablespoons mayonnaise

¼   teaspoon salt

¼   teaspoon cayenne pepper

4   skinless, boneless chicken breast halves (about 1¼ pounds total)
    Salt and black pepper

⅓   cup mole sauce

4   4- to 6-inch ciabata buns, split and toasted
    Tomato slices
    Baby romaine lettuce or other lettuce leaves

① In a small bowl stir together avocado, mayonnaise, ¼ teaspoon salt, and cayenne pepper. Cover and chill until ready to serve.

② Sprinkle chicken with additional salt and black pepper. Using a sharp knife, cut a horizontal slit two-thirds through each chicken piece. Open each piece and spread with 1 tablespoon of the mole sauce; fold closed.

③ For a charcoal grill, grill chicken on the rack of an uncovered grill directly over medium coals for 12 to 15 minutes or until chicken is no longer pink (170°F), turning once halfway through grilling and brushing with the remaining mole sauce during the last 3 minutes of grilling. (For a gas grill, preheat grill. Reduce heat to medium. Place chicken on grill rack over heat. Cover and grill as directed.)

④ Cut chicken diagonally into ¼- to ½-inch slices. Spread avocado mixture on bottoms of buns. Layer with chicken, tomato, and lettuce. Replace tops of buns.

PER SANDWICH 624 calories; 18 g total fat (3 g sat. fat); 85 mg cholesterol; 1,101 mg sodium; 67 g carbohydrate; 7 g fiber; 46 g protein

Chicken with Roquefort ♥

Combining rich blue cheese with fat-free yogurt gives you the best of two worlds—luxurious flavor without the high-calorie price tag.

MAKES 4 servings **PREP** 20 minutes **GRILL** 12 minutes

1   6-ounce carton plain fat-free yogurt

½   cup chopped red onion

2   tablespoons crumbled Roquefort or other blue cheese

1   tablespoon snipped fresh chives

⅛   teaspoon black pepper

2   medium pears, halved lengthwise, cored, and stemmed
    Lemon juice

4   skinless, boneless chicken breast halves (1 to 1¼ pounds total)

½   teaspoon dried Italian seasoning, crushed

¼   teaspoon salt

① For sauce, in a small bowl combine yogurt, red onion, Roquefort cheese, chives, and pepper. Cover and chill until ready to serve. Brush cut sides of pears with lemon juice. Set aside.

② Sprinkle chicken with Italian seasoning and salt. For a charcoal grill, place chicken on the rack of an uncovered grill directly over medium coals. Grill for 5 minutes. Turn chicken. Place pears on grill, cut sides down. Grill chicken and pears for 7 to 10 minutes or until chicken is no longer pink (170°F) and pears are just tender. (For a gas grill, preheat grill. Reduce heat to medium. Place chicken, then pears on grill rack over heat. Cover and grill as directed.) Serve sauce with chicken and pears.

PER SERVING 218 calories; 3 g total fat (1 g sat. fat); 70 mg cholesterol; 297 mg sodium; 18 g carbohydrate; 3 g fiber; 30 g protein

Cajun Turkey Cutlets with Melon and Blueberries

If you cannot find farmer cheese, dry cottage cheese or crumbled goat cheese will do the trick.

MAKES 4 servings **START TO FINISH** 20 minutes

- 2 turkey breast tenderloins, cut in half horizontally (about 1 pound)
- 1 tablespoon olive oil
- 1½ teaspoons Cajun seasoning
- 6 cups torn mixed greens
- 1½ cups sliced cantaloupe
- 1 cup fresh blueberries

  Crumbled farmer cheese (optional)

  Purchased salad dressing

① Brush turkey with oil. Sprinkle with Cajun seasoning. For a charcoal grill, place turkey portions on the rack of an uncovered grill directly over medium coals. Grill for 12 to 15 minutes or until turkey is no longer pink (170°F), turning once halfway through grilling. (For a gas grill, preheat grill. Reduce heat to medium. Place turkey on grill rack over heat. Cover; grill as above.) Slice turkey.

② Arrange greens on a serving platter along with the turkey, cantaloupe, and berries. If desired, top with farmer cheese. Serve with salad dressing.

PER SERVING 359 calories; 22 g total fat (4 g sat. fat); 68 mg cholesterol; 161 mg sodium; 14 g carbohydrate; 3 g fiber; 29 g protein

Cajun Turkey Cutlets with Melon and Blueberries

Chicken Caesar Burgers

There are two distinctively different versions of bread crumbs. Dry bread crumbs are the kind that come packed in cylindrical cartons at the grocery store. Fresh or soft bread crumbs—the moist variety—are simple to make at home. Just cube a few slices of bread and give the cubes a whirl in a food processor or blender.

MAKES 4 burgers **PREP** 15 minutes **GRILL** 12 minutes

- 1 egg, lightly beaten
- 1 cup soft bread crumbs (2 slices)
- ¼ cup grated Parmesan cheese
- 2 teaspoons anchovy paste
- 1 teaspoon lemon juice
- 1 teaspoon Worcestershire sauce
- 1 clove garlic, minced
- ¼ teaspoon black pepper
- 1 pound uncooked ground chicken
- ½ cup sour cream
- ½ cup bottled Caesar salad dressing
- 4 small pita bread rounds, split open one-third around

  Shredded romaine lettuce

  Tomato slices (optional)

① In a large bowl combine egg, bread crumbs, Parmesan cheese, anchovy paste, lemon juice, Worcestershire sauce, garlic, and pepper. Add chicken; mix well. Shape chicken mixture into four ½-inch-thick patties.

② For a charcoal grill, grill patties on the lightly greased rack of an uncovered grill directly over medium coals for 12 to 14 minutes or until no longer pink (165°F), turning once halfway through grilling. (For a gas grill, preheat grill. Reduce heat to medium. Place patties on lightly greased grill rack over heat. Cover; grill as directed.)

③ Meanwhile, in small bowl stir together sour cream and dressing. Serve burgers on pitas with some of the sour cream mixture, lettuce, and, if desired, tomato slices.

PER BURGER 538 calories; 28 g total fat (7 g sat. fat); 167 mg cholesterol; 1,328 mg sodium; 36 g carbohydrate; 2 g fiber; 34 g protein

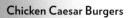

Turkey Pizza Burgers

Turkey Pizza Burgers ♥

These zesty, low-cholesterol burgers will be a hit with kids and grown-ups alike.

MAKES 4 servings **START TO FINISH** 30 minutes

1   egg, lightly beaten
¼   cup quick-cooking rolled oats
4   teaspoons snipped fresh oregano
⅛   teaspoon salt
⅛   teaspoon black pepper
1   pound uncooked ground turkey breast
4   slices provolone cheese (2 ounces)
½   cup reduced-sodium red pasta sauce
4   whole wheat hamburger buns, split and toasted

① In a medium bowl combine egg, oats, 2 teaspoons of the oregano, the salt, and pepper. Add ground turkey; mix well. Shape turkey mixture into four ¾-inch-thick patties.

② For a charcoal grill, grill patties on the rack of an uncovered grill directly over medium coals for 14 to 18 minutes or until no longer pink (165°F), turning once halfway through grilling and adding cheese for the last 1 minute of grilling. (For a gas grill, preheat grill. Reduce heat to medium. Place patties on grill rack over heat. Cover and grill as directed.)

③ Meanwhile, in a small saucepan cook pasta sauce until heated through.

④ Place burgers on bottoms of buns. Top with pasta sauce and the remaining 2 teaspoons oregano. Replace tops of buns.

PER SERVING 354 calories; 9 g total fat (3 g sat. fat); 133 mg cholesterol; 487 mg sodium; 28 g carbohydrate; 3 g fiber; 38 g protein

Turkey Tenderloin Tandoori ♥

Make it easy on yourself—sliced ripe tomatoes and cucumbers are all you need to accompany these India-inspired turkey tenderloins.

MAKES 4 servings **PREP** 15 minutes **GRILL** 12 minutes

2   turkey breast tenderloins (1 to 1½ pounds)
1½ teaspoons ground cumin
1½ teaspoons coriander seeds, crushed
1   teaspoon finely shredded lime peel
¾   teaspoon kosher salt
¾   teaspoon ground ginger
½   teaspoon crushed red pepper
½   cup plain low-fat yogurt
2   tablespoons lime juice
    Lime wedges (optional)

① Cut each turkey tenderloin in half horizontally to make 4 steaks; set aside. For rub, in a small bowl stir together cumin, coriander seeds, lime peel, salt, ginger, and crushed red pepper. Set aside ½ teaspoon of the spice mixture for sauce. Sprinkle the remaining spice mixture evenly over turkey steaks; rub in with your fingers.

② For a charcoal grill, grill turkey on the rack of an uncovered grill directly over medium coals for 12 to 15 minutes or until turkey is no longer pink (170°F), turning once halfway through grilling. (For a gas grill, preheat grill. Reduce heat to medium. Place turkey on grill rack over heat. Cover and grill as directed.)

③ Meanwhile, for sauce, in a small bowl stir together yogurt, lime juice, and the reserved ½ teaspoon spice mixture. Serve turkey with sauce and, if desired, lime wedges.

PER SERVING 158 calories; 2 g total fat (1 g sat. fat); 70 mg cholesterol; 439 mg sodium; 4 g carbohydrate; 1 g fiber; 29 g protein

> ❮ High in protein, low in fat, and always affordable, turkey is a tasty alternative for summertime grilling. ❯

Brats with Jalapeño-Green Apple Kraut

Jalapeños add some serious kick to the tasty brat topper. Pack up your mini grill and make these bodacious brats your tailgating specialty.

MAKES 6 sandwiches **PREP** 7 minutes **COOK** 20 minutes **GRILL** 3 minutes

- 6 uncooked bratwurst (about 1¼ pounds)
- 3 cups apple juice or apple cider
- ⅓ cup apple jelly
- 1 8-ounce can sauerkraut, drained
- 1 tart green apple, cored and cut into thin bite-size pieces
- 2 to 3 fresh jalapeños, seeded and cut into thin strips (see quick tip, page 28)
- 6 bratwurst or hot dog buns, split and toasted

① Use the tines of a fork to pierce the skin of each bratwurst several times. In a Dutch oven combine bratwurst and apple juice. Bring to boiling; reduce heat. Simmer, covered, about 20 minutes or until bratwurst are no longer pink and juices run clear (160°F); drain.

② Meanwhile, in a small saucepan melt apple jelly over low heat. In a medium bowl combine 2 tablespoons of the melted jelly, the sauerkraut, apple, and jalapeños. Set aside remaining melted jelly to brush on bratwurst.

③ Fold a 30 x 18-inch piece of heavy foil in half to make a 15 x 18-inch rectangle. Mound sauerkraut mixture in center of foil. Bring up 2 opposite edges of foil; seal with a double foil. Fold remaining edges to completely enclose sauerkraut mixture, leaving space for steam to build.

④ For a charcoal grill, grill bratwurst and foil packet on the rack of an uncovered grill directly over medium coals for 3 to 7 minutes or until bratwurst are browned, turning bratwurst and foil packet once halfway through grilling and brushing bratwurst with the reserved melted jelly during the last 2 minutes of grilling. (For a gas grill, preheat grill. Reduce heat to medium. Place bratwurst and foil packet on grill rack over heat. Cover; grill as directed.)

⑤ Serve bratwurst in toasted buns topped with sauerkraut mixture.

PER SANDWICH 737 calories; 48 g total fat (21 g sat. fat); 101 mg cholesterol; 2,014 mg sodium; 42 g carbohydrate; 3 g fiber; 34 g protein

Pizza Burgers

Grill all the flavors that your family loves in less time than it takes for pizza to be delivered to your door.

MAKES 4 burgers **PREP** 15 minutes **GRILL** 14 minutes

- 1 egg, lightly beaten
- ⅓ cup canned mushroom stems and pieces, drained and chopped
- ¼ cup seasoned fine dry bread crumbs
- 2 tablespoons milk
- 1 teaspoon dried Italian seasoning, crushed
- ¼ teaspoon salt
- 1 pound lean ground pork
- 4 slices French bread (½-inch-thick slices)
- 1 8-ounce can pizza sauce
- ¼ cup sliced pitted ripe olives
- ¼ cup shredded mozzarella cheese (1 ounce)

① In a large bowl combine egg, mushrooms, bread crumbs, milk, Italian seasoning, and salt. Add pork; mix well. Shape meat mixture into four ¾-inch-thick patties.

② For a charcoal grill, grill patties on the rack of an uncovered grill directly over medium coals for 14 to 18 minutes or until done (160°F), turning once halfway through grilling. Toast bread slices on the grill. (For a gas grill, preheat grill. Reduce heat to medium. Place patties, then bread slices, on grill rack over heat. Cover; grill as directed.)

③ Meanwhile, in a small saucepan combine pizza sauce and olives; heat through over low heat.

④ Serve burgers on toasted bread slices; spoon sauce on burger. Sprinkle with cheese.

PER BURGER 546 calories; 23 g total fat (9 g sat. fat); 133 mg cholesterol; 1,133 mg sodium; 48 g carbohydrate; 4 g fiber; 37 g protein

Grilled Italian Panini

Grilled Italian Panini

Assemble this boat-size sandwich in the morning before work. Its flavors will meld together as it rests in the refrigerator, and it will be ready to go when you get home.

MAKES 4 sandwiches **PREP** 20 minutes **GRILL** 8 minutes

- 1 16-ounce loaf unsliced ciabatta or Italian bread
- 6 ounces thinly sliced provolone cheese
- ¼ cup mayonnaise
- 1 tablespoon purchased basil pesto
- 4 ounces thinly sliced capocollo or cooked ham
- 4 ounces thinly sliced salami
- 1 recipe Red Onion Relish
- 1 cup arugula
- 1 tablespoon olive oil

① Carefully trim off and discard the top crust of the bread to make a flat surface. Turn bread over; trim off and discard bottom crust. Cut remaining bread in half horizontally to form two ½-inch-thick slices.

② Place half of the provolone cheese on 1 slice of bread. In a small bowl stir together mayonnaise and pesto; spread over cheese. Top with capocollo, salami, Red Onion Relish, arugula, the remaining cheese, and the other slice of bread. Brush both sides of sandwich evenly with oil.

③ For a charcoal grill, place sandwich on the lightly greased grill rack of an uncovered grill directly over medium coals. Place a 13 x 9 x 2-inch baking pan on top of sandwich; weight pan with several baking potatoes or a brick. Grill about 5 minutes or until sandwich is lightly browned. Use hot pads to remove baking pan. Use a spatula to carefully turn over sandwich. Place weighted pan back on sandwich; grill about 3 minutes more or until cheese melts. (For a gas grill, preheat grill. Reduce heat to medium. Place sandwich on lightly greased grill rack over heat. Grill as directed.)

Red Onion Relish: In a small bowl combine 1 medium red onion, halved and thinly sliced; 2 tablespoons olive oil; 1 tablespoon red wine vinegar; and 1 teaspoon snipped fresh oregano. Season to taste with salt and black pepper. Cover and let stand at room temperature up to 2 hours.

PER SANDWICH 840 calories; 51 g total fat (15 g sat. fat); 77 mg cholesterol; 2,118 mg sodium; 62 g carbohydrate; 4 g fiber; 33 g protein

Cuban Panini

When a classic Cuban sandwich and an Italian pressing technique go hand in hand, as they do in this extraordinary grilled sandwich, multiculturalism tastes magnificent.

MAKES 4 sandwiches **PREP** 25 minutes **GRILL** 6 minutes

- 1 cup thinly sliced cucumber
- ¼ cup thinly sliced red onion
- 1 tablespoon lime juice
- 1 teaspoon snipped fresh oregano
- 1 teaspoon sugar
- 1 1-pound loaf country-style bread
- 4 ounces sliced Swiss cheese
- 6 ounces thinly sliced cooked pork loin
- 2 tablespoons olive oil

① In a small bowl combine cucumber, onion, lime juice, oregano, and sugar; set aside.

② Cut two ¾-inch-thick horizontal slices from the bread. (Reserve remaining bread for anther use.) Top 1 slice of bread with half of the cheese and all of the pork. Remove cucumber with a slotted spoon and place on pork. Top with remaining cheese and second bread slice. Brush sandwich with olive oil.

③ Arrange medium-hot coals around the outside edge of a charcoal grill. Test for medium heat in the center of the grill. Place sandwich on a grill rack in the center of the grill. Place a baking sheet on top of the sandwich and weight it with 2 bricks. Cover and grill 6 to 8 minutes, turning once (see quick tip, below) or until bread is golden brown and cheese melts. (For a gas grill, preheat grill. Reduce heat to medium. Adjust for indirect grilling. Wait 2 minutes to allow the grill rack to cool slightly. Place sandwich on a grill rack away from heat. Grill as directed.)

PER SANDWICH 309 calories; 19 g total fat (8 g sat. fat); 61 mg cholesterol; 168 mg sodium; 12 g carbohydrate; 1 g fiber; 21 g protein

quick tip To turn the panini, remove bricks and baking sheet. Slide the baking sheet under the sandwich to help turn it over.

Pork and Apple Sandwiches with Honey-Pecan Glaze

If you don't see tenderized chops in your grocer's meat case, ring the bell and ask the clerk to run some chops thorough the tenderizer for you. It only takes a minutes.

MAKES 4 sandwiches **PREP** 23 minutes **GRILL** 7 minutes

- 2 tenderized butterflied pork chops, halved, or 4 tenderized boneless pork loin slices (1¼ pounds total)
  Salt and black pepper
- 1 large tart apple, cored and cut crosswise into 4 rings
- 1 recipe Honey-Pecan Glaze
- 4 1-ounce slices provolone cheese
- ⅓ cup sour cream
- ⅓ cup mayonnaise
- 2 teaspoons prepared horseradish
- 4 kaiser rolls, split and toasted

① Lightly sprinkle chops with salt and pepper. For a charcoal grill, grill chops and apple rings on the rack of an uncovered grill directly over medium coals for 7 to 9 minutes or until chops are slightly pink in center (160°F) and apples are tender, turning once halfway through grilling and brushing with Honey-Pecan Glaze during the last 3 minutes of grilling. Add provolone cheese to chops the last 1 minute of grilling. (For a gas grill, preheat grill. Reduce heat to medium. Place chops and apple rings on grill rack over heat. Cover and grill as directed.)

② Meanwhile, in a small bowl stir together sour cream, mayonnaise, and horseradish; spread on cut sides of toasted rolls. Place a chop and an apple slice on each roll bottom; add roll tops.

Honey-Pecan Glaze: In a small saucepan combine ¼ cup honey; ¼ cup chopped pecans, toasted; 2 tablespoons butter or margarine; and ½ teaspoon finely shredded lemon peel. Heat and stir until butter melts.

PER SANDWICH 822 calories; 46 g total fat (16 g sat. fat); 126 mg cholesterol; 936 mg sodium; 55 g carbohydrate; 3 g fiber; 46 g protein

Antipasto Panini

Placing provolone cheese under and over the riot of Italian meats that fill this sandwich glues everything into its gooey, delicious place.

MAKES 4 sandwiches **START TO FINISH** 30 minutes

- 1 9- to 10-inch Italian flatbread (focaccia)
- ¼ cup olive tapenade and/or pesto
- 4 ounces sliced provolone cheese
- 3 ounces sliced salami
- 3 ounces sliced capocollo
- 4 pepperoncini salad peppers
- 6 large fresh basil leaves
- 2 tablespoons butter, softened

① Using a serrated knife, cut focaccia in half horizontally. If necessary, trim off tops or bottoms of focaccia halves to make each about ¾ inch thick. Spread cut sides of focaccia with tapenade.

② Arrange half of the cheese on one of the focaccia halves. Layer with salami, capicola, pepperoncini peppers, and basil. Top with the remaining cheese and the remaining focaccia half, tapenade side down. Spread butter on both sides of sandwich.

③ For a charcoal grill, arrange medium-hot coals around edge of grill. Test for medium heat above center of grill. Place sandwich on grill rack over center of grill. Weight sandwich down with a baking sheet topped with 2 bricks. Cover and grill for 6 to 8 minutes or until golden brown. Turn sandwich over. Place weighted pan back on sandwich. Cover and grill for 6 to 8 minutes more or until golden brown and cheese is melted. (For a gas grill, preheat grill. Reduce heat to medium. Adjust for indirect cooking. Grill as above.)

PER SANDWICH 604 calories; 35 g total fat (13 g sat. fat); 78 mg cholesterol; 1,912 mg sodium; 51 g carbohydrate; 3 g fiber; 25 g protein

Grilled Fish with Moroccan Vinaigrette

Grilled Fish with Moroccan Vinaigrette

North African cuisine is filled with flavor combinations that amaze American palates. This Moroccan-inspired grilled fish dish is a great way to introduce your family to eye-opening flavors from this part of the world.

MAKES 4 servings **PREP** 20 minutes **GRILL** 6 minutes

- 1¼ to 1½ pounds fresh or frozen skinless red snapper, sea bass, grouper, or tuna fillets, ¾ inch thick
- 4 tablespoons olive oil
- ¼ teaspoon kosher salt or sea salt
- ¼ teaspoon black pepper
- ½ cup red wine vinegar
- 2 tablespoons snipped fresh Italian parsley
- 2 tablespoons snipped fresh cilantro
- 1 tablespoon fresh lemon juice
- 3 tablespoons finely chopped shallot (1 large)
- 1 clove garlic, minced
- ½ teaspoon kosher salt or sea salt
- ½ teaspoon paprika
- ¼ teaspoon cayenne pepper
- ¼ teaspoon ground cumin
  Hot cooked couscous

① Thaw fish, if frozen. Rinse fish; pat dry with paper towels. Cut fish into 4 portions. Brush both sides of fish evenly with 2 tablespoons of the olive oil. Sprinkle both sides of fish with the ¼ teaspoon salt and the ¼ teaspoon black pepper.

② For vinaigrette, in a screw-top jar combine vinegar, parsley, cilantro, the remaining 2 tablespoons olive oil, the lemon juice, shallot, garlic, the ½ teaspoon salt, paprika, cayenne pepper, and cumin. Cover and shake well. Set aside.

③ For a charcoal grill, grill fish on the greased rack of an uncovered grill directly over medium coals for 6 to 8 minutes or until fish begins to flake when tested with a fork, turning fish once and brushing with the remaining oil halfway through grilling. (For a gas grill, preheat grill. Reduce heat to medium. Place fish on greased grill rack over heat. Cover and grill as directed.)

④ To serve, shake vinaigrette. Using a wide spatula, transfer fish to plates with couscous. Drizzle vinaigrette over fish.

PER SERVING 261 calories; 15 g total fat (2 g sat. fat); 35 mg cholesterol; 366 mg sodium; 3 g carbohydrate; 0 g fiber; 29 g protein

Red Snapper with Herb-Pecan Crust ♥

Grilling infuses the crunchy pecan crust with a provocative hint of smoky flavor.

MAKES 4 servings **PREP** 15 minutes **GRILL** 4 minutes

- 4 5- to 6-ounce fresh or frozen red snapper fillets, ½ to 1 inch thick
- ⅓ cup finely chopped pecans
- 2 tablespoons fine dry bread crumbs
- 2 tablespoons butter, softened
- 1 teaspoon finely shredded lemon peel
- 1 tablespoon snipped fresh parsley
- ¼ teaspoon salt
- ⅛ teaspoon black pepper
  Dash cayenne pepper
- 2 cloves garlic, minced
  Snipped fresh parsley (optional)
  Lemon wedges (optional)

① Thaw fish, if frozen. Rinse fish; pat dry with paper towels. Measure thickness of fish; set aside. In a small bowl combine pecans, bread crumbs, butter, lemon peel, the 1 tablespoon parsley, salt, black pepper, cayenne pepper, and garlic. Set aside.

② For a charcoal grill, grill fish, skin sides down, on the greased rack of an uncovered grill directly over medium coals. Spoon the pecan mixture on top of fillets; spread slightly. Grill until fish begins to flake when tested with a fork. Allow 4 to 6 minutes per ½-inch thickness of fish. (For a gas grill, preheat grill. Reduce heat to medium. Place fish on greased grill rack over heat. Spoon pecan mixture on top of fillets. Cover and grill as directed.) If desired, sprinkle fish with additional snipped parsley and serve with lemon wedges.

PER SERVING 268 calories; 14 g total fat (4 g sat. fat); 67 mg cholesterol; 287 mg sodium; 7 g carbohydrate; 8 g fiber; 30 g protein

Grilled Salmon and Asparagus with Garden Mayonnaise

Healthful, versatile salmon swims onto the grill in a terrifically tasty way.

MAKES 4 servings **PREP** 10 minutes **GRILL** 8 minutes

4	6- to 8-ounce fresh or frozen skinless salmon fillets, about 1 inch thick
1	pound asparagus spears
1	tablespoon olive oil
	Sea salt or salt and freshly ground black pepper
½	cup finely chopped celery (1 stalk)
⅓	cup mayonnaise
¼	cup thinly sliced green onions (2)
1	tablespoon lemon juice
2	teaspoons snipped fresh tarragon or ½ teaspoon dried tarragon, crushed
	Lemon wedges (optional)

① Thaw fish, if frozen. Rinse fish; pat dry with paper towels. Snap off and discard woody bases from asparagus. Brush both sides of fish and asparagus lightly with olive oil. Sprinkle fish and asparagus with salt and pepper.

② For a charcoal grill, place fish on the greased rack of an uncovered grill directly over medium coals. Place asparagus on grill rack next to salmon. Grill for 8 to 12 minutes or until fish begins to flake when tested with a fork and asparagus is tender, turning fish once halfway through grilling and turning asparagus occasionally. (For a gas grill, preheat grill. Reduce heat to medium. Place fish and asparagus on a greased grill rack over heat. Cover and grill as above.)

③ Meanwhile, for garden mayonnaise, in a small bowl stir together celery, mayonnaise, green onions, lemon juice, and tarragon. Chill until serving time.

④ To serve, arrange fish and asparagus on 4 dinner plates. Top fish with garden mayonnaise. If desired, serve with lemon wedges.

PER SERVING 545 calories; 41 g total fat (8 g sat. fat); 100 mg cholesterol; 314 mg sodium; 6 g carbohydrate; 3 g fiber; 37 g protein

Barbecued Salmon with Corn Relish

Jalapeño gives the fresh corn relish for this yummy barbecued salmon a real kick. Serve it with cooling and creamy coleslaw and some crusty sourdough bread.

MAKES 4 servings **START TO FINISH** 30 minutes

1	jalapeño (see quick tip, page 28)
1	red sweet pepper, chopped
2	fresh ears of corn, husked
4	5-to 6-ounce skinless salmon fillets, ½ to 1 inch thick
	Salt and freshly ground black pepper
½	cup bottled barbecue sauce
2	teaspoons olive oil
¼	teaspoon salt
¼	teaspoon black pepper
	Fresh marjoram or oregano (optional)

① Thinly slice half the jalapeño; seed and finely chop the remaining half. In a bowl combine chopped jalapeño and sweet pepper; set aside.

② Place corn on grill rack directly over medium heat; grill, turning occasionally, 10 to 15 minutes or until crisp-tender. Transfer corn to cutting board; cool slightly.

③ Meanwhile, rinse salmon and pat dry; sprinkle with salt and pepper. Add to grill. Grill 4 to 6 minutes or until fish flakes easily when tested with a fork, turning once. Cover salmon to keep warm. Cut corn from cob. Add to chopped peppers with 1 tablespoon of the barbecue sauce, the olive oil, salt, and black pepper.

④ Serve salmon with corn and relish. Top with remaining barbecue sauce and, if desired, fresh herbs.

PER SERVING 395 calories; 22 g total fat (5 g sat. fat); 78 mg cholesterol; 470 mg sodium; 18 g carbohydrate; 2 g fiber; 31 g protein

Barbecued Salmon with Corn Relish

Salmon Caesar Salad

Salmon Caesar Salad

To check salmon for pin bones, run your fingers along the flesh from top to bottom. The bones pull out easily with tweezers.

MAKES 4 servings **PREP** 20 minutes **GRILL** 8 minutes

- 1 pound fresh or frozen skinless salmon fillets, about 1 inch thick
- 1 tablespoon olive oil
- 1 teaspoon finely shredded lemon peel
- 1 tablespoon lemon juice
- ¼ teaspoon black pepper
- 1 pound fresh asparagus spears, trimmed
- 2 cups sliced hearts of romaine lettuce
- 2 cups torn curly endive
- ½ of a medium cucumber, thinly sliced
- ½ cup bottled Caesar salad dressing
  Finely shredded Parmesan cheese (optional)
  Thin slices baguette-style French bread, toasted (optional)

① Thaw fish, if frozen. Rinse fish; pat dry with paper towels. In a small bowl stir together oil, lemon peel, lemon juice, and pepper. Brush both sides fish with lemon mixture; set aside.

② In a large skillet cook asparagus, covered, in a small amount of boiling water for 3 minutes; drain. Place asparagus in a grill wok.

③ For a charcoal grill, grill fish on the greased rack of an uncovered grill directly over medium coals for 8 to 12 minutes or until fish begins to flake when tested with a fork, turning once halfway through grilling. Add asparagus in wok to grill during the last 3 to 5 minutes of grilling or until asparagus browns, turning once halfway through grilling. (For a gas grill, preheat grill. Reduce heat to medium. Place fish, then asparagus in wok on greased grill rack over heat. Cover and grill as directed.)

④ In a large bowl combine lettuce, endive, and cucumber. Divide evenly among serving plates. Using a fork, flake fish into bite-size pieces. Arrange fish and asparagus on lettuce mixture. Drizzle salads with dressing. If desired, sprinkle with cheese and serve with toasted baguette slices.

PER SERVING 351 calories; 25 g total fat (4 g sat. fat); 59 mg cholesterol; 418 mg sodium; 5 g carbohydrate; 3 g fiber; 26 g protein

Fish Tacos with Chipotle Cream ♥

Fish tacos often appear when you're California dreaming. Make it real with this extraordinary recipe.

MAKES 12 tacos **PREP** 20 minutes **GRILL** 4 minutes

- 4 4- to 5-ounce fresh or frozen skinless red snapper, tilapia, or sole fillets, ½ inch thick
- 1 tablespoon cooking oil
- 1 teaspoon ancho chili powder
- ½ teaspoon ground cumin
- ¼ teaspoon salt
- ¼ teaspoon black pepper
- ½ cup sour cream
- 1 teaspoon finely chopped canned chipotle pepper in adobo sauce (see quick tip, page 28)
- 12 6-inch corn or flour tortillas
- 2 cups shredded cabbage or romaine lettuce
- 1 ripe avocado, halved, seeded, peeled, and cut into thin slices (optional)
- 1 cup refrigerated fresh salsa
- 1 lime, cut into wedges
  Snipped cilantro (optional)

① Thaw fish, if frozen. Rinse fish; pat dry with paper towels. Brush oil evenly on both sides of fish. For rub, in a small bowl stir together chili powder, cumin, salt, and pepper. Sprinkle rub over both sides of fish; rub in with your fingers.

② For chipotle cream, in another small bowl stir together sour cream and chopped chipotle pepper; set aside. Wrap tortillas tightly in foil.

③ For a charcoal grill, grill fish and tortilla packet on the greased rack of an uncovered grill directly over medium coals for 4 to 6 minutes or until fish begins to flake when tested with a fork and tortillas are heated through, turning fish and tortilla packet once halfway through grilling. (For a gas grill, preheat grill. Reduce heat to medium. Place fish and tortilla packet on greased grill rack over heat. Cover and grill as directed.)

④ Using a fork, break fish into pieces. Fill warm tortillas evenly with cabbage, fish, and if desired, avocado slices. Serve with fresh salsa, chipotle cream, lime wedges, and, if desired, cilantro.

PER 2 tacos 293 calories; 9 g total fat (3 g sat. fat); 35 mg cholesterol; 493 mg sodium; 34 g carbohydrate; 4 g fiber; 19 g protein

Garlic-Buttered Shrimp ♥

Make the side as quick and simple as the shrimp—simply place the kabobs on a bed of fluffy cooked wild and long grain rice mix.

MAKES 4 servings **START TO FINISH** 25 minutes

- 1 pound fresh or frozen large shrimp in shells
- 2 tablespoons butter
- 2 cloves garlic, minced, or 1 teaspoon bottled minced garlic
- 1 tablespoon snipped fresh parsley
   Dash cayenne pepper (optional)
- 2 tablespoons dry white wine

① Thaw shrimp, if frozen. Peel and devein shrimp, keeping tails intact. Rinse shrimp; pat dry with paper towels. Thread shrimp onto 4 long metal skewers; set aside.

② For sauce, in a small saucepan melt butter. Stir in garlic, parsley, and, if desired, cayenne pepper. Cook for 1 minute. Stir in wine; heat through. Set sauce aside.

③ For a charcoal grill, grill kabobs on the greased grill rack of an uncovered grill directly over medium coals for 6 to 10 minutes or until shrimp turn opaque, turning once and brushing frequently with sauce. (For a gas grill, preheat grill. Reduce heat to medium. Place kabobs on greased grill rack over heat. Cover and grill as directed.)

PER SERVING 159 calories; 8 g total fat (4 g sat. fat); 156 mg cholesterol; 199 mg sodium; 1 g carbohydrate; 0 g fiber; 19 g protein

Garlic-Buttered Shrimp

Grilled Shrimp and Pineapple Kabobs ♥

Choose pineapples that are slightly soft to the touch and whose skins are golden not green.

MAKES 4 servings **PREP** 20 minutes **GRILL** 7 minutes

- 12 ounces fresh or frozen peeled and deveined jumbo shrimp
- ½ of a fresh pineapple
- ½ cup water
- 6 tablespoons orange marmalade
- 1 tablespoon soy sauce
- 1 8.8-ounce pouch cooked long grain rice
- ¼ cup fresh cilantro

① Thaw shrimp, if frozen. Rinse shrimp; pat dry with paper towels. Thread shrimp onto 4 skewers (see quick tip, below). Cut pineapple into 4 slices; core slices and cut each slice into quarters to make 16 small wedges. Thread pineapple wedges into 4 skewers.

② In a small saucepan combine the water, 4 tablespoons of the marmalade, and the soy sauce. Brush the shrimp and pineapple with some of the soy sauce mixture.

③ For a charcoal grill, grill shrimp on the rack of an uncovered grill directly over medium-hot coals for 7 to 9 minutes or until shrimp are opaque and pineapple wedges are heated through, turning once halfway through grilling. (For a gas grill, preheat grill. Reduce heat to medium. Place shrimp and pineapple skewers on grill rack over heat. Cover and grill as directed.) Remove from grill; cover and keep warm.

④ In a small saucepan bring the remaining soy sauce mixture to a boil; transfer to a small serving bowl. Heat rice in the microwave according to package directions. Transfer rice to a serving bowl; stir in the remaining 2 tablespoons marmalade and cilantro. Serve shrimp and pineapple skewers with rice and the remaining soy mixture.

PER KABOB 322 calories; 8 g total fat (0 g sat. fat); 172 mg cholesterol; 451 mg sodium; 49 g carbohydrate; 2 g fiber; 25 g protein.

quick tip If using wooden skewers, soak skewers in water for at least 30 minutes. Drain before using.

Open-Face Veggie Melts

Open-Face Veggie Melts

If you do not have a grilling basket, simply wrap the mushrooms and sweet pepper in foil, then follow the rest of the recipe.

MAKES 6 servings **PREP** 25 minutes **GRILL** 14 minutes

- 1 tablespoon balsamic vinegar
- 1 clove garlic, finely chopped
- ½ teaspoon Dijon mustard
- 1½ teaspoons packed brown sugar
- ¼ cup olive oil
- 6 slices eggplant (½ inch thick)
- 6 slices yellow summer squash (½ inch thick)
- 2 slices red onion (½ inch thick)
- 1 8-ounce package whole white mushrooms
- 1 large red sweet pepper, seeded and cut into ½-inch slices
- ¼ cup vegetable oil
- 1 16-ounce round loaf crusty bread, cut into six 1-inch-thick slices
- 1 large clove garlic, peeled and halved
- 2 cups shredded fontina cheese (8 ounces)

① For dressing, whisk together vinegar, garlic, ⅛ teaspoon *salt*, ⅛ teaspoon *black pepper*, mustard, and sugar. Gradually whisk in ¼ cup olive oil. Set aside.

② In a bowl combine eggplant, squash, onion, mushrooms, sweet pepper, vegetable oil, ½ teaspoon *salt*, and ¼ teaspoon *black pepper*; toss to coat.

③ For a charcoal grill, place eggplant, squash, and onion on the lightly greased rack of an uncovered grill directly over medium-hot coals. Grill for 6 to 8 minutes or until crisp-tender, turning once halfway through grilling. Transfer to bowl; keep warm. Place mushrooms and sweet peppers in a grilling basket. Place grill basket on grill rack over coals. Grill for 6 to 8 minutes or until tender. Add to eggplant mixture. Brush cut sides of bread with additional olive oil. Rub bread with garlic. Place bread on the grill rack over coals. Grill for 2 to 3 minutes or until light brown, turning once halfway through grilling. (For a gas grill, preheat grill. Reduce heat to medium-high Place vegetables, then bread on lightly greased grill rack over heat. Cover and grill as directed.)

④ Pour dressing over vegetables; toss to coat. Divide vegetable mixture among bread slices. Top with cheese. Serve warm.

PER SANDWICH 520 calories; 30 g total fat (9 g sat. fat); 44 mg cholesterol; 890 mg sodium; 47 g carbohydrate; 7 g fiber; 18 g protein

Grilled Sweet Pepper and Eggplant Sandwiches

Eggplant's peak season is in August and September, making this healthful sandwich perfect for late-summer meals. When you purchase eggplant, do use it within just a few days, however—the voluptuous purple fruits tend to taste bitter when stored for much longer.

MAKES 4 servings **START TO FINISH** 30 minutes

- 2 medium green, red, and/or yellow sweet peppers
- 1 medium eggplant (about 12 ounces)
- 1 tablespoon olive oil
- 8 ½-inch slices French bread
- 4 ounces soft goat cheese (chèvre)
- ¼ cup Dijon mustard

① Quarter the sweet peppers lengthwise; remove stems, seeds, and membranes. Cut eggplant crosswise into 8 slices. Brush sweet pepper quarters and eggplant slices lightly with oil.

② Place sweet pepper quarters and eggplant slices on the rack of an uncovered grill over medium heat. Grill for 8 to 10 minutes or until sweet peppers are slightly charred and eggplant is tender, turning once. Remove vegetables from grill; set aside.

③ Spread one side of each bread slice with goat cheese and mustard. Place 2 sweet pepper quarters and 2 eggplant slices on 4 of the bread slices. Top with remaining bread slices.

PER SERVING 292 calories; 11 g total fat (5 g sat. fat); 13 mg cholesterol; 757 mg sodium; 34 g carbohydrate; 4 g fiber; 11 g protein

quick tip When it comes to eggplant, bigger is not necessarily better. Large eggplants are pretty and impressive but are often bitter. For the most pleasing texture and flavor, aim for eggplants that weigh 12 ounces or less.

Grilled Veggie Sandwiches

This sandwich comes from the hallowed halls of the Mediterranean diet, a simple, vegetable-focussed eating style filled with bold, fresh flavors.

MAKES 4 sandwiches **PREP** 26 minutes **GRILL** 4 minutes

- 2 tablespoons olive oil
- 4 ciabatta rolls or other hearty rolls, split
- 1 lemon, halved and seeded
- 1 tablespoon balsamic vinegar
- 3 small zucchini and/or yellow summer squash, cut lengthwise into ¼-inch-thick slices
- 1 small red onion, cut into ¼-inch-thick slices
  Salt and black pepper
- 2 ounces feta cheese, crumbled
  Fresh mint leaves (optional)

① Lightly brush 1 tablespoon of the oil on the cut sides of rolls and the cut sides of the lemon halves; set aside. In a small bowl combine the remaining 1 tablespoon oil and the vinegar. Brush zucchini and onion slices with some of the oil-vinegar mixture; sprinkle with salt and pepper.

② For charcoal grill, place vegetables and lemon on the rack of an uncovered grill directly over medium-hot coals. Grill for 4 to 6 minutes or until tender, turning once halfway through grilling. Add rolls, cut sides down, during last 3 minutes of grilling. (For a gas grill, preheat grill. Reduce heat to medium-hot. Place vegetables and lemon on grill rack over heat. Cover; grill as above. Add rolls, cut sides down, during last 3 minutes of grilling.)

③ Arrange vegetables on roll bottoms. Top with feta cheese and, if desired, mint. Drizzle with remaining oil-vinegar mixture. Squeeze juice from lemon over all. Add roll tops.

PER SANDWICH 294 calories; 11 g total fat (3 g sat. fat); 13 mg cholesterol; 684 mg sodium; 41 g carbohydrate; 4 g fiber; 10 g protein

Southwestern Black Bean Cakes with Guacamole

Filling, flavorful, fiber-filled, and affordable—these bean patties have it all!

MAKES 4 servings **PREP** 20 minutes **GRILL** 8 minutes

- 2 slices whole wheat bread, torn
- ¼ cup fresh cilantro leaves
- 2 cloves garlic
- 1 15-ounce can black beans, rinsed and drained
- 1 canned chipotle pepper in adobo sauce
- 1 to 2 teaspoons adobo sauce
- 1 teaspoon ground cumin
- 1 egg
  Olive oil
- ½ of a medium avocado, seeded and peeled
- 1 tablespoon lime juice
  Salt and black pepper
- 4 hamburger buns (optional)
- 1 small plum tomato, chopped
  Salsa (optional)
  Sour cream (optional)

① Place torn bread in a food processor. Cover and process until bread resembles coarse crumbs; transfer to a large bowl and set aside. Place cilantro and garlic in the food processor; cover and process until finely chopped. Add beans, chipotle pepper, adobo sauce, and cumin; process with several on/off turns until beans are coarsely chopped and mixture begins to pull away from sides. Add mixture to bread crumbs in bowl. Add egg to bean mixture; mix well and shape into four ½-inch-thick patties. Brush patties lightly with olive oil.

② Grill patties on the lightly greased rack of an uncovered grill directly over medium coals for 8 to 10 minutes or until patties are heated through (160°F), turning once.

③ Meanwhile, for guacamole, in a small bowl mash avocado. Stir in lime juice; season with salt and pepper. If desired, serve patties in hamburger buns with guacamole, tomato, salsa, and sour cream.

PER SERVING 168 calories; 6 g total fat (1 g sat. fat); 53 mg cholesterol; 536 mg sodium; 25 g carbohydrate; 8 g fiber; 10 g protein

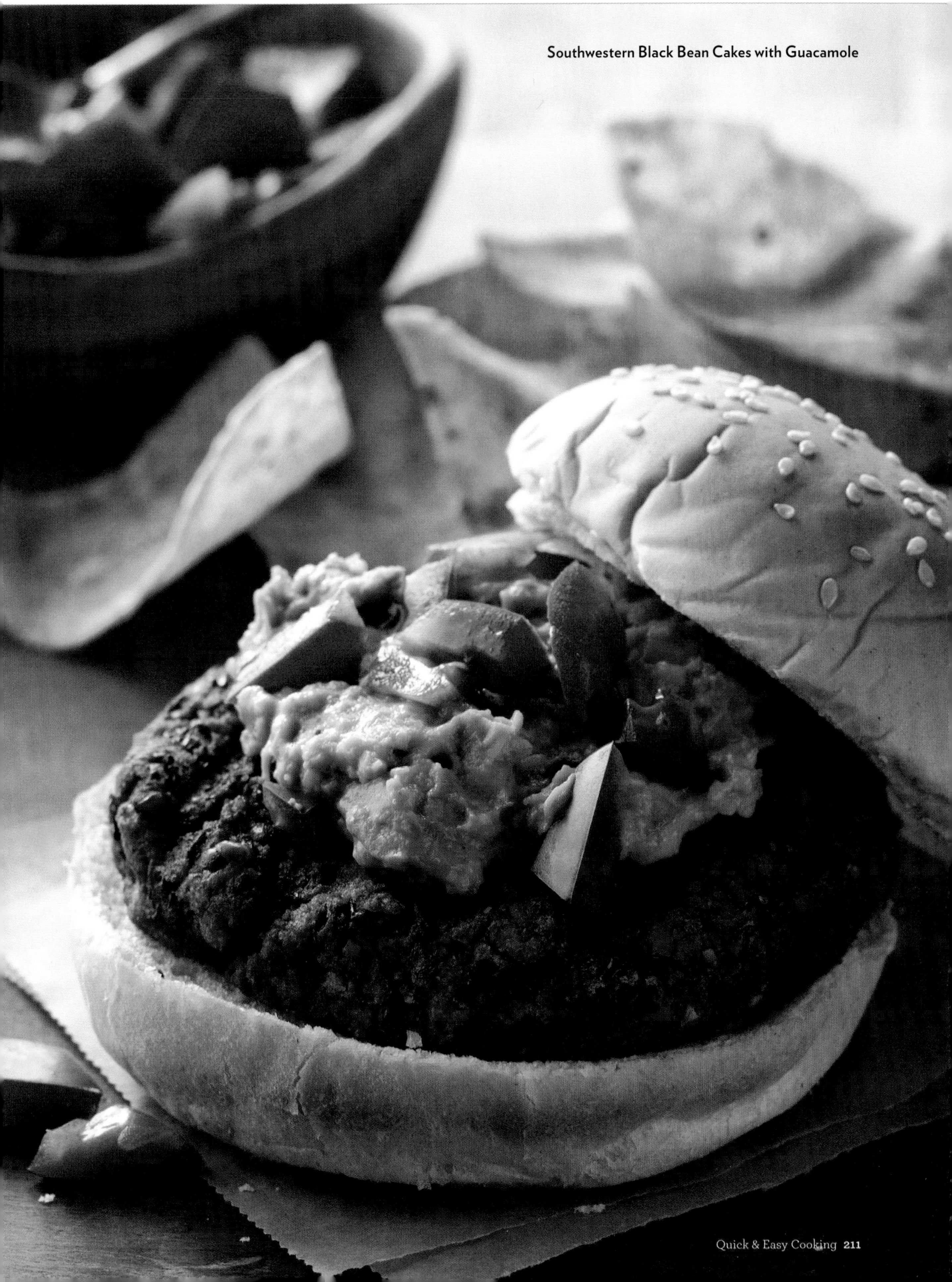

Southwestern Black Bean Cakes with Guacamole

The adjectives slow and simple may not describe your life. But with a trusty slow cooker as your sous-chef, they'll perfectly describe the ease of meal preparation.

220

232

234

SLOW & SIMPLE

Barbecued Brisket

When huge beef briskets are cut into smaller pieces for the retail market, two cuts are created—the "point" and the "flat." The point, which is somewhat triangular, is fatty, but most flavorful. The flat, which is square or rectangular, yields a greater amount of deliciously lean meat. Both cuts work wonderfully in the slow cooker.

MAKES 12 servings **PREP** 15 minutes
COOK 12 to 14 hours (low) or 6 to 7 hours (high)

- 1   **4- to 4½-pound fresh beef brisket**
      Black pepper
- 1   **16-ounce package peeled fresh baby carrots**
- 2   **stalks celery, cut into ½-inch thick slices**
- 1½   **cups bottled smoke-flavor barbecue sauce**
- 2   **tablespoons quick-cooking tapioca, crushed**
- 2   **tablespoons Dijon mustard**
- 1   **tablespoon Worcestershire sauce**
- 4   **cups mashed potatoes or hot cooked noodles**

① Trim fat from brisket. If necessary, cut brisket in half to fit into a 5- to 6-quart slow cooker. Season brisket with pepper. In the slow cooker combine carrots and celery. Place brisket on vegetables. In a small bowl combine barbecue sauce, tapioca, mustard, and Worcestershire sauce; pour over brisket.

② Cover and cook on low-heat setting for 12 to 14 hours or on high-heat setting for 6 to 7 hours.

③ Transfer brisket to cutting board. Thinly slice brisket across the grain. Skim fat from cooking liquid. Serve cooking liquid with sliced brisket and vegetables over mashed potatoes.

PER SERVING 441 calories; 7 g total fat (3 g sat. fat); 65 mg cholesterol; 1,580 mg sodium; 54 g carbohydrate; 5 g fiber; 37 g protein

Asian Flank Steak

To make slow cooking even more convenient and trouble-free, try the nylon slow cooker liners now on the market. When you use a liner, there is no need to soak and scrub the ceramic liner—just lift it out and toss the mess away.

MAKES 6 servings **PREP** 30 minutes **COOK** 8 to 9 hours (low) or 4 to 4½ hours (high) + 30 minutes (high)

- 3   **pounds beef flank steak**
- ¾   **cup hoisin sauce**
- ¾   **cup orange juice**
- ¾   **cup beef broth**
- ¼   **cup dry sherry or orange juice**
- 2   **tablespoons bottled minced garlic (12 cloves)**
- 1   **teaspoon ground ginger**
- 2   **tablespoons quick-cooking tapioca**
- 1½   **cups diagonally sliced carrots (3 medium)**
- 1   **large onion, thinly sliced**
- 1½   **cups fresh snow pea pods, trimmed**
- 1½   **cups red sweet pepper strips (2 medium)**
- 3   **cups hot cooked white or brown rice**

① Trim fat from meat. If necessary, cut meat to fit into a 4- to 5-quart slow cooker; set aside. In the cooker stir together hoisin sauce, orange juice, broth, sherry, garlic, and ginger. Sprinkle with tapioca. Stir in carrots and onion; add meat.

② Cover and cook on low-heat setting for 8 to 9 hours or on high-heat setting for 4 to 4½ hours.

③ If using low-heat setting, turn to high-heat setting. Stir in pea pods and sweet peppers. Cover and cook for 30 minutes more.

④ Remove meat from cooker. Thinly slice across the grain. Serve meat, vegetables, and cooking liquid over hot cooked rice.

PER SERVING 568 calories; 16 g total fat (6 g sat. fat); 85 mg cholesterol; 647 mg sodium; 48 g carbohydrate; 3 g fiber; 52 g protein

> ❮ Flank steak and brisket melt into total tenderness in the slow cooker. ❯

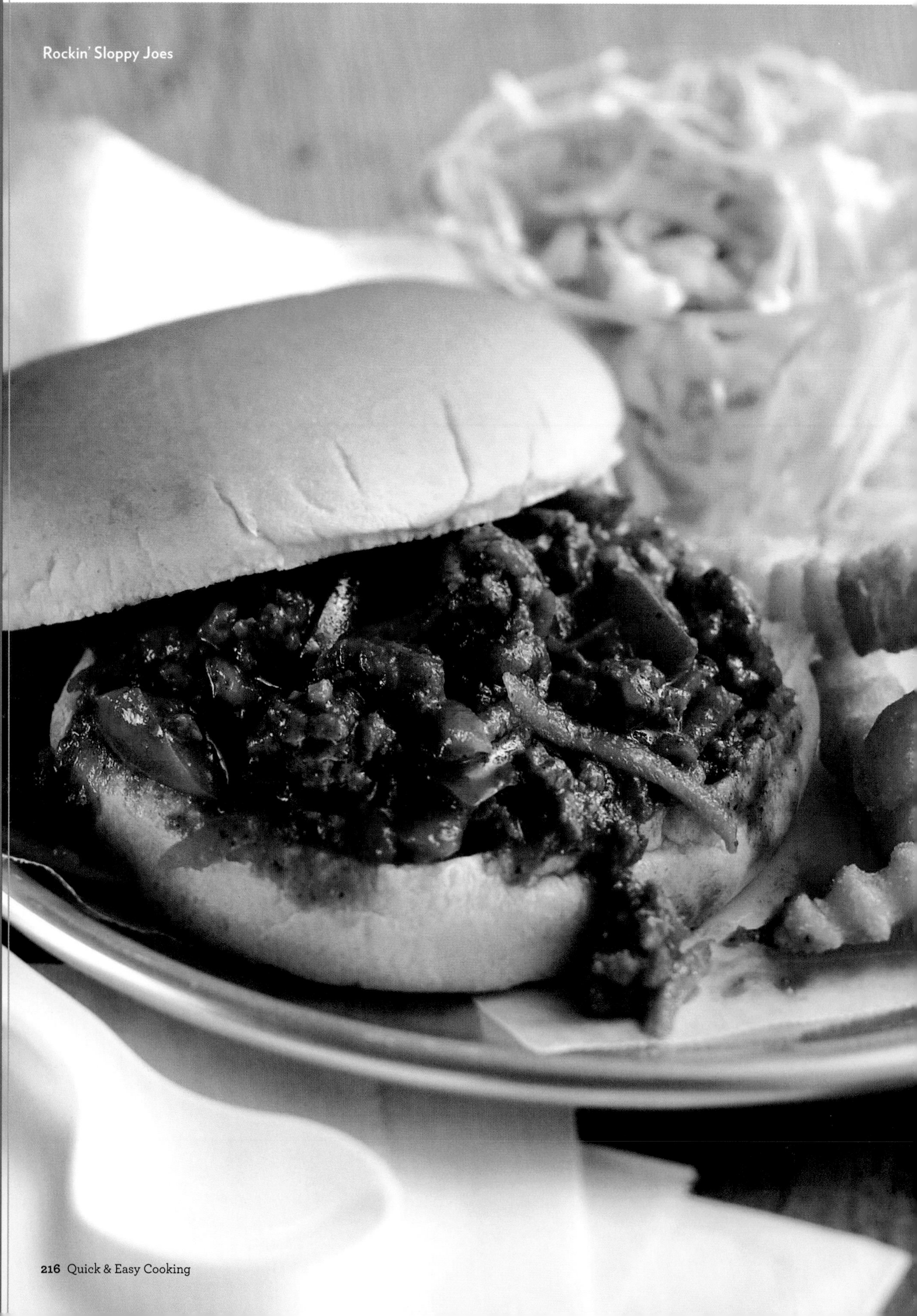

Rockin' Sloppy Joes

Rockin' Sloppy Joes

Whoa, baby—this recipe takes plain old sloppy joes and turns them on their heads. Serve some cool carrot and celery sticks on the side.

MAKES 8 servings **PREP** 30 minutes
COOK 6 to 8 hours (low) or 3 to 4 hours (high)

1½	pounds ground beef
1	large onion, chopped
2	cloves garlic, minced
1	large red sweet pepper, chopped
2	medium carrots, shredded
1	4-ounce can diced green chiles
1	5.5-ounce can hot-style vegetable juice or vegetable juice
½	cup ketchup
1	tablespoon brown sugar
1	tablespoon yellow mustard
2	teaspoons chili powder
1	teaspoon cider vinegar
8	hamburger buns, split and toasted

① In a large skillet cook ground beef, onion, and garlic over medium heat until meat is browned and onion is tender. Drain off fat.

② In a 3½- or 4-quart slow cooker combine meat mixture, sweet pepper, carrots, green chiles, vegetable juice, ketchup, brown sugar, mustard, chili powder, and vinegar.

③ Cover; cook on low-heat setting for 6 to 8 hours or on high-heat setting for 3 to 4 hours. Serve on toasted buns.

PER SERVING 354 calories; 15 g total fat (6 g sat. fat); 58 mg cholesterol; 572 mg sodium; 33 g carbohydrate; 3 g fiber; 21 g protein

Peppery Italian Beef Sandwiches

Few things in a cook's life are as rewarding as having the dish he or she delivered be the first food to disappear from the potluck buffet. This is exactly what will happen if you bring the fixings for Peppery Italian Beef Sandwiches.

MAKES 8 servings **PREP** 30 minutes
COOK 10 hours (low) or 5 hours (high)

1	2½- to 3-pound boneless beef chuck pot roast
4	teaspoons garlic pepper seasoning
1	tablespoon vegetable oil
1	14.5-ounce can beef broth
1	0.7-ounce envelope Italian dry salad dressing mix
1	teaspoon onion salt
1	teaspoon dried oregano, crushed
1	teaspoon dried basil, crushed
1	teaspoon dried parsley
1	12- to 16-ounce jar pepperoncini salad peppers, drained
8	hoagie buns or kaiser rolls, split and toasted
2	cups shredded mozzarella cheese (8 ounces)

① Trim fat from meat. Coat meat with garlic pepper seasoning. In a Dutch oven brown meat on all sides in hot oil.

② If necessary cut meat to fit into a 3½ or 4-quart slow cooker. Place meat in cooker. In a medium bowl whisk together beef broth, dressing mix, onion salt, oregano, basil, and parsley. Pour over meat in cooker. Top with peppers.

③ Cover and cook on low-heat setting for 10 hours or on high-heat setting for 5 hours. Transfer meat to a cutting board. Using 2 forks, pull meat apart into shreds. Using a slotted spoon, remove peppers from cooking liquid and transfer to a serving bowl. Skim fat from cooking liquid and transfer cooking liquid to a serving bowl.

④ To serve, spoon some shredded meat on the bottom halves of buns. If desired, spoon some of the cooking liquid on meat. Sprinkle with cheese. Top with peppers and bun tops.

PER SERVING 579 calories; 21 g total fat (8 g sat. fat); 105 mg cholesterol; 2,390 mg sodium; 54 g carbohydrate; 2 g fiber; 42 g protein

Round Steak with Vegetables

Serve this steamy sensation over an effortless side dish such as rice or couscous.

MAKES 4 servings **PREP** 20 minutes
COOK 8 to 9 hours (low) or 4 to 4½ hours (high)

- 1½ pounds boneless beef round steak, cut ¾ to 1 inch thick
- ¼ teaspoon black pepper
- ⅛ teaspoon salt
- 2 cups packaged peeled baby carrots
- 2 cups sliced fresh mushrooms
- 1 large onion, cut into wedges
- 1 14½-ounce can diced tomatoes with basil, garlic, and oregano, undrained
- 3 tablespoons tomato paste with Italian seasonings
- 1 tablespoon Worcestershire sauce
- 1 medium zucchini, halved lengthwise and sliced

① Trim fat from steak. Cut steak into 4 serving-size pieces; season with pepper and salt. Place meat in a 3½- or 4-quart slow cooker. Top with carrots, mushrooms, and onion.

② In a medium bowl stir together undrained tomatoes, tomato paste, and Worcestershire sauce. Pour tomato mixture over vegetables.

③ Cover and cook on low-heat setting for 8 to 9 hours or on high-heat setting for 4 to 4½ hours. Add zucchini during the last 20 minutes of cooking.

PER SERVING 335 calories; 6 g total fat (2 g sat. fat); 78 mg cholesterol; 901 mg sodium; 26 g carbohydrate; 4 g fiber; 44 g protein

quick tip To make the most of pricey cans of tomato paste, try this: Remove both the top and the bottom of the can with a can opener. Using one of the metal lids, press the cylinder of paste out of the can. Cut the cylinder into ½-inch—or tablespoon-size—slices. Use what you need, then wrap the remaining slices individually in plastic wrap and place in the freezer. Use the frozen disks whenever you need just a tablespoon or so of tomato paste.

Russian Braised Brisket ♥

To make sure that spices you don't use very much—such as caraway seeds—are still full of flavor, rub them firmly between your thumb and forefinger.

MAKES 6 servings **PREP** 20 minutes **COOK** 10 hours (low) or 5 hours (high) + 30 to 60 minutes (high)

- 1 2- to 3-pound beef brisket
   Salt and black pepper
- 1 tablespoon cooking oil
- 1 large onion, cut into wedges
- 2 medium parsnips, cut into 2-inch pieces
- 2 medium carrots, cut into 2-inch pieces
- ½ teaspoon dill seeds
- ½ teaspoon caraway seeds
- ¼ teaspoon salt
- 1½ cups beef broth
- ¼ cup vodka (optional)
- 1 8-ounce carton sour cream
- ⅓ cup all-purpose flour
- ¼ cup water
- 2 teaspoons dried dill weed
- 2 teaspoons horseradish mustard
- 2 cups finely shredded cabbage
- 1 cup sliced fresh mushrooms
   Hot mashed potatoes (optional)

① Trim fat from brisket. Cut brisket to fit into a 3½- or 4-quart slow cooker; season with salt and pepper. In a skillet brown brisket in hot oil over medium-high heat.

② In the slow cooker place onion, parsnips, and carrots. Sprinkle with dill seeds, caraway seeds, and salt. Top with brisket. Pour beef broth and vodka, if using, over all.

③ Cover; cook on low-heat setting for 10 hours or on high-heat setting for 5 hours.

④ If using low-heat setting, turn to high-heat setting. In a bowl stir together sour cream, flour, water, dill weed, and mustard. Stir 1 cup hot cooking liquid into the sour cream mixture. Return all to cooker; stir to combine. Add cabbage and mushrooms. Cover; cook 30 to 60 minutes more or until vegetables are tender and liquid is thickened.

⑤ Transfer brisket to a cutting board and slice thinly across the grain. Serve with sauce, vegetables, and, if desired, mashed potatoes.

PER SERVING 379 calories; 17 g total fat (7 g sat. fat); 79 mg cholesterol; 589 mg sodium; 20 g carbohydrate; 4 g fiber; 37 g protein

Russian Braised Brisket

So-Easy Pepper Steak

So-Easy Pepper Steak ♥

All it takes to vary this recipe is to use a different variety of tomatoes.

MAKES 6 servings **PREP** 15 minutes
COOK 9 to 10 hours (low) or 4½ to 5 hours (high)

- 1   2-pound boneless beef round steak, cut ¾ to 1 inch thick
- ½   teaspoon salt
- ¼   teaspoon black pepper
- 1   14.5-ounce can Cajun-, Mexican-, or Italian-style stewed tomatoes, undrained
- ⅓   cup tomato paste
- ½   teaspoon bottled hot pepper sauce (optional)
- 1   16-ounce package frozen pepper stir-fry vegetables (yellow, green, and red peppers and onion)
- 4   cups hot cooked whole wheat pasta (optional)

① Trim fat from steak. Cut steak into 6 serving-size pieces. Sprinkle meat with salt and black pepper. Place in a 3½- or 4-quart slow cooker. In a medium bowl combine undrained tomatoes, tomato paste, and, if desired, hot pepper sauce. Pour over meat in cooker. Top with frozen vegetables.

② Cover and cook on low-heat setting for 9 to 10 hours or on high-heat setting for 4½ to 5 hours. If desired, serve with hot cooked pasta.

PER SERVING 258 calories; 6 g total fat (2 g sat. fat); 83 mg cholesterol; 644 mg sodium; 12 g carbohydrate; 2 g fiber; 37 g protein

Spicy Steak and Beans ♥

Fill your bread basket with warm corn tortillas—they're perfect for mopping up the spicy sauce.

MAKES 6 servings **PREP** 25 minutes
COOK 7 to 9 hours (low) or 3½ to 4½ (high) + 30 minutes (high)

- 1½   pounds beef flank steak
- 1   10-ounce can chopped tomatoes with green chile peppers, undrained
- ½   cup chopped onion
- 2   cloves garlic, minced
- 1   tablespoon snipped fresh oregano or 1 teaspoon dried oregano, crushed
- 1   teaspoon chili powder
- 1   teaspoon ground cumin
- ¼   teaspoon salt
- ¼   teaspoon black pepper
- 2   small green, red, and/or yellow sweet peppers, cut into strips
- 1   15-ounce can pinto beans, rinsed and drained
- 2   cups hot cooked brown rice (optional)
     Crumbled queso fresco or feta cheese (optional)

① Trim fat from meat. Place meat in a 3½- or 4-quart slow cooker. In a bowl stir together undrained tomatoes, onion, garlic, dried oregano (if using), chili powder, cumin, salt, and black pepper. Pour over meat.

② Cover and cook on low-heat setting for 7 to 9 hours or on high-heat setting for 3½ to 4½ hours.

③ If using low-heat setting, turn to high-heat setting. Stir in sweet pepper strips and pinto beans. Cover and cook for 30 minutes. Remove meat; cool slightly. Shred or thinly slice meat across the grain. Stir fresh oregano (if using) into bean mixture.

④ If desired, spoon rice into shallow bowls. Serve meat on rice; spoon bean mixture over all. If desired, sprinkle with cheese.

PER SERVING 262 calories; 8 g total fat (3 g sat. fat); 45 mg cholesterol; 452 mg sodium; 17 g carbohydrate; 4 g fiber; 29 g protein

Beef in Red Wine Gravy ♥

Tapioca thickens the aromatic red wine gravy. To crush tapioca granules, place the granules in a large skillet, then press and grind them with the bottom a smaller skillet. Or give them a few twirls in your coffee or spice grinder.

MAKES 6 servings **PREP** 15 minutes
COOK 8 to 10 hours (low) or 4 to 5 hours (high)

- 1½ pounds boneless beef chuck, cut into 1-inch cubes
- 1 16-ounce package frozen sliced carrots
- 1 16-ounce package frozen small whole onions
- 3 tablespoons quick-cooking tapioca, crushed
- 2 teaspoons beef bouillon granules
- ½ teaspoon black pepper
- ¼ teaspoon salt
- 1½ cups dry red wine
- 6 ounces dried noodles, cooked and drained

① In a 3½- or 4-quart slow cooker stir together meat, carrots, and onions. Sprinkle tapioca, bouillon, pepper, and salt over mixture. Pour red wine over mixture in cooker; stir gently to combine.

② Cover and cook on low-heat setting for 8 to 10 hours or on high-heat setting for 4 to 5 hours. Serve over hot cooked noodles.

PER SERVING 375 calories; 6 g total fat (2 g sat. fat); 91 mg cholesterol; 494 mg sodium; 39 g carbohydrate; 5 g fiber; 30 g protein

Beef in Red Wine Gravy

Steak with Tuscan Tomato Sauce

When your slow cooker is done braising the herb-enhanced round steak, it will be so tender you can eat it with a spoon.

MAKES 4 servings **PREP** 25 minutes
COOK 8 to 10 hours (low) or 4 to 5 (high)

- 1 pound boneless beef round steak, cut 1 inch thick
   Nonstick cooking spray
- 1 medium onion, sliced and separated into rings
- 2 tablespoons quick-cooking tapioca
- 1 teaspoon dried thyme, crushed
- ¼ teaspoon pepper
- ⅛ teaspoon salt
- 1 14½-ounce can diced tomatoes with basil, garlic, and oregano
   Hot cooked noodles or rice (optional)

① Trim fat from meat. Cut meat into 4 serving-size pieces. Lightly coat a large skillet with cooking spray; heat over medium heat. Add meat; cook on both sides until browned.

② Place onion in a 3½- or 4-quart slow cooker. Sprinkle with tapioca, thyme, pepper, and salt. Pour undrained tomatoes over onion. Top with meat.

③ Cover and cook on low-heat setting for 8 to 10 hours or on high-heat setting for 4 to 5 hours. If desired, serve with hot cooked noodles.

PER SERVING 205 calories; 2 g total fat (1 g sat. fat); 49 mg cholesterol; 667 mg sodium; 16 g carbohydrate; 1 g fiber; 28 g protein

quick tip Cooking a double batch of rice does not take longer than cooking a single batch, so consider doubling up and freezing rice you will need for another meal. Just cool the rice completely after cooking, transfer it to plastic freezer bags in 1- or 2-cup increments, and toss them in the freezer. The rice will reheat in the microwave in minutes, cutting 20 minutes from the preparation time of a future meal.

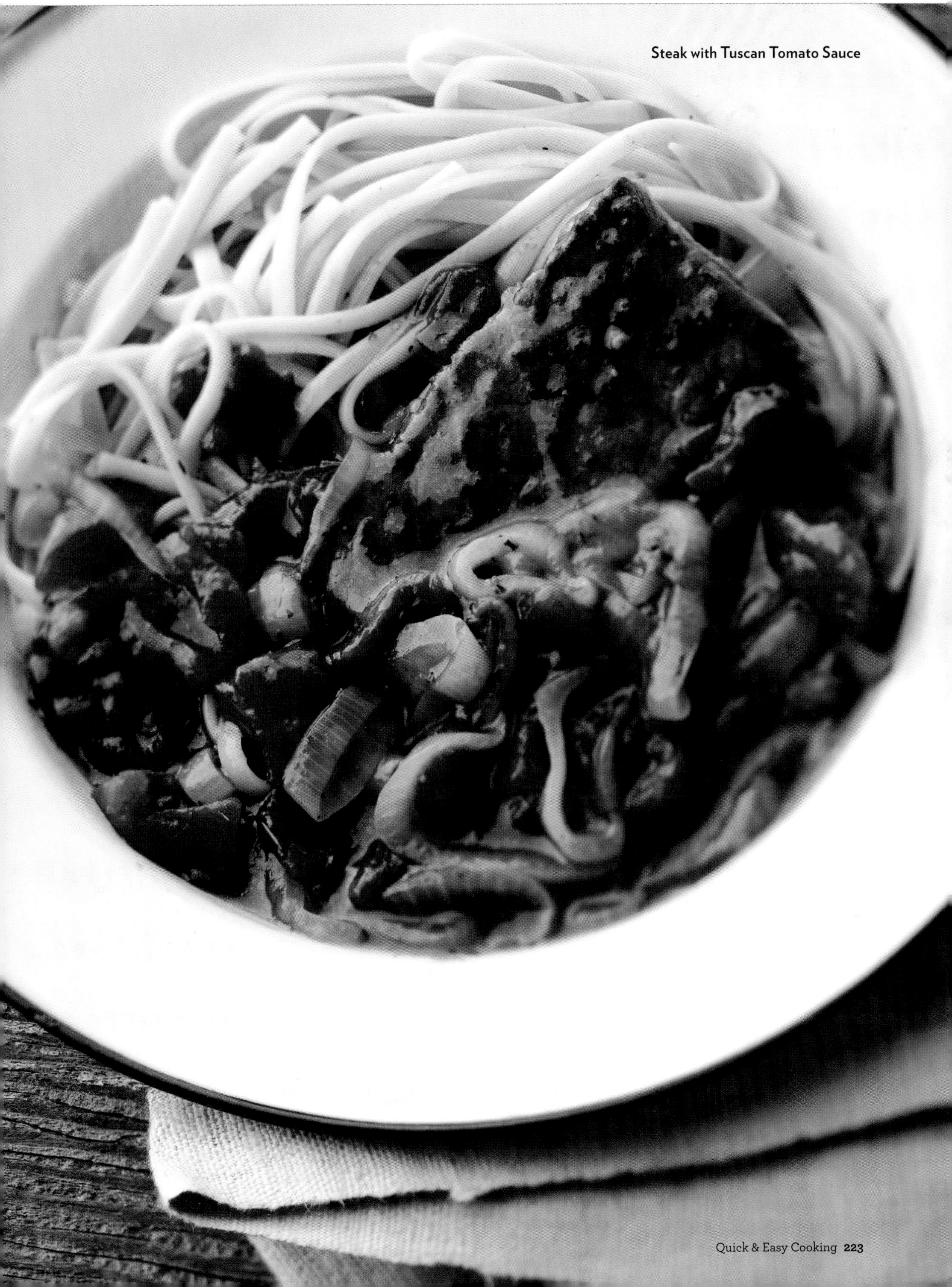

Steak with Tuscan Tomato Sauce

Chicken and Noodles with Vegetables

Chicken and Noodles with Vegetables

Chicken and Noodles may be the quintessential comfort food.

MAKES 6 servings **PREP** 30 minutes
COOK 8 to 9 hours (low) or 4 to 4½ hours (high)

- 2 cups sliced carrots (4 medium)
- 1½ cups chopped onions (3 medium)
- 1 cup sliced celery (2 stalks)
- 1 bay leaf
- 4 medium chicken legs (drumstick-thigh portion) (about 2½ pounds total), skinned
- 2 10.75-ounce cans reduced-fat and reduced-sodium condensed cream of chicken soup
- ½ cup water
- 1 teaspoon salt
- 1 teaspoon dried thyme, crushed
- ¼ teaspoon black pepper
- 8 ounces dried wide noodles (about 4 cups)
- 1 cup frozen peas

① In a 3½- or 4-quart slow cooker stir together carrots, onions, celery, and bay leaf. Place chicken on vegetables. In a large bowl stir together soup, the water, salt, thyme, and pepper. Pour over chicken in cooker. Cover and cook on low-heat setting for 8 to 9 hours or on high-heat setting for 4 to 4½ hours.

② Remove chicken from slow cooker; cool slightly. Discard bay leaf. Cook noodles according to package directions; drain. Meanwhile, stir frozen peas into mixture in cooker. Remove chicken from bones; discard bones. Shred or chop meat; stir into mixture in cooker.

③ To serve, in a large serving bowl stir together chicken, vegetables, and noodles.

PER SERVING 388 calories; 8 g total fat (2 g sat. fat); 122 mg cholesterol; 928 mg sodium; 48 g carbohydrate; 5 g fiber; 31 g protein

Chicken with Artichokes and Olives ♥

Turmeric—a ground tuber—gives curry powder its golden-yellow color.

MAKES 8 servings **PREP** 15 minutes **COOK** 7½ hours to 8 hours (low) or 3½ to 4 hours (high) + 15 minutes (high)

- 2 cups sliced fresh mushrooms
- 1 14.5-ounce can diced tomatoes, undrained
- 1 cup reduced-sodium chicken broth
- ½ cup chopped onion (1 medium)
- ¼ cup dry white wine or reduced-sodium chicken broth
- 1 2¼-ounce can sliced pitted ripe olives or ¼ cup capers, drained
- 2 to 3 teaspoons curry powder
- 1 teaspoon dried thyme, crushed
- ¼ teaspoon salt
- ¼ teaspoon black pepper
- 1 8- or 9-ounce package frozen artichoke hearts
- 2½ pounds skinless, boneless chicken breast halves and/or thighs
- 3 tablespoons cornstarch
- 3 tablespoons cold water

① In a 4- to 5-quart slow cooker combine mushrooms, undrained tomatoes, chicken broth, onion, wine, olives, curry powder, thyme, salt, and pepper. Add artichoke hearts. Place chicken on top; spoon some of the tomato mixture over the chicken.

② Cover and cook on low-heat setting for 7 to 8 hours or on high-heat setting for 3½ to 4 hours.

③ Using a slotted spoon, transfer chicken and artichokes to a serving bowl; cover with foil to keep warm.

④ If using low-heat setting, turn to high-heat setting. In a small bowl combine cornstarch and the water. Stir into mixture in cooker. Cover and cook about 15 minutes more or until thickened. Spoon tomato mixture over chicken and artichokes.

PER SERVING 229 calories; 4 g total fat (1 g sat. fat); 82 mg cholesterol; 396 mg sodium; 10 g carbohydrate; 3 g fiber; 35 g protein

Chicken in Wine Sauce ♥

Chicken and hearty vegetables are simmered in a delicate wine-flavor sauce. Choose dark meat chicken—legs, thighs, or drumsticks—for this dish.

MAKES 6 servings **PREP** 30 minutes
COOK 7 to 8 hours (low) to 3½ to 4 hours (high)

- 4 medium round red potatoes, quartered
- 4 medium carrots, cut into ½-inch pieces
- 2 stalks celery, cut into 1-inch pieces
- 1 small onion, sliced
- 3 pounds chicken thighs or drumsticks, skinned
- 1 tablespoon snipped fresh parsley
- ½ teaspoon salt
- ½ teaspoon dried rosemary, crushed
- ½ teaspoon dried thyme, crushed
- ¼ teaspoon black pepper
- 1 clove garlic, minced
- 1 cup reduced-sodium chicken broth
- ½ cup dry white wine
- 3 tablespoons butter
- 3 tablespoons all-purpose flour
  Snipped fresh thyme (optional)

① In a 5- to 6-quart slow cooker place potatoes, carrots, celery, and onion. Place chicken pieces on vegetables. Sprinkle with parsley, salt, rosemary, dried thyme, pepper, and garlic; add broth and wine.

② Cover and cook on low-heat setting for 7 to 8 hours or on high-heat setting for 3½ to 4 hours. Using a slotted spoon, transfer chicken and vegetables to a serving platter; cover with foil to keep warm.

③ For gravy, skim fat from cooking juices; strain juices. In a large saucepan melt butter. Stir in flour and cook for 1 minute. Add cooking juices. Cook and stir until thickened and bubbly. Cook and stir 1 minute more. If desired, sprinkle chicken and vegetables with snipped thyme. Pass gravy with the chicken and vegetables.

PER SERVING 321 calories; 11 g total fat (5 g sat. fat); 122 mg cholesterol; 463 mg sodium; 23 g carbohydrate; 3 g fiber; 29 g protein

Chinese Red-Cooked Chicken

No cheesecloth for making the spice bag? A large coffee filter, secured at the top with string, makes a last-minute stand-in.

MAKES 6 servings **PREP** 25 minutes
COOK 6 to 7 hours (low) or 3 to 3½ hours (high)

- 2½ to 3 pounds chicken drumsticks and/or thighs, skin removed
- 5 whole star anise
- 2 3-inch-long strips orange peel (see quick tip)
- 1 2-inch piece fresh ginger, thinly sliced
- 3 inches stick cinnamon
- 2 cloves garlic, smashed
- 1 teaspoon whole Szechwan peppercorns
- 2 14.5-ounce cans reduced-sodium chicken broth
- ¾ cup soy sauce
- ¼ cup packed brown sugar
- 1 tablespoon dry sherry
- 4 green onions (white and green parts), cut into 2-inch pieces
- 1 8-ounce package Chinese egg noodles
- 1 teaspoon sesame oil
- 2 tablespoons fresh cilantro

① Place chicken in a 3½- or 4-quart slow cooker. For a spice bag, place star anise, orange peel, ginger, cinnamon, garlic, and peppercorns in the center of a double-thick, 8-inch square of 100%-cotton cheesecloth. Tie closed with clean 100%-cotton kitchen string. Add bag to slow cooker with chicken. In a bowl combine broth, soy sauce, brown sugar, sherry, and green onions. Pour over chicken.

② Cover; cook on low-heat setting for 6 to 7 hours or on high-heat setting for 3 to 3½ hours.

③ Meanwhile, prepare noodles according to package directions. Remove chicken from cooking liquid. Strain liquid, discarding spice bag and solids; skim off any extra fat. Serve chicken over noodles. Drizzle chicken with sesame oil and garnish with cilantro leaves. If desired, drizzle with cooking liquid.

PER SERVING 404 calories; 16 g total fat (3 g sat. fat); 85 mg cholesterol; 2,608 mg sodium; 36 g carbohydrate; 2 g fiber; 29 g protein

quick tip Use a vegetable peeler to remove 3-inch strips of peel from an orange, avoiding the bitter white pith just beneath the skin.

Country Captain

Country Captain ♥

When nuts toast in the oven, it is easy to walk away and forget about them. To toast the almonds for this recipe more vigilantly, simply drop them into a dry skillet and shake the skillet back and forth over medium heat until the nuts become golden brown and fragrant. Remove nuts from heat immediately.

MAKES 6 servings **PREP** 25 minutes
COOK 5 to 6 hours (low) or 2½ to 3 hours (high)

- 1   medium sweet onion, cut into thin wedges
- 3   pounds chicken drumsticks and/or thighs, skin removed
- 1   medium green sweet pepper, cut into thin strips
- 1   medium yellow sweet pepper, cut into thin strips
- ¼   cup currants or golden raisins
- 2   cloves garlic, minced
- 1   14-ounce can diced tomatoes, undrained
- 2   tablespoons quick cooking tapioca, crushed
- 2   to 3 teaspoons curry powder
- ½   teaspoon salt
- ½   teaspoon ground cumin
- ¼   teaspoon ground mace
     Hot cooked rice
- 2   tablespoons chopped green onion
- 2   tablespoons sliced almonds, toasted

① In a 3½- or 4-quart slow cooker place onion, chicken, sweet peppers, currants, and garlic. In a large bowl combine undrained tomatoes, tapioca, curry powder, salt, cumin, and mace. Pour over all.

② Cover; cook on low-heat setting for 5 to 6 hours or on high-heat setting for 2½ to 3 hours.

③ Serve chicken mixture over rice. Sprinkle with green onion and almonds.

PER SERVING 338 calories; 6 g total fat (1 g sat. fat); 98 mg cholesterol; 446 mg sodium; 40 g carbohydrate; 4 g fiber; 31 g protein

Curried Chicken

You may notice that many slow cooker recipes call for low-sodium broth rather than its saltier cousins. This is because when foods braise in an enclosed pot, their natural flavors concentrate, largely eliminating the need for extra salt.

MAKES 4 servings **PREP** 20 minutes **COOK** 8½ to 9 hours (low) or 4 to 4½ hours (high) + 15 minutes (high)

- 1¼   pounds skinless, boneless chicken thighs
- 1   medium red sweet pepper, chopped
- 1   medium yellow sweet pepper, chopped
- 1   small onion, sliced
- 1   fresh jalapeño, seeded and finely chopped (see Quick Tip, page 28)
- 2   cloves garlic, minced
- 1   cup reduced-sodium chicken broth
- ½   cup golden raisins
- ½   cup shredded coconut
- 3   tablespoons curry powder
- 1   teaspoon salt
- ¼   teaspoon ground cinnamon
- ¼   teaspoon cayenne pepper (optional)
- ½   cup unsweetened coconut milk
- 1   tablespoon cornstarch
      Hot cooked rice (optional)
- ¾   cup coarsely chopped lightly salted cashews

① In a 3½- or 4-quart slow cooker place chicken, sweet peppers, onion, jalapeño, garlic, broth, raisins, coconut, curry powder, salt, cinnamon, and, if using, cayenne pepper.

② Cover; cook on low-heat setting for 8½ to 9 hours or on high-heat setting for 4 to 4½ hours.

③ Stir together coconut milk and cornstarch until smooth. Stir into chicken mixture. If cooking on low-heat setting, turn to high-heat setting. Cover; cook for 15 to 20 minutes more or until slightly thickened. If desired, serve with rice. Sprinkle with cashews.

PER SERVING 489 calories; 23 g total fat (8 g sat. fat); 118 mg cholesterol; 868 mg sodium; 39 g carbohydrate; 6 g fiber; 35 g protein

Barbecued Turkey Thighs ♥

The days after Thanksgiving you are most likely to find cut-up turkey parts in your grocer's meat case. Grab a few packages of thighs and toss them in the freezer—the economical cuts are one of the best candidates for slow cooking.

MAKES 4 to 6 servings **PREP** 15 minutes
COOK 10 to 12 hours (low) or 5 to 6 (high)

- ½   cup ketchup
- 2   tablespoons sugar
- 1   tablespoon quick-cooking tapioca
- 1   tablespoon vinegar
- 1   teaspoon Worcestershire sauce
- ¼   teaspoon ground cinnamon
- ¼   teaspoon crushed red pepper
- 2   to 2½ pounds turkey thighs (about 2 thighs) or meaty chicken pieces (breasts, thighs, and drumsticks), skinned

      Hot cooked brown rice or whole wheat pasta (optional)

① In a 3½- or 4-quart slow cooker combine ketchup, sugar, tapioca, vinegar, Worcestershire sauce, cinnamon, and red pepper. Place turkey thighs, meaty sides down, on sauce.

② Cover and cook on low-heat setting for 10 to 12 hours or high-heat setting for 5 to 6 hours. Transfer turkey to a serving dish. Pour cooking juices into a small bowl; skim off fat. Serve turkey with cooking juices and, if desired, hot cooked rice.

PER SERVING 225 calories; 6 g total fat (2 g sat. fat); 100 mg cholesterol; 444 mg sodium; 12 g carbohydrate; 1 g fiber; 30 g protein

quick tip Crushing dried herbs between your fingertips releases the herbs' potent oils, which makes your dishes even more delicious.

Turkey and Dumplings

Light and airy clouds of tender dumplings make this dish an often-requested family favorite.

MAKES 6 servings **PREP** 20 minutes **COOK** 6 to 7 hours (low) or 3 to 3½ hours (high) + 45 minutes (high)
STAND 15 minutes

- 1½   cups thinly sliced carrots (3 medium)
- 1½   cups thinly sliced celery (3 stalks)
- 1   medium onion, cut into very thin wedges
- 1¼   pounds turkey breast tenderloin, cut into ¾-inch cubes
- 1   14.5-ounce can reduced-sodium chicken broth
- 1   10.75-ounce can condensed cream of chicken soup
- 2   teaspoons dried leaf sage, crushed
- ¼   teaspoon black pepper
- 1   cup all-purpose flour
- 1   teaspoon baking powder
- ½   teaspoon salt
- 2   tablespoons shortening
- ½   cup milk
- ¼   cup all-purpose flour

① In a 3½- or 4-quart slow cooker combine carrots, celery, and onion; stir in turkey. Set aside ½ cup of the broth. In a medium bowl combine remaining broth, the soup, sage, and pepper; stir into mixture in cooker.

② Cover and cook on low-heat setting for 6 to 7 hours or on high-heat setting for 3 to 3½ hours.

③ For biscuits, stir together 1 cup flour, baking powder, and salt. Use a pastry blender to cut in shortening until mixture resembles coarse crumbs. Add milk and stir just until moistened.

④ If using low-heat setting, turn cooker to high-heat setting. In a small bowl whisk together reserved ½ cup broth and ¼ cup flour; stir into mixture in cooker. Drop biscuit dough by small spoonfuls on top of turkey in cooker. Cover and cook for 45 minutes.

⑤ Remove ceramic liner from cooker or turn off cooker. Let stand, covered, for 15 minutes before serving.

PER SERVING 320 calories; 8 g total fat (2 g sat. fat); 64 mg cholesterol; 809 mg sodium; 30 g carbohydrate; 2 g fiber; 29 g protein

Carnitas with Sweet Corn Polenta

Carnitas with Sweet Corn Polenta

This is comfort food Mexican-style.

MAKES 10 to 12 servings **PREP** 25 minutes
COOK 8 to 10 hours (low) or 4 to 5 hours (high)

- 1½ teaspoons garlic powder
- 1 teaspoon salt
- ¾ teaspoon dried oregano, crushed
- ¾ teaspoon ground coriander
- ¾ teaspoon ground ancho chile pepper
- ¼ teaspoon ground cinnamon
- 1 5-pound boneless pork shoulder roast
- 2 tablespoons vegetable oil
- 2 bay leaves
- 1 cup chicken broth
- 1 recipe Sweet Corn Polenta
  Snipped fresh oregano (optional)

① In a large bowl combine garlic powder, salt, dried oregano, coriander, ground chile pepper, and cinnamon; set aside.

② Trim fat from meat. Cut meat into 2-inch pieces. Add meat to spice mixture; toss gently to coat.

③ In a large skillet heat oil over medium-high heat. Cook meat, one-third at a time, in hot oil until brown. Using a slotted spoon, transfer meat to a 4- or 4½-quart slow cooker. Add bay leaves. Pour broth over meat.

④ Cover and cook on low-heat setting for 8 to 10 hours or on high-heat setting for 4 to 5 hours. Remove bay leaves. Serve meat and cooking liquid with Sweet Corn Polenta. If desired, sprinkle with fresh oregano.

Sweet Corn Polenta: In a large pot combine 4 cups chicken broth; two 12-ounce cans evaporated milk; two 4-ounce cans diced green chile peppers, undrained; 2 teaspoons dried oregano, crushed; 2 teaspoons garlic powder; and 1 teaspoon salt. Bring to boiling. Gradually add 2 cups quick-cooking polenta mix or coarse cornmeal, stirring constantly. Reduce heat to low. Cook, uncovered, for 5 to 10 minutes or until thickened. Stir in 2 cups frozen whole kernel corn and, if desired, 1½ cups shredded Monterey Jack cheese (6 ounces). Remove from heat. Let stand for 5 minutes before serving.

PER SERVING 674 calories; 22 g total fat (8 g sat. fat); 168 mg cholesterol; 1,270 mg sodium; 59 g carbohydrate; 7 g fiber; 56 g protein

Red Beans and Rice

If you can find it, Cajun-style andouille—which is highly spiced and smoked over pecan wood and sugarcane stalks—will make your red beans and rice truly authentic.

MAKES 6 servings **PREP** 30 minutes **STAND** 1 hour
COOK 9 to 10 hours (low) or 4½ to 5 hours (high)
+ 30 minutes (high)

- 1 cup dry red kidney beans
- 1 smoked pork hock
- 12 ounces andouille sausage or cooked kielbasa, cut into ½-inch pieces
- 2½ cups reduced-sodium chicken broth
- ½ cup chopped onion (1 medium)
- ½ cup chopped celery (1 stalk)
- 1 tablespoon tomato paste
- 2 cloves garlic, minced
- ½ teaspoon dried thyme, crushed
- ½ teaspoon dried oregano, crushed
- ⅛ to ¼ teaspoon cayenne pepper
- 1 8.8-ounce pouch cooked long grain rice
- ½ cup chopped red or yellow sweet pepper

① Rinse beans with cold water; drain. In a large saucepan combine beans and 6 cups water. Bring to boiling; reduce heat. Simmer, uncovered, for 10 minutes. Remove from heat. Cover and let stand for 1 hour. Drain and rinse beans.

② In a 3½- or 4-quart slow cooker combine beans, pork hock, sausage, broth, onion, celery, tomato paste, garlic, thyme, oregano, and cayenne pepper.

③ Cover and cook on low-heat setting for 9 to 10 hours or on high-heat setting for 4½ to 5 hours.

④ Remove pork hock. When cool enough to handle, cut meat off bone; cut meat into bite-size pieces. Discard bone. Stir meat, rice, and sweet pepper into bean mixture in cooker. If using low-heat setting, turn cooker to high-heat setting. Cover and cook for 30 minutes more or until heated through.

PER SERVING 429 calories; 22 g total fat (9 g sat. fat); 40 mg cholesterol; 766 mg sodium; 37 g carbohydrate; 6 g fiber; 21 g protein

Creamy Ham and Potatoes

Cream cheese is the secret to making this old-time dish extra creamy and rich.

MAKES 4 servings **PREP** 15 minutes
COOK 6 to 8 hours (low) or 3 to 4 hours (high)

- 1½   pounds Yukon gold potatoes
- 8   ounces sliced cooked ham, coarsely chopped
- 1   cup shredded Gruyère cheese or Swiss cheese (4 ounces)
- 1   medium onion, chopped
- 1   3-ounce package cream cheese, cut up
- 1   10-ounce package refrigerated Alfredo pasta sauce
- 2   tablespoons Dijon mustard
- 1   teaspoon dried thyme, crushed
- 2   cloves garlic, minced
      Fresh thyme sprigs (optional)

① Scrub potatoes; halve lengthwise and slice ¼ inch thick. In a 3½- or 4-quart slow cooker combine potatoes, ham, Gruyère cheese, onion, and cream cheese. In a small bowl combine pasta sauce, mustard, thyme, and garlic. Pour sauce over potato mixture.

② Cover; cook on low-heat setting for 6 to 8 hours or on high-heat setting for 3 to 4 hours. Stir before serving. If desired, garnish with fresh thyme.

PER SERVING 602 calories; 36 g total fat (20 g sat. fat); 128 mg cholesterol; 1,597 mg sodium; 42 g carbohydrate; 5 g fiber; 27 g protein

Creamy Ham and Potatoes

Spicy Pulled Pork

Should you be fortunate enough to have leftover pork, toss the meat in the juices from the bottom of the slow cooker and refrigerate—the pork will absorb the flavorful juices and become even tastier.

MAKES 8 servings **PREP** 15 minutes
COOK 8 to 10 hours (low) or 4 to 5 hours (high)

- 2   to 2½ pounds boneless pork shoulder
      Salt and black pepper
- 1   large sweet onion, cut into thin wedges
- 1   18- to 20-ounce bottle hot-style barbecue sauce (about 1¾ cups)
- 1   cup Dr Pepper carbonated beverage (see quick tip, below)
- 8   hamburger buns or 16 baguette slices, toasted
      Sliced pickles (optional)

① Trim fat from meat. If necessary, cut meat to fit in a 3½- or 4-quart slow cooker. Sprinkle meat with salt and pepper.

② Place onion in the slow cooker. Top with meat. In a medium bowl stir together barbecue sauce and carbonated beverage. Pour sauce mixture over meat.

③ Cover and cook on low-heat setting for 8 to 10 hours or on high-heat setting for 4 to 5 hours.

④ Transfer meat to a cutting board. Using 2 forks, shred the meat. Place meat in a large bowl. With a slotted spoon remove onion from the cooking liquid and add to meat. Skim fat from the cooking liquid. Stir enough of the remaining cooking liquid into meat mixture to moisten.

⑤ Using a slotted spoon, divide meat mixture among buns or half the baguette slices. Top with remaining baguette slices and secure with wooden picks. If desired, serve sandwiches with sliced pickles.

PER SERVING 378 calories; 8 g total fat (3 g sat. fat); 73 mg cholesterol; 1,355 mg sodium; 45 g carbohydrate; 1 g fiber; 27 g protein

quick tip Do not use diet Dr Pepper. The artificial sweeteners in the diet version will not stand up to cooking and will give the pork an off flavor.

Vegetable Casserole .

Ratatouille

A specialty from the South of France, versatile ratatouille can be served warm or at room temperature as a side dish or as an appetizer.

MAKES 6 servings **PREP** 20 minutes **COOK** 5½ to 7½ hours (low) or 2½ to 3½ (high) + 30 minutes (high)

- 4 cups peeled, cubed eggplant (1 small)
- 1 14.5-ounce can diced tomatoes with green pepper and onion, undrained
- 1 15-ounce can tomato puree
- 1 large red sweet pepper, chopped
- 1 large yellow sweet pepper, chopped
- 5 cloves garlic, minced
- 1 teaspoon salt
- 1 teaspoon dried oregano, crushed
- 1 teaspoon dried basil, crushed
- ¼ teaspoon black pepper
- 2 medium zucchini and/or summer squash, halved lengthwise and cut into ¼-inch slices (2½ cups)
- 3 cups hot cooked couscous
- ½ cup finely shredded Parmesan cheese (2 ounces)

① In a 4- to 5-quart slow cooker combine eggplant, undrained tomatoes, tomato puree, sweet peppers, garlic, salt, oregano, basil, and black pepper.

② Cover; cook on low-heat setting for 5½ to 7½ hours or high-heat setting for 2½ to 3½ hours.

③ If using low-heat setting, turn to high-heat setting. Add zucchini. Cover; cook about 30 minutes more or until vegetables are tender.

④ Serve ratatouille over hot cooked couscous; sprinkle servings with cheese.

PER SERVING 210 calories; 2 g total fat (1 g sat. fat); 5 mg cholesterol; 1,058 mg sodium; 40 g carbohydrate; 7 g fiber; 9 g protein

Vegetable Casserole

Although assertive and a bit bitter when fresh, radicchio becomes mellow and sweet when cooked slowly.

MAKES 8 servings **PREP** 20 minutes
COOK 4 to 6 hours (low) or 2 to 2½ hours (high)
STAND 5 minutes

- 2 19-ounce cans cannellini beans (white kidney beans), rinsed and drained
- 1 19-ounce can garbanzo beans (chickpeas) or fava beans, rinsed and drained
- ½ cup chopped onion (1 medium)
- ¼ cup basil pesto
- 4 cloves garlic, minced
- 1½ teaspoons dried Italian seasoning, crushed
- 1 16-ounce tube refrigerated cooked polenta, cut into ½-inch slices
- 2 cups finely shredded Italian cheese blend (8 ounces)
- 1 large tomato, thinly sliced
- 2 cups fresh spinach leaves
- 1 cup torn radicchio
- 1 tablespoon water

① In a large bowl combine drained cannellini beans, drained garbanzo beans, onion, 2 tablespoons of the pesto, the garlic, and Italian seasoning.

② In a 4- to 5-quart slow cooker layer half the bean mixture, half the polenta, and half the cheese. Add the remaining bean mixture and the remaining polenta. Cover and cook on low-heat setting for 4 to 6 hours or on high-heat setting for 2 to 2½ hours.

③ Add tomato slices and the remaining cheese; top with spinach and radicchio. In a small bowl combine the remaining 2 tablespoons pesto and the water; drizzle over greens. Let stand, uncovered, for 5 minutes.

PER SERVING 360 calories; 12 g total fat (6 g sat. fat); 26 mg cholesterol; 926 mg sodium; 46 g carbohydrate; 10 g fiber; 21 g protein

Pick one—or better yet, pick them all. Look through this pil
of pizzas and stack of sandwiches to find a month's worth o
handheld meals. In a hurry? Don't worry. And every one, of
course, will be ready PDQ (pretty darn quick).

244

248

260

SANDWICHES & PIZZAS

256

Tapenade Beef Burgers

Tapenade—a South of France specialty—is a relish made with olives, capers, lemon juice, olive oil, and occasionally anchovies.

MAKES 4 servings   **START TO FINISH** 30 minutes

- ¼   **cup purchased black or green olive tapenade**
- ⅓   **cup chopped tomato**
- ½   **teaspoon black pepper**
- 1   **clove garlic, minced**
- 1   **pound lean ground beef**
- 4   **slices mozzarella cheese**
      Purchased black or green olive tapenade
- 4   **hamburger buns, split and, if desired, toasted,**

① Preheat broiler. In a medium bowl combine tapenade, tomato, pepper, and garlic. Add beef; mix well. Shape beef mixture into four ¾-inch-thick patties.

② Place patties on the unheated rack of a broiler pan. Broil 3 to 4 inches from the heat for 12 to 14 minutes or until done (160°F), turning once. Place a cheese slice on top of each patty. Broil for 1 minute more or until cheese melts. Top with additional tapenade. Serve patties on buns.

PER SERVING 542 calories; 34 g total fat (12 g sat. fat); 100 mg cholesterol; 865 mg sodium; 24 g carbohydrate; 2 g fiber; 32 g protein

Tapenade Beef Burgers

Italian Sausage Burgers

Combining ground meats makes for interesting burgers. This one, made from pork and beef, is marvelously juicy and moist.

MAKES 4 servings   **START TO FINISH** 30 minutes

- 1   **cup marinara sauce**
- ¼   **cup finely shredded Parmesan cheese (1 ounce)**
- 2   **tablespoons snipped fresh basil or 2 teaspoons dried basil, crushed**
- 1   **pound ground beef**
- 4   **ounces bulk pork sausage**
- 4   **slices Italian bread, toasted**
- ¼   **to ½ cup shredded provolone or mozzarella cheese (1 to 2 ounces)**
      Shredded fresh basil (optional)

① In a large bowl combine 2 tablespoons of the marinara sauce, the Parmesan cheese, and snipped or dried basil. Add ground beef and sausage; mix well. Shape meat mixture into four ¾-inch-thick patties.

② For a charcoal grill, grill patties on the rack of an uncovered grill directly over medium coals for 14 to 18 minutes or until done (160°F), turning once halfway through grilling. (For a gas grill, preheat grill. Reduce heat to medium. Place patties on grill rack over heat. Cover and grill as above.)

③ Serve burgers on toasted bread. Heat the remaining marinara sauce; spoon over burgers. Sprinkle with provolone cheese and, if desired, top with shredded basil.

PER SERVING 548 calories; 34 g total fat (14 g sat. fat); 109 mg cholesterol; 796 mg sodium; 24 g carbohydrate; 2 g fiber; 31 g protein

quick tip When combining ground beef with ground pork—as in Italian Sausage Burgers—purchase ground beef that contains less than 20 percent fat. Ground pork contains enough extra fat to ensure that your burgers are juicy.

Open-Face Italian Beef Sandwiches

Open-Face Italian Beef Sandwiches

Open-face sandwiches are extra appealing—the flavor of the topping shines through without all of the bread.

MAKES 4 servings **START TO FINISH** 20 minutes

- ¼ cup white wine or cider vinegar
- 1 teaspoon sugar
- ½ teaspoon salt
- ½ teaspoon black pepper
- 1 cup sliced baby or regular sweet pepper
- 1 17-ounce package refrigerated cooked Italian style herbed beef roast in au jus
- 4 1-ounce slices provolone cheese
- 2 square whole grain ciabatta rolls or whole grain buns
- 2 tablespoons snipped fresh parsley
  Snipped fresh parsley (optional)

① Preheat broiler. In a large skillet combine vinegar, sugar, salt, and pepper. Stir in sliced peppers and undrained beef.

② Cover and cook on high for 4 minutes. Using a fork, coarsely shred the beef.

③ Meanwhile, split rolls. Place rolls, cut sides up, on baking sheet. Broil 3 to 4 inches from heat for 1 minute or until bread is lightly toasted. Top cut sides with a slice of cheese. Broil 1 to 2 minutes or until cheese is melted.

④ Stir 2 tablespoons parsley into meat mixture. With a slotted spoon, spoon beef mixture on toasted bread pieces.

⑤ If desired, top with additional snipped parsley. Serve with any remaining cooking liquid.

PER SERVING 341 calories; 15 g total fat (8 g sat. fat); 78 mg cholesterol; 774 mg sodium; 22 g carbohydrate; 2 g fiber; 31 g protein

Apple-Bacon Burgers

Mixing chopped apples into the ground meat mixture makes these innovative burgers incredibly moist.

MAKES 4 servings **START TO FINISH** 30 minutes

- 6 slices bacon
- 2 small green apples
- 8 ounces bulk Italian sausage
- 8 ounces ground beef
- 2 tablespoons mayonnaise
- 1 tablespoon Dijon mustard
- 1 teaspoon honey
- 4 kaiser rolls, split and toasted

① In a very large skillet cook bacon over medium heat until crisp. Remove bacon and drain on paper towels. Halve bacon crosswise; set aside.

② Core and finely chop 1 of the apples. In a large bowl combine the chopped apple, sausage, and ground beef; mix well. Shape meat mixture into four ½-inch-thick patties.

③ For a charcoal grill, grill patties on the rack of an uncovered grill directly over medium-hot coals for 8 to 10 minutes or until done (160°F), turning once halfway through grilling. (For a gas grill, preheat grill. Reduce heat to medium-high. Place patties on grill rack over heat. Cover and grill as above.)

④ Meanwhile, in a small bowl combine mayonnaise, mustard, and honey. Core and slice the remaining apple.

⑤ Layer apple slices and burgers on bottoms of rolls; add bacon. Generously spread tops of rolls with mayonnaise mixture; replace tops of rolls.

PER SERVING 659 calories; 42 g total fat (14 g sat. fat); 99 mg cholesterol; 1,164 mg sodium; 40 g carbohydrate; 3 g fiber; 28 g protein

Garlic-Mustard Steak Sandwiches ♥

By making shallow diagonal cuts in the flank steak before broiling, you will help it remain flat and cook evenly.

MAKES 4 sandwiches **START TO FINISH** 30 minutes

8	½-inch slices French bread
1	tablespoon honey mustard
2	cloves garlic, minced
½	teaspoon dried marjoram or thyme, crushed
¼	teaspoon coarsely ground black pepper
12	ounces beef flank steak
1	large red onion, cut into ½-inch slices
2	tablespoons light sour cream
2	ounces thinly sliced reduced-fat Swiss cheese

① Preheat broiler. Place bread slices on the unheated rack of a broiler pan. Broil 4 to 5 inches from the heat for 2 to 4 minutes or until toasted, turning once halfway through broiling. Transfer to a wire rack; set aside. In a small bowl stir together honey mustard, garlic, marjoram, and pepper; set aside.

② Trim fat from meat. Score both sides of meat in a diamond pattern by making shallow diagonal cuts at 1-inch intervals. Place meat on one side of the broiler pan. Spread half the mustard mixture on meat. Place onion slices beside meat on broiler pan.

③ Broil 4 to 5 inches from the heat for 15 to 18 minutes or until meat is medium (160°F) and onion is crisp-tender, turning onion slices once halfway through broiling (do not turn meat). Thinly slice meat diagonally across the grain. Separate onion slices into rings.

④ In a bowl stir together sour cream and the remaining mustard mixture. Spread sour cream mixture on half the bread slices; top with meat, onion, and cheese. Return to the broiler pan. Broil about 1 minute or until cheese is melted. Top with the remaining bread slices.

PER SANDWICH 334 calories; 9 g total fat (4 g sat. fat); 38 mg cholesterol; 425 mg sodium; 35 g carbohydrate; 2 g fiber; 30 g protein

Cajun Steak Sandwich with Sweet Potato Fries

Baked sweet potato fries are a nutritious alternative to regular fries—sweet potatoes are loaded with vitamins, minerals, and fiber.

MAKES 4 servings **START TO FINISH** 25 minutes

1	20-ounce package frozen french-fried sweet potatoes
	Salt and freshly ground black pepper
2	8-ounce trimmed ribeye steaks or boneless beef top steak, cut ½ inch thick
3	teaspoons Cajun or blackening seasoning
¼	cup mayonnaise
1	tablespoon ketchup
1	teaspoon molasses
2	ciabatta rolls, split and toasted
1	tomato, sliced
	Sliced green onions (optional)

① Heat oven to 400°F. Spread sweet potatoes in a 15 x 10 x 1-inch baking pan. Season lightly with salt and pepper. Bake 18 to 20 minutes.

② Meanwhile, cut steaks in half crosswise. Coat both sides of steaks with 1½ teaspoons seasoning. Heat a cast-iron or heavy skillet over medium-high heat. Cook steaks in hot skillet for 3 to 5 minutes on each side.

③ In a small bowl combine mayonnaise, ketchup, molasses, and remaining seasoning.

④ Place 1 steak on each roll half. Top with some of the sauce, tomato slice, and green onions. Serve remaining sauce with fries.

PER SERVING 583 calories; 29 g total fat (6 g sat. fat); 55 mg cholesterol; 856 mg sodium; 59 g carbohydrate; 6 g fiber; 24 g protein

Asian-Style Pork Burgers

Asian-Style Pork Burgers

The unique, assertive flavors of this Asian-influenced burger make it a wonderful change from the everyday burger.

MAKES 4 servings **START TO FINISH** 30 minutes

- ¼ cup sliced green onions
- 1 tablespoon soy sauce
- 1½ teaspoons grated fresh ginger or ¾ teaspoon ground ginger
- 1 teaspoon toasted sesame oil
- 1 clove garlic, minced
- 1 pound ground pork
- ⅓ cup mayonnaise or salad dressing
- 1 tablespoon sliced green onion
- 1 small clove garlic, minced
- ¼ teaspoon grated fresh ginger or ⅛ teaspoon ground ginger
- 1½ cups packaged shredded cabbage with carrot (coleslaw mix)
- 4 burger buns, split and, if desired, toasted
  Toasted sesame seeds (optional)

① Preheat broiler. In a large bowl combine ¼ cup green onions, soy sauce, 1½ teaspoons ginger, sesame oil, and 1 clove garlic; add pork and mix well. Shape mixture into four ½-inch-thick patties. Place on the unheated rack of a broiler pan. Broil 3 to 4 inches from the heat for 10 to 12 minutes or until juice runs clear (160°F).

② Meanwhile, in a medium bowl combine mayonnaise, 1 tablespoon green onion, small clove garlic, and ¼ teaspoon ginger. Add coleslaw mix; toss to coat well.

③ Place pork burgers on bun bottoms. Top with coleslaw mixture, toasted sesame seeds (if desired), and bun tops.

PER SERVING 547 calories; 42 g total fat (12 g sat. fat); 88 mg cholesterol; 630 mg sodium; 24 g carbohydrate; 2 g fiber; 24 g protein

Italian-Style Muffuletta

This masterpiece is the signature sandwich of New Orleans.

MAKES 6 servings **START TO FINISH** 30 minutes

- 1 16-ounce jar pickled mixed vegetables
- ¼ cup chopped pimiento-stuffed green olives and/or pitted ripe olives
- 1 clove garlic, minced
- 1 tablespoon olive oil
- 1 16-ounce loaf ciabatta or unsliced French bread
- 6 lettuce leaves
- 3 ounces thinly sliced salami, pepperoni, or summer sausage
- 3 ounces thinly sliced cooked ham or turkey
- 6 ounces thinly sliced provolone, Swiss, or mozzarella cheese
- ½ cup crumbled feta cheese (2 ounces)
- 1 or 2 medium tomatoes, thinly sliced
- ⅛ teaspoon coarsely ground black pepper

① Drain the mixed vegetables, reserving liquid. Chop the vegetables, removing any pepperoncini stems. In a medium bowl combine the chopped vegetables, 2 tablespoons of the reserved liquid, garlic, and olive oil

② Horizontally split the bread loaf and hollow out the inside of the top half, leaving a ¾-inch shell. Layer the bottom half of the bread with lettuce, meats, cheese, and tomato; sprinkle with pepper. Stir vegetable mixture and spoon on the tomato. Add the top of the bread.

③ To serve, cut into 6 portions.

PER SERVING 409 calories; 19 g total fat (8 g sat. fat); 43 mg cholesterol; 2,008 mg sodium; 41 g carbohydrate; 2 g fiber; 20 g protein

Make All-American burgers a cross-cultural treat.

Double Pork Cuban Sandwiches

The popularity of El Cubano—Cuba's iconic sandwich—has reached new heights in the United States and will win rave reviews at your own table.

MAKES 4 servings **START TO FINISH** 30 minutes

- 2 tablespoons Dijon mustard
- 2 tablespoons mayonnaise or salad dressing
- 1 teaspoon lime juice
- 1/8 teaspoon ground cumin
- 4 English muffins or ciabatta rolls, split
- 8 ounces thinly sliced smoked ham
- 8 slices packaged ready-to-serve cooked bacon
- 8 lengthwise sandwich pickle slices
- 4 slices provolone or Swiss cheese (4 ounces)
- 1 tablespoon butter, softened

① Preheat an electric sandwich press, covered indoor grill, grill pan, or skillet. In a small bowl combine mustard, mayonnaise, lime juice, and cumin. Spread evenly on the cut sides of the English muffins. Layer ham, bacon, pickle slices, and cheese on spread sides of muffin bottoms. Top with muffin tops, spread sides down. Spread butter on tops and bottoms of sandwiches.

② Place sandwiches (2 at a time if necessary) in the sandwich press or indoor grill; cover and cook for 7 to 9 minutes or until bread is toasted and cheese melts. (If using a grill pan or skillet, weight sandwiches with a heavy skillet; cook about 2 minutes or until bread is lightly toasted. Turn sandwiches over, weight, and cook until remaining side is lightly toasted.)

PER SERVING 426 calories; 22 g total fat (10 g sat. fat); 65 mg cholesterol; 1,755 mg sodium; 29 g carbohydrate; 2 g fiber; 24 g protein

Pork Tenderloin Sandwiches

Pork tenderloin sandwiches are classic fare in the Midwest, where restaurants and fast-food joints compete to serve the biggest pork patty.

MAKES 4 sandwiches **START TO FINISH** 30 minutes

- 1 pound pork tenderloin
- 1/4 cup all-purpose flour
- 1/4 teaspoon garlic salt
- 1/4 teaspoon black pepper
- 1 egg
- 1 tablespoon milk
- 1/2 cup seasoned fine dry bread crumbs
- 2 tablespoons vegetable oil
- 4 large hamburger buns or kaiser rolls, split and toasted

  Ketchup, mustard, onion slices, and/or dill pickle slices

① Trim fat from meat. Cut meat crosswise into 4 pieces. Place each piece between 2 pieces of plastic wrap. Using the flat side of a meat mallet, pound the pork lightly to about 1/4-inch thickness. Remove plastic wrap.

② In a shallow bowl combine flour, garlic salt, and pepper. In an another shallow bowl whisk together egg and milk. In a third bowl place bread crumbs. Dip pork into flour mixture to coat. Dip into egg mixture; coat with bread crumbs.

③ In a large heavy skillet cook pork in hot oil over medium heat for 6 to 8 minutes or until browned and meat is slightly pink in center, turning once (see quick tip, below).

④ Serve tenderloin slices on warm buns with ketchup, mustard, onion slices, and/or dill pickle slices.

PER SANDWICH 424 calories; 13 g total fat (3 g sat. fat); 127 mg cholesterol; 776 mg sodium; 42 g carbohydrate; 2 g fiber; 33 g protein

quick tip If necessary, cook two tenderloin slices at a time. Keep warm on a baking sheet in a 300°F oven until all four are done. Add additional oil to pan if needed.

Stuffed Focaccia

Stuffed Focaccia

Mascarpone is a buttery-rich double-cream cheese born in Italy. The cheese is one-of-a-kind, but if you cannot find it, whipped cream cheese works wonderfully in this recipe.

MAKES 3 servings **START TO FINISH** 20 minutes

- ½ of a 9- to 10-inch whole wheat, garlic, onion, or plain Italian flatbread (focaccia)
- ½ of an 8-ounce carton mascarpone cheese
- 1 6-ounce jar marinated artichoke hearts, drained and chopped
- 1 tablespoon drained capers (optional)
- 4 ounces thinly sliced Genoa salami
- 1 cup arugula leaves

① Using a serrated knife, cut focaccia in half horizontally. Spread cut sides of focaccia with mascarpone cheese. Sprinkle bottom half of focaccia with artichoke hearts and, if desired, capers; top with salami and arugula. Replace top half of focaccia, spread side down.

PER SERVING 545 calories; 36 g total fat (16 g sat. fat); 83 mg cholesterol; 970 mg sodium; 43 g carbohydrate; 3 g fiber; 23 g protein

Apple, Ham, and Brie Panini

To slice soft Brie easily, spray a little nonstick cooking spray on a serrated knife and slice away—it will slice like butter.

MAKES 4 sandwiches **START TO FINISH** 20 minutes

- 8 ½-inch slices sourdough bread
- 2 ounces low-fat, reduced-sodium sliced cooked ham, cut into bite-size strips
- 1½ ounces brie cheese, sliced
- 2 medium tart apples, cored and thinly sliced
- ½ cup whole cranberry sauce
- 2 tablespoons olive oil

① On 4 of the bread slices layer ham, cheese, and apples. Spread the remaining 4 bread slices with cranberry sauce; place on apples, cranberry sides down. Brush sandwiches with oil. Preheat a panini press or large skillet. Place sandwiches in press. Cover and cook about 6 minutes or until golden brown. (If using a skillet, weight sandwiches with a heavy skillet; cook for 2 minutes. Turn sandwiches over, weight, and cook about 2 minutes more or until golden brown and cheese is melted.)

PER SANDWICH 333 calories; 11 g total fat (3 g sat. fat); 18 mg cholesterol; 505 mg sodium; 49 g carbohydrate; 3 g fiber; 10 g protein

Tote-and-Slice Salami and Cheese Loaf

This sumptuous sandwich belongs in a picnic basket along with a bunch of grapes, a jar of marinated vegetables, and a bottle of wine.

MAKES 6 sandwiches **START TO FINISH** 25 minutes

- ¾ cup dried tomatoes (not oil pack)
- 1 16-ounce loaf unsliced Italian or French bread
- ½ of an 8-ounce package cream cheese, softened
- ⅓ cup basil pesto
- 8 ounces thinly sliced provolone cheese
- 8 ounces thinly sliced peppered or regular salami
- 1 medium fresh banana chile pepper or 8 bottled banana chile peppers, stemmed, seeded, and sliced (see quick tip, page 28)
- ½ of a medium red onion, thinly sliced

  Small bottled pepperoncini salad peppers and/or pimiento-stuffed green olives (optional)

① In a small bowl combine dried tomatoes and enough boiling water to cover. Let stand for 10 minutes; drain. Place tomatoes in a food processor. Cover and process until finely chopped. (Or finely chop drained tomatoes by hand.)

② Using a serrated knife, cut bread in half horizontally. Remove some of the soft bread from bottom half of loaf, leaving a ½-inch shell.

③ Spread cream cheese on cut sides of bread. Spread top half with finely chopped tomatoes and bottom half with pesto. On the bottom half layer half the provolone cheese, the salami, banana pepper, red onion, and the remaining provolone cheese. Replace top half of bread, spread side down.

④ If toting, tightly wrap loaf in plastic wrap. Tote in an insulated cooler with ice packs.

⑤ To serve, slice loaf crosswise into 6 sandwiches. If desired, secure with long wooden picks threaded with pepperoncini peppers and/or olives.

PER SANDWICH 588 calories; 34 g total fat (14 g sat. fat); 69 mg cholesterol; 1,645 mg sodium; 46 g carbohydrate; 4 g fiber; 24 g protein

Barbecue-Ranch Chicken Sandwiches

Italian bread shells make sandwiches special. Their shelf life is lengthy too, making them a perfect pantry staple.

MAKES 4 sandwiches **START TO FINISH** 30 minutes
OVEN 450°F

- 1 10-ounce (12-inch) Italian bread shell
  Nonstick cooking spray
- 1½ cups shredded Colby-Jack cheese (6 ounces)
- 1 cup cooked shredded chicken
- 2 tablespoons barbecue sauce
- 6 slices packaged ready-to-serve cooked bacon
- 1½ cups shredded lettuce
- 2 tablespoons finely chopped sweet onion
- 1 tablespoon bottled ranch salad dressing
- 1 medium tomato, sliced

① Preheat oven to 450°F. Place bread shell on baking sheet, bottom side up. Coat bread shell with cooking spray. With pizza cutter, cut bread in half. Sprinkle cheese evenly over bread halves. In a small bowl combine chicken and barbecue sauce. Top 1 bread half with chicken mixture and the bacon slices.

② Bake for 7 to 9 minutes or until cheese is melted and bacon is crisp. Cool on baking sheet for 2 minutes. Meanwhile, in a small bowl combine lettuce, onion, and ranch salad dressing.

③ To serve, cut each half into quarters to make 8 wedges. Evenly layer lettuce mixture on wedges with chicken. Top with tomato slices. Top with remaining wedges.

PER SANDWICH 608 calories; 27 g total fat (11 g sat. fat); 86 mg cholesterol; 1,196 mg sodium; 56 g carbohydrate; 1 g fiber; 35 g protein

Open-Face Chicken and Basil Sandwiches

To snip basil, arrange several leaves into a stack. Roll the stack tightly—as if you were rolling a cigar—and then snip across the roll with kitchen shears.

MAKES 8 sandwiches **START TO FINISH** 30 minutes

- 1 8-ounce container whipped cream cheese
- ½ cup snipped fresh basil
- 3 tablespoons bottled ranch salad dressing
- 2 6-ounce packages refrigerated chopped cooked chicken breast
- 1 cup chopped roma tomatoes (3 medium)
- 2 tablespoons snipped fresh basil
- 8 ½-inch slices French or Italian bread, toasted
- ½ cup finely shredded Parmesan cheese (2 ounces)

① Preheat broiler. In a small bowl combine cream cheese, ½ cup basil, and salad dressing; set aside. In a medium bowl combine chicken, tomatoes, and 2 tablespoons basil.

② Spread 1 side of toast with cream cheese mixture; place on a baking sheet. Top with chicken mixture; sprinkle with cheese. Broil 3 to 4 inches from the heat for 1 to 2 minutes or until heated through and cheese is melted.

PER SANDWICH 268 calories; 15 g total fat (7 g sat. fat); 62 mg cholesterol; 795 mg sodium; 17 g carbohydrate; 1 g fiber; 17 g protein

Rosemary Chicken and Brie Burgers

Rosemary Chicken and Brie Burgers

The powdery white rind of Brie cheese will trim off most easily if you place the wheel in the freezer for 45 minutes before trimming.

MAKES 4 servings **START TO FINISH** 30 minutes

- ⅓ cup fine dry bread crumbs
- ¼ cup finely shredded Parmesan cheese (1 ounce)
- 2 tablespoons snipped fresh parsley
- 2 teaspoons snipped fresh rosemary
- ¼ teaspoon salt
- ¼ teaspoon black pepper
- 1¼ pounds uncooked ground chicken
  Nonstick cooking spray
- 3 ounces Brie cheese, rind removed and thinly sliced
- 4 kaiser rolls, split and toasted
- 2 tablespoons mayonnaise
- 4 lettuce leaves
  Quick Tomato Relish (optional)

① In a large bowl combine bread crumbs, Parmesan cheese, parsley, rosemary, salt, and pepper. Add ground chicken; mix well. Shape chicken mixture into four ½-inch-thick patties.

② Lightly coat a grill pan or large skillet with cooking spray; heat grill pan over medium heat. Add patties; cook for 10 to 12 minutes or until no longer pink (165°F), turning once halfway through cooking and topping with Brie cheese during the last 1 minute of cooking.

③ Spread bottom halves of rolls with mayonnaise; top with lettuce and burgers. Replace tops of rolls. If desired, serve with Quick Tomato Relish.

PER SERVING 623 calories; 35 g total fat (6 g sat. fat); 28 mg cholesterol; 871 mg sodium; 38 g carbohydrate; 2 g fiber; 38 g protein

Tomato Relish: In a medium bowl combine 1 teaspoon snipped fresh rosemary, ½ teaspoon salt, 1 tablespoon olive oil, and 1½ cups quartered cherry tomatoes. Gently toss to coat.

Tomato-Basil Turkey Burgers

To store fresh basil, remove it from its package, trim ¼ inch of its stems, place in a glass filled with a inch of water, and cover the glass loosely with a plastic bag.

MAKES 8 servings **START TO FINISH** 30 minutes

- 2 pounds uncooked ground turkey breast
- 2 tablespoons finely chopped oil-pack dried tomato
- 2 tablespoons snipped fresh basil
- 1 teaspoon sea salt
- ½ teaspoon freshly ground black pepper
- 4 ounces smoked or fresh mozzarella cheese, thinly sliced
- 2 cups lightly packed arugula or watercress
- 8 sourdough or other hamburger buns, split and toasted
- 1 large yellow sweet pepper, roasted and cut into strips, or ¾ cup roasted red sweet pepper strips (optional)
- 1 recipe Pesto Mayonnaise (optional)

① In a large bowl combine ground turkey, dried tomato, basil, salt, and black pepper; mix well. Shape turkey mixture into eight ½-inch-thick patties.

② For a charcoal grill, grill patties on the rack of an uncovered grill directly over medium coals for 10 to 13 minutes or until no longer pink (165°F), turning once halfway through grilling and adding cheese for the last 1 to 2 minutes of grilling. (For a gas grill, preheat grill. Reduce heat to medium. Place patties on grill rack over heat. Cover and grill as directed.)

③ Place arugula on bottoms of toasted buns; add burgers. If desired, top with roasted pepper strips and Pesto Mayonnaise. Replace tops of buns.

PER SERVING 328 calories; 5 g total fat (2 g sat. fat); 65 mg cholesterol; 700 mg sodium; 33 g carbohydrate; 2 g fiber; 35 g protein

Pesto Mayonnaise: In a small bowl stir together ⅓ cup fat-free mayonnaise and ¼ cup basil pesto. Season to taste with salt, black pepper, and bottled hot pepper sauce.

Mexican Tuna Melt

Seldom is canned tuna treated to more than mayo and pickle relish. This unique south-of-the-border sandwich is a true fiesta on the plate.

MAKES 4 sandwiches **START TO FINISH** 20 minutes

- 2 6-ounce cans chunk white tuna (water pack), drained
- ¼ cup mayonnaise or salad dressing
- 2 tablespoons toasted pumpkin seeds (pepitas) (see quick tip, below) or dry-roasted sunflower kernels
- 1 tablespoon finely chopped red onion
- ½ teaspoon finely shredded lime peel
- 1 tablespoon lime juice
- 1 teaspoon finely chopped chipotle pepper in adobo sauce (see quick tip, page 28) (optional)
- 8 slices whole wheat bread
- 1 cup shredded Monterey Jack cheese with jalapeños (4 ounces)
- 1 small tomato, thinly sliced
- 1 cup shredded iceberg lettuce

① Preheat broiler. In a medium bowl combine tuna, mayonnaise, pumpkin seeds, red onion, lime peel, lime juice, and, if desired, chipotle pepper. Place 4 of the bread slices on a baking sheet. Spread tuna mixture on bread slices; top with cheese.

② Broil 4 to 5 inches from the heat for 1½ to 3 minutes or until cheese is melted. Top with tomato, lettuce, and the remaining 4 bread slices.

PER SANDWICH 467 calories; 26 g total fat (9 g sat. fat); 73 mg cholesterol; 883 mg sodium; 24 g carbohydrate; 4 g fiber; 36 g protein

quick tip To toast pumpkin seeds, spread them in a shallow baking pan. Bake in a 350°F oven for 7 to 10 minutes or until light brown. Cool.

Shrimp Po'Boy

To keep shrimp moist and tender, cook them carefully. They are ready at the very moment they turn pink.

MAKES 4 servings **START TO FINISH** 30 minutes

- 1 1-pound package frozen medium shrimp
- 2 teaspoons Old Bay seasoning
- ¼ teaspoon black pepper
- 1 tablespoon cooking oil
- 1 cup purchased deli coleslaw
- 2 teaspoons prepared horseradish
- ½ teaspoon bottled hot pepper sauce
- 4 French or hoagie rolls, split and toasted
   Potato chips (optional)

① Place shrimp in a medium bowl half-filled with cool water. Let stand for 5 minutes; drain. Remove tails if present. In the same bowl toss shrimp with Old Bay seasoning and pepper. In a large skillet cook shrimp in hot oil over medium-high heat for 3 minutes or until opaque.

② In a small mixing bowl combine coleslaw, horseradish, and hot pepper sauce. To serve, divide shrimp and coleslaw mixture between rolls. If desired, serve with potato chips.

PER SERVING 545 calories; 14 g total fat (3 g sat. fat); 132 mg cholesterol; 1,158 mg sodium; 77 g carbohydrate; 4 g fiber; 29 g protein

quick tip The choice is yours. Both cabbage concoctions—the classic, creamy-style coleslaw or North Carolina's clear vinaigrette-dressed slaw—taste terrific on this sensational sub from New Orleans.

Tuna and White Bean Panini

Tuna and White Bean Panini

In Italy, the name "panini" refers to two or more pressed sandwiches, while the word panino is singular.

MAKES 4 sandwiches **START TO FINISH** 30 minutes

- 1   15-ounce can cannellini beans (white kidney beans), rinsed, drained, and slightly mashed
- 2   7.1-ounce packages albacore tuna (water pack), drained and slightly flaked
- ¼   cup finely chopped red onion
- 2   cloves garlic, minced
- ¼   cup mayonnaise
- 8   ½-inch slices crusty country Italian or sourdough bread, or white or whole wheat sandwich bread
- 3   tablespoons butter, softened
      Garlic-flavor oil (optional)
- 2   medium tomatoes, thinly sliced
- 1   cup lightly packed large fresh basil leaves
- 4   ounces sliced provolone cheese
      Cherry tomatoes (optional)

① In a medium bowl combine beans, tuna, red onion, and garlic. Stir in mayonnaise. Set aside.

② Spread 1 side of bread slices with butter; if desired, brush the opposite sides with garlic-flavor oil. Spread tuna mixture on the unbuttered sides of 4 of the bread slices. Layer with tomatoes, basil, and cheese. Top with the remaining bread slices, buttered sides up.

③ Preheat a covered indoor grill, panini press, grill pan, or large skillet. Place sandwiches, half at a time if necessary, in grill or panini press. Cover and cook about 6 minutes or until golden brown and cheese is melted. (If using a grill pan or skillet, place sandwiches on grill pan or skillet. Weight sandwiches with a heavy skillet [add food cans for more weight] and cook for 2 minutes. Turn sandwiches over, weight, and cook about 2 minutes more or until golden brown and cheese is melted.)

④ If desired, garnish each sandwich with a wooden pick threaded with a cherry tomato.

PER SANDWICH 630 calories; 33 g total fat (8 g sat. fat); 93 mg cholesterol; 1,090 mg sodium; 45 g carbohydrate; 8 g fiber; 43 g protein

Eggplant Parmesan Heroes

The best way to pick a fresh eggplant is by looking at its blossom end. The blossom and stem should be moist and green, never shriveled and brown.

MAKES 4 sandwiches **START TO FINISH** 30 minutes
OVEN 400°F

      Nonstick cooking spray
- 1   medium eggplant (about 1 pound)
- 1   cup seasoned croutons
- ⅓   cup shredded Parmesan cheese
- 1   cup bottled marinara sauce
- 4   bratwurst buns, split
      Fresh basil leaves (optional)

① Preheat oven to 400°F. Lightly coat a baking sheet with cooking spray. Peel eggplant, if desired, and slice lengthwise into ¼-inch slices.

② Crush croutons; in a shallow dish combine croutons with ¼ cup of the cheese. Place marinara sauce in another shallow dish. Dip eggplant slices in marinara sauce and then into croutons, pressing lightly to coat. Place on prepared baking sheet. Lightly coat with cooking spray.

③ Bake for 15 minutes or until breading is browned and eggplant is tender. If desired, place buns, cut sides up, on a baking sheet. Remove eggplant from oven. Bake or broil buns for 2 minutes or until toasted.

④ Meanwhile, heat remaining sauce in a small saucepan or in a small microwave-safe bowl in the microwave on high for 30 seconds. Place eggplant slices on buns and top with remaining sauce and cheese. Garnish with fresh basil, if desired.

PER SANDWICH 423 calories; 9 g total fat (3 g sat. fat); 7 mg cholesterol; 1,011 mg sodium; 73 g carbohydrate; 9 g fiber; 13 g protein

Falafel Patty Melt

Falafels come from the Mideast, where they are as common—and as loved—as hot dogs are here in the United States.

MAKES 4 servings **START TO FINISH** 25 minutes
OVEN 400 °F

- ½ cup frozen peas
- 1 16-ounce can garbanzo beans (chickpeas), rinsed and drained
- 1 medium carrot, shredded
- 2 tablespoons all-purpose flour
- 2 tablespoons olive oil
- ½ teaspoon salt
- ¼ teaspoon black pepper
- 4 flatbreads or pita bread
- 8 slices dilled Havarti cheese (4 to 6 ounces)
  Romaine leaves and sliced tomato (optional)

① Preheat oven to 400°F. Place peas in a 1-quart microwave-safe dish. Cover and microwave on high for 2 minutes. In food processor or with an immersion blender puree garbanzo beans, carrot, flour, 1 tablespoon of the olive oil, salt, and pepper. Stir in peas. Form mixture into 8 patties.

② Heat remaining oil in a large nonstick skillet over medium-high heat. Add patties. Cook 2 to 3 minutes per side or until browned and heated through.

③ Meanwhile, place flatbreads on a baking sheet. Place 2 slices of cheese on each flatbread. Bake 5 minutes or until cheese is melted. Place 2 patties on each flatbread; fold over. Cut each in half; serve with romaine and tomato, if desired.

PER SERVING 508 calories; 17 g total fat (7 g sat. fat); 21 mg cholesterol; 1,006 mg sodium; 66 g carbohydrate; 8 g fiber; 18 g protein

Artichoke Flatbreads

Save the marinade when draining artichoke hearts. It makes a delightful drizzle for almost any kind of steamed vegetable. Try it as an ingredient in pasta, chicken, or tuna salads, or spoon it over tomato slices for a simple side dish.

MAKES 4 servings **START TO FINISH** 20 minutes

- 4 whole wheat flatbreads (naan)
- 3 tablespoons olive oil
- 6 cups fresh spinach leaves
- 6 ounces garlic-and-herb-flavor goat cheese, crumbled
- 2 6-ounce jars marinated artichoke hearts, drained and cut up
- ½ cup chopped tomato
- ½ teaspoon salt
- ¼ teaspoon black pepper
  Pizza seasoning and/or snipped fresh herbs (optional)

① Brush both sides of each flatbread lightly with some of the oil. For a charcoal grill, grill the flatbreads on the rack of an uncovered grill directly over medium coals about 2 minutes or until golden. (For a gas grill, preheat grill. Reduce heat to medium. Add flatbreads to grill rack. Cover and grill as above.) Remove from heat.

② Top the grilled side of each flatbread with spinach, cheese, artichoke hearts, and tomato. Sprinkle with salt and pepper. Grill about 2 minutes more or until bottoms are browned and toppings are heated through. If desired, sprinkle with pizza seasoning and/or fresh herbs.

PER SERVING 720 calories; 43 g total fat (15 g sat. fat); 44 mg cholesterol; 1,559 mg sodium; 65 g carbohydrate; 7 g fiber; 21 g protein

〈 Sandwiches appear all over the world. These two are fashioned after sandwiches served on the streets of Cairo and Rome. 〉

Artichoke Flatbreads

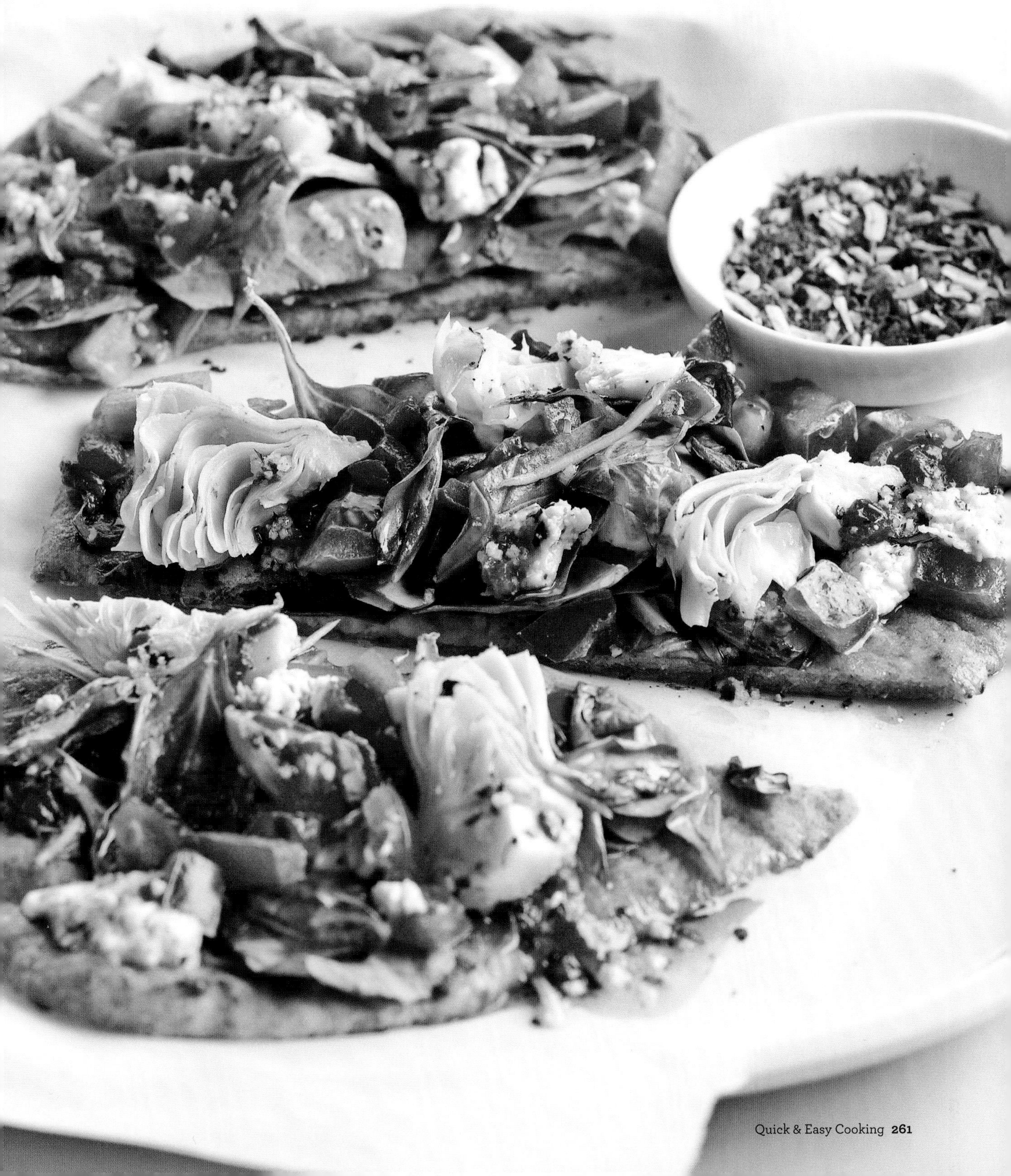

Focaccia Topped with Veggies and Goat Cheese

Focaccia Topped with Vegetables and Goat Cheese

Diners adore individual portions, and these bright, healthful mini focaccia make a great just-for-you impression.

MAKES 4 servings **START TO FINISH** 30 minutes

- ⅓ cup olive oil
- 1 medium yellow summer squash, quartered lengthwise and sliced (about 1¼ cups)
- ½ cup chopped carrot (1 medium)
- ½ cup chopped green sweet pepper (1 small)
- ½ cup chopped red sweet pepper (1 small)
- ½ cup broccoli florets
- ½ of a small red onion, sliced
- 4 cloves garlic, minced
- ⅔ cup chopped roma tomatoes (2 medium)
- 12 pimiento-stuffed green olives, halved
- 1 tablespoon olive liquid from jar
- 4 6- to 7½-inch individual focaccia
- 2 cups crumbled goat cheese (chèvre) (8 ounces)
  Sea salt
  Freshly ground black pepper

① Preheat broiler. In a very large skillet heat 2 tablespoons of the oil over medium-high heat. Add squash, carrot, sweet peppers, broccoli, red onion, and garlic. Cook and stir for 3 minutes. Add tomatoes, olives, and olive liquid. Cook about 2 minutes more or until vegetables are tender, stirring occasionally.

② Lightly brush both sides of each focaccia with some of the remaining oil. Place on an extra-large baking sheet (see quick tip, below). Broil about 4 inches from the heat for 2 to 4 minutes or until lightly browned, turning once halfway through broiling. Remove from broiler.

③ Using a slotted spoon, divide vegetable mixture among focaccia; sprinkle with cheese. Broil about 2 minutes more or until cheese is softened. Drizzle with any remaining oil and sprinkle with salt and black pepper.

PER SERVING 611 calories; 40 g total fat (15 g sat. fat); 45 mg cholesterol; 894 mg sodium; 45 g carbohydrate; 5 g fiber; 20 g protein

quick tip If necessary, divide focaccia between two baking sheets and broil in batches.

Portobello Focaccia Sandwiches

To remove gills from the undersides of a portobello mushrooms run a spoon around the stem to scrape them out.

MAKES 4 sandwiches **START TO FINISH** 25 minutes

- 1 12-inch round garlic Italian flatbread (focaccia)
- 4 large portobello mushroom caps, stems and gills removed
- 2 tablespoons olive oil
- 2 tablespoons balsamic vinegar
- ¼ cup purchased basil pesto
- 2 to 4 tablespoons mayonnaise
- ⅛ teaspoon black pepper
- 1 cup bottled roasted red pepper strips, drained (optional)
- 3 ounces fontina cheese, thinly sliced
- 2 cups arugula or fresh spinach

① Preheat broiler. Split focaccia in half horizontally. Place bread halves, cut sides up, on large baking sheet. Broil 4 to 5 inches from the heat for 3 to 4 minutes or until lightly toasted. Cool slightly.

② Arrange mushroom caps on unheated rack of broiler pan. In a small bowl whisk together oil and vinegar. Brush over both sides of mushroom caps. Broil for 8 to 10 minutes or until tender, turning once halfway through broiling time; cool slightly.

③ Meanwhile, spread cut side of the bottom bread half with pesto. Spread cut side of top bread half with mayonnaise. Sprinkle mayonnaise with black pepper.

④ Transfer mushrooms to cutting board. Cut each mushroom into quarters; arrange quarters on pesto-spread bread. Top with roasted red pepper strips, then cheese. If desired, return to broiler; broil about 1 minute or until cheese melts. Add arugula and top bread half. Cut flatbread into 4 sandwiches.

PER SANDWICH 572 calories; 31 g total fat (10 g sat. fat); 31 mg cholesterol; 308 mg sodium; 57 g carbohydrate; 6 g fiber; 21 g protein

Veggie Grilled Cheese

To choose a ball of fresh mozzarella cheese, give it a squeeze. It should feel as soft and pliable as a ball of children's clay.

MAKES 4 sandwiches **START TO FINISH** 20 minutes

- 2 cups jarred pickled mixed vegetables (giardiniera)
- 3 cups packed fresh baby spinach leaves
- 6 ounces fresh mozzarella cheese, chopped
- ½ cup oil-packed dried tomatoes, snipped
- 1 teaspoon fresh chopped or dried minced garlic
- ½ teaspoon black pepper
- 12 slices whole grain bread, toasted

① Rinse and drain the pickled vegetables well. In a large microwave-safe bowl combine all ingredients except the bread. Microwave, uncovered, about 2 minutes or just until the mixture is warm, the spinach is wilted, and the cheese is beginning to melt.

② To assemble sandwiches, layer half of the cheese and vegetable mixture on 4 slices of bread. Add another slice of bread; top with the remaining cheese mixture and another slice of bread. Slice diagonally.

PER SANDWICH 359 calories; 14 g total fat (7 g sat. fat); 30 mg cholesterol; 782 mg sodium; 42 g carbohydrate; 7 g fiber; 17 g protein

Olive and Arugula Flatbread

This Mediterranean-inspired sandwich makes a hearty appetizer, as well.

MAKES 4 servings **START TO FINISH** 25 minutes

- 2 to 3 tablespoons olive oil
- 1 teaspoon lemon juice
- 1 teaspoon red wine vinegar
- ¼ teaspoon salt
- ⅛ teaspoon cracked black pepper
- 2 cups baby arugula leaves
- 1 14 x 12-inch Italian flatbread (focaccia) or one 12-inch thin Italian bread shell
- 2 teaspoons olive oil
- ¼ cup purchased olive pesto or tapenade
- 18 to 20 pimiento-stuffed green olives
- ¼ cup shaved Parmesan cheese (1 ounce) (see quick tip, below)

① For dressing, in a screw-top jar combine 2 to 3 tablespoons oil, lemon juice, vinegar, salt, and pepper. Cover and shake well. Place arugula in a medium bowl. Drizzle with dressing; toss gently to coat.

② Brush flatbread with 2 teaspoons oil. For a charcoal grill, grill flatbread on the rack of an uncovered grill directly over medium coals for 1 to 2 minutes or just until golden brown, turning once halfway through grilling. (For a gas grill, preheat grill. Reduce heat to medium. Place flatbread on grill rack over heat. Cover and grill as above.)

③ Spread flatbread with pesto. Top with dressed arugula, olives, and cheese.

PER SERVING 472 calories; 26 g total fat (6 g sat. fat); 4 mg cholesterol; 879 mg sodium; 50 g carbohydrate; 5 g fiber; 12 g protein

quick tip To shave the cheese, use a vegetable peeler or a grater with large holes.

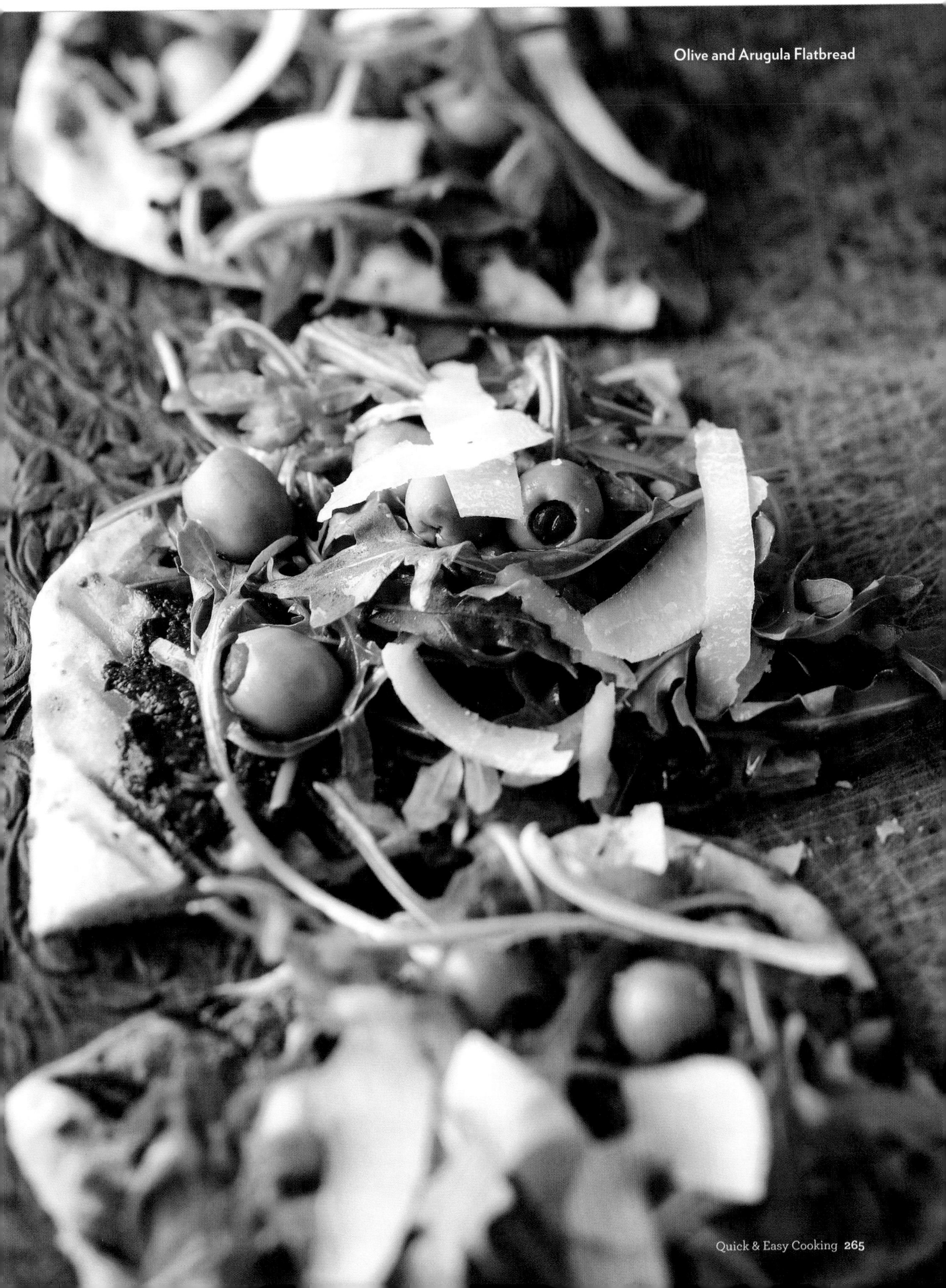
Olive and Arugula Flatbread

Lemony Garbanzo Bean Sandwich

Lemony Garbanzo Bean Sandwich ♥

It is no longer unusual to have a vegetarian at the table. This healthful, hearty sandwich is just the kind of fare that herbivores love—and will love you for making.

MAKES 4 sandwiches **START TO FINISH** 20 minutes

- 1 15-ounce can no-salt-added organic garbanzo beans (chickpeas), rinsed and drained
- 3 tablespoons snipped fresh parsley
- 1 teaspoon finely shredded lemon peel
- 2 tablespoons lemon juice
- 1 tablespoon finely chopped red onion
- 1 tablespoon olive oil
- ⅛ teaspoon black pepper
- ½ of a large cucumber, peeled, quartered, and sliced (about 1 cup)
- ½ cup watercress or arugula
- ⅓ cup bottled roasted red sweet pepper strips
- 1 1-pound loaf focaccia bread, quartered

① In a medium bowl combine garbanzo beans, parsley, lemon peel, lemon juice, red onion, oil, and black pepper. Using a potato masher or fork, mash the garbanzo bean mixture until the beans are in coarse chunks. Add cucumber, watercress, and sweet pepper strips. Toss to combine.

② Split each focaccia portion. Fill with garbanzo bean-cucumber mixture.

PER SANDWICH 401 calories; 8 g total fat (0 g sat. fat); 10 mg cholesterol; 472 mg sodium; 71 g carbohydrate; 5 g fiber; 16 g protein

Barbecued Chicken, Onion, and Apple Pizza ♥

Tart cooking apples include the varieties Rome, McIntosh, Jonathan, and Granny Smith.

MAKES 32 wedges **START TO FINISH** 20 minutes
OVEN 425°F

- 1 medium sweet onion, halved and thinly sliced
- 1 tart cooking apple, cored and thinly sliced
- 2 tablespoons butter or margarine
- 2 10-ounce packages 8-inch Italian bread shells (4 shells) or four 8-inch Italian flatbreads (focaccia)
- ½ cup bottled barbecue sauce
- 2 cups shredded cooked chicken
- 1 tablespoon snipped fresh oregano or thyme
- 1½ cups shredded Gouda or fontina cheese (6 ounces)

① Preheat oven to 425°F. In a large skillet cook onion and apple in hot butter over medium heat, stirring occasionally, just until onion and apple are tender. Remove from heat.

② Place bread shells on 2 large baking sheets. Spread barbecue sauce over bread shells. Divide chicken evenly among bread shells. Arrange onion and apple slices over top. Sprinkle with oregano and cheese.

③ Bake, 1 sheet at a time, about 10 minutes or until edges are lightly browned and chicken is hot. Cut each pizza into 8 wedges.

PER WEDGE 95 calories; 4 g total fat (1 g sat. fat); 17 mg cholesterol; 185 mg sodium; 9 g carbohydrate; 0 g fiber; 6 g protein

> Focaccia and Italian bread shells are two yeasty ways to take sandwiches from ho-hum to "Give me some!"

Grilled Vegetable Pizzas

If you've ever tried to grill fresh dough-bottom pizzas on the grill and failed, you are not alone. This version, which uses failproof pita bread for the crust, is sensational—and perfectly stress-free.

MAKES 4 pizzas **START TO FINISH** 30 minutes

1	medium zucchini, quartered lengthwise
1	small yellow summer squash, quartered lengthwise
1	small red sweet pepper, seeded and quartered lengthwise
2	tablespoons olive oil
¼	teaspoon salt
⅛	teaspoon black pepper
1	large ripe tomato, seeded and chopped
¼	cup mayonnaise or salad dressing
3	tablespoons basil pesto
4	6- to 7-inch pita bread rounds or Italian bread shells
1	cup shredded mozzarella or smoked provolone cheese (4 ounces)

① Brush zucchini, yellow squash, and sweet pepper with oil; sprinkle with salt and black pepper. For a charcoal grill, with a cover, grill vegetables, uncovered, on the grill rack directly over medium coals until crisp-tender, turning once halfway through grilling. Allow 5 to 6 minutes for zucchini and yellow squash and 8 to 10 minutes for sweet pepper. (For a gas grill, preheat grill. Reduce heat to medium. Place vegetables on grill rack over heat. Cover and grill as above.) Remove vegetables from grill.

② Chop grilled vegetables. In a medium bowl combine chopped vegetables, tomato, mayonnaise, and pesto. Spread vegetable mixture over pita rounds. Sprinkle with cheese.

③ Return vegetable-topped pita rounds to grill. Cover and grill for 2 to 3 minutes or until pita rounds are light brown, vegetables are heated through, and cheese is melted.

PER PIZZA 513 calories; 33 g total fat (6 g sat. fat); 34 mg cholesterol; 821 mg sodium; 41 g carbohydrate; 3 g fiber; 14 g protein

---

quick tip For a crispy crust, grill untopped pita rounds on the grill rack directly over medium coals for 1 to 2 minutes or until light brown. Turn pita rounds over and spread with vegetable mixture. Continue as directed.

Chicken Taco Pizzas ♥

Combine the look of pizza with cheesy Mexican ingredients and you have an instant kid-pleasing meal.

MAKES 4 servings **START TO FINISH** 25 minutes
OVEN 425°F

2	whole wheat pita bread rounds, split horizontally
1	teaspoon olive oil or canola oil
2	5-ounce cans no-salt-added chunk chicken breast, drained
¼	cup bottled salsa
1	cup shredded reduced-fat Monterey Jack and/or cheddar cheese (4 ounces)
1½	cups shredded lettuce
⅔	cup halved grape tomatoes or chopped tomato
1	recipe Light Sour Cream Drizzle

① Preheat oven to 425°F. Place pita bread pieces, cut sides up, on an ungreased baking sheet. Lightly brush cut sides of each piece with oil. Bake about 4 minutes or until lightly browned and crisp.

② Meanwhile, in a small bowl stir together drained chicken and salsa. Evenly spoon chicken mixture over pita bread pieces. Sprinkle with cheese.

③ Bake about 5 minutes more or until chicken is heated through and cheese melts.

④ To serve, top with lettuce and grape tomatoes. Drizzle with Light Sour Cream Drizzle.

Light Sour Cream Drizzle: In a small bowl stir together ¼ cup light sour cream and 1 to 2 teaspoons fat-free milk. If desired, transfer mixture to a small resealable plastic bag. Snip off one corner and squeeze onto pizzas.

PER SERVING 248 calories; 9 g total fat (4 g sat. fat); 69 mg cholesterol; 483 mg sodium; 22 g carbohydrate; 3 g fiber; 23 g protein

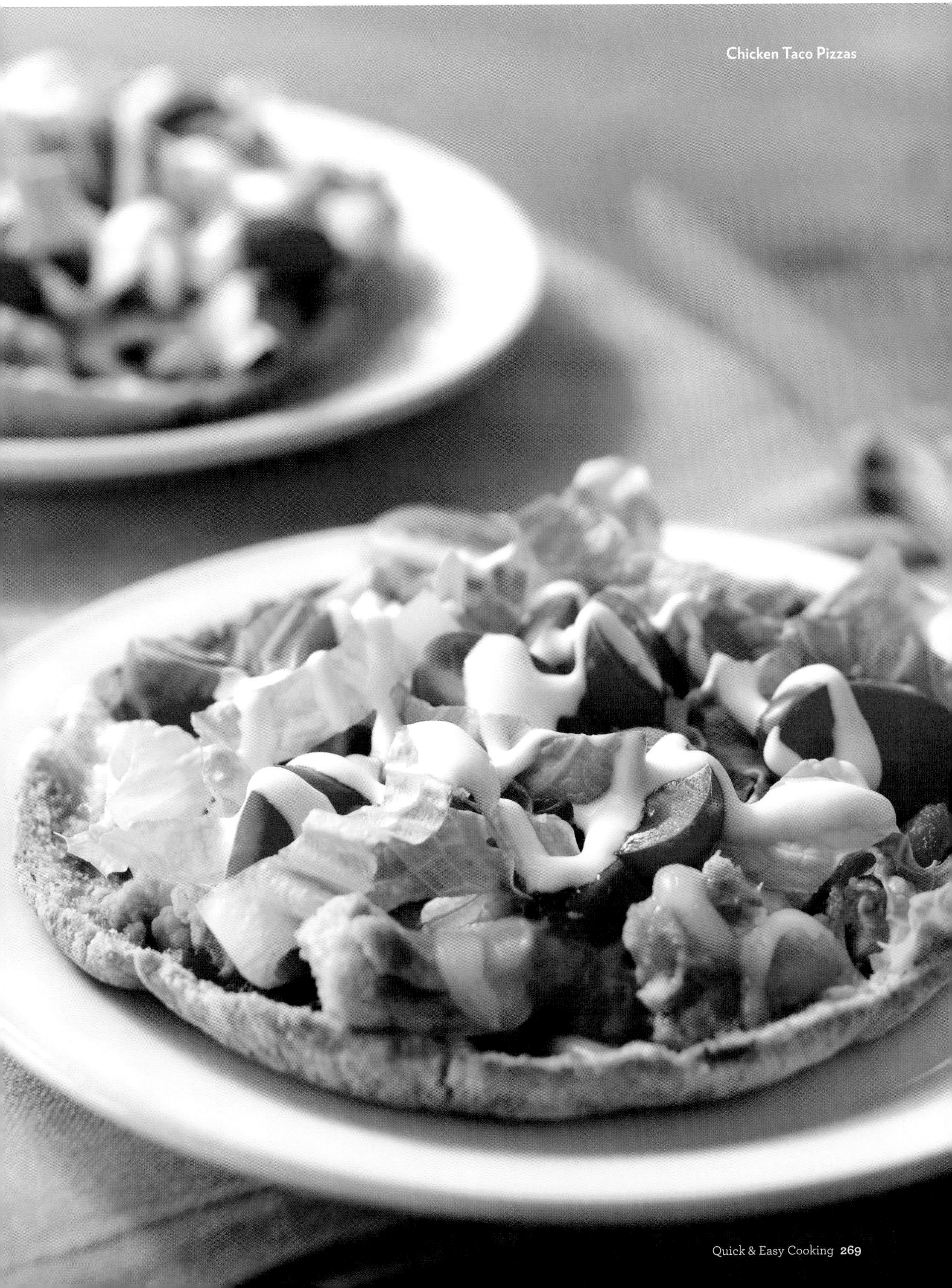

Chicken Taco Pizzas

Think of these ABC-easy side dishes as the supporting cast in a dinnertime drama—they may not be the stars of the show, but the show could not go on without them.

279 **284** **291**

TASTY SIDE DISHES

287

Apple-Thyme Saute 🍲

Shallots are favored for their mild onion flavor and can be used in the same manner as onions.

MAKES 4 servings **START TO FINISH** 15 minutes

- 1 tablespoon butter
- 2 medium Granny Smith and/or Rome Beauty apples, cored and cut into ½-inch wedges (about 2½ cups)
- ⅓ cup sliced shallots (3)
- 1 tablespoon snipped fresh thyme or 1 teaspoon dried thyme, crushed
- 1 tablespoon lemon juice
- ¼ teaspoon salt
- ⅛ teaspoon black pepper

① In a large skillet melt butter over medium heat. Add apples, shallots, and thyme. Cover and cook about 5 minutes or just until apples are tender, stirring occasionally. Stir in lemon juice, salt, and pepper.

PER SERVING 84 calories; 3 g total fat (2 g sat. fat); 8 mg cholesterol; 168 mg sodium; 15 g carbohydrate; 2 g fiber; 1 g protein

Fruited Spinach Salad with Currant Vinaigrette

If you're looking for the perfect salad to serve with Asian-flavor premarinated pork tenderloins, look no further than this one.

MAKES 8 servings **START TO FINISH** 10 minutes

- ¼ cup currant jelly
- 3 tablespoons red wine vinegar
- 1 9- to 10-ounce package fresh spinach (about 8 cups)
- 1 medium red apple, cored and sliced
- 1 11-ounce can mandarin orange sections, drained
- 4 green onions, sliced (½ cup)
- ⅓ cup butter toffee-glazed sliced almonds

① For vinaigrette, in a blender combine currant jelly and vinegar; cover and blend until smooth.

② Meanwhile, in a large salad bowl combine spinach, apple slices, orange sections, and green onions. Drizzle vinaigrette over spinach mixture; toss to coat. Top with almonds.

PER SERVING 89 calories; 2 g total fat (0 g sat. fat); 0 mg cholesterol; 52 mg sodium; 17 g carbohydrate; 2 g fiber; 2 g protein

Waldorf Salad 🍲

High fiber and fantastic flavors—this crunchy concoction delivers both.

MAKES 8 to 10 servings **PREP** 20 minutes **CHILL** 8 hours

- 4 cups chopped apples and/or pears
- 4 teaspoons lemon juice
- ½ cup chopped celery
- ½ cup chopped walnuts or pecans, toasted (see quick tip, below)
- ½ cup dried tart cherries, raisins, or snipped pitted whole dates
- ½ cup seedless green grapes, halved
- ⅔ cup mayonnaise or salad dressing

① In a medium bowl toss apples with lemon juice. Stir in celery, nuts, cherries, and grapes. Stir in mayonnaise until combined. Serve immediately or cover and chill up to 8 hours.

PER SERVING 245 calories; 20 g total fat (3 g sat. fat); 7 mg cholesterol; 107 mg sodium; 18 g carbohydrate; 2 g fiber; 2 g protein

Fluffy Waldorf Salad: Prepare as above, except substitute 1½ cups frozen whipped dessert topping, thawed, for the mayonnaise. Stir in 1 cup tiny marshmallows. Serve immediately or cover and chill up to 8 hours.

PER SERVING: 174 calories.; 7 g total fat (3 g saturated fat); 0 mg cholesterol; 16 mg sodium; 27 g carbohydrate; 2 g fiber; 2 g protein

quick tip To toast chopped nuts or seeds, place them in a dry skillet over medium heat, stirring often so they don't burn. To toast coconut and whole or broken nuts, spread them in a shallow baking pan and bake for 5 to 10 minutes, shaking the pan once or twice.

Greek Salad

Greek Salad

To make this colorful salad into a one-dish meal, simply toss in 2 cups of cubed cooked chicken or 12 ounces of peeled and deveined cooked shrimp.

MAKES 6 side-dish servings **START TO FINISH** 15 minutes

- 6 cups torn romaine mixed salad greens
- 8 cherry tomatoes or 2 medium tomatoes, cut into wedges
- 1 small cucumber, halved lengthwise and thinly sliced
- 1 small red onion, cut into thin wedges
- ½ cup pitted kalamata olives
- ½ cup crumbled feta cheese (2 ounces)
- 1 recipe Greek Vinaigrette
- 2 small pita bread rounds, cut into wedges (optional)

① In a salad bowl combine salad greens, tomatoes, cucumber, onion, olives, and crumbled cheese. Drizzle Greek Vinaigrette; toss to coat. If desired, serve with pita bread wedges.

Greek Vinaigrette: In a screw-top jar combine 2 tablespoons olive oil or salad oil; 2 tablespoons lemon juice; 2 teaspoons snipped fresh oregano or ½ teaspoon dried oregano, crushed; ⅛ teaspoon salt; and ⅛ teaspoon black pepper. Cover and shake well.

PER SERVING 109 calories; 8 g total fat (2 g sat. fat); 8 mg cholesterol; 289 mg sodium; 7 g carbohydrate; 2 g fiber; 3 g protein

Wilted Spinach Salad

Consider this dish as a beautiful bed for simple broiled or grilled chicken breasts.

MAKES 4 side-dish servings **START TO FINISH** 25 minutes

- 8 cups fresh baby spinach or torn spinach (5 ounces)
- 1 cup sliced fresh mushrooms
- ¼ cup thinly sliced green onions (2)
  Dash black pepper (optional)
- 3 slices bacon
- ¼ cup vinegar
- 2 teaspoons sugar
- ½ teaspoon dry mustard
- 1 hard-cooked egg, chopped

① In a large bowl combine spinach, mushrooms, and green onions. If desired, sprinkle with pepper; set aside.

② For dressing, in a very large skillet cook bacon until crisp. Remove bacon, reserving 2 tablespoons drippings in skillet (add salad oil if necessary). Or, if desired, substitute 2 tablespoons salad oil for bacon drippings. Crumble bacon; set aside. Stir vinegar, sugar, and dry mustard into drippings. Bring to boiling; remove from heat. Add the spinach mixture; toss in skillet for 30 to 60 seconds or just until spinach is wilted.

③ Transfer spinach mixture to a salad bowl. Add chopped egg and crumbled bacon; toss to combine. Serve immediately.

PER SERVING 145 calories; 11 g total fat (4 g sat. fat); 64 mg cholesterol; 161 mg sodium; 6 g carbohydrate; 2 g fiber; 6 g protein

Wilted Garden Greens Salad: Prepare recipe as above, except omit the spinach and use 8 cups (5 ounces) arugula or torn leaf lettuce. Omit hard-cooked egg.

Wilted Spinach Salad

Mediterranean Salad ♨

Reserve the strained marinade from the artichokes—it will make a superlative, ready-to-go marinade for chicken breasts later in the week.

MAKES 6 servings **START TO FINISH** 10 minutes

- 1 6.5-ounce jar marinated artichoke hearts, drained
- 1 15-ounce can three-bean salad, drained
- 1 large tomato, seeded and chopped
- 1 tablespoon snipped fresh basil or ½ teaspoon dried basil, crushed
- ¼ cup Italian salad dressing
   Lettuce leaves (optional)

① Halve any large artichoke hearts. In a medium bowl combine artichoke hearts, three-bean salad, tomato, and basil. Drizzle Italian dressing over bean mixture; toss gently to coat. If desired, serve on lettuce leaves.

PER SERVING 109 calories; 5 g total fat (0 g sat. fat); 0 mg cholesterol; 538 mg sodium; 16 g carbohydrate; 3 g fiber; 3 g protein

Festive Fall Salad ♨

This autumnal delight makes an amazing accompaniment to roast pork.

MAKES 6 servings **START TO FINISH** 15 minutes

- 1 5- to 8-ounce package mixed salad greens
- ⅓ cup dried cranberries
- ⅓ cup broken pecans, toasted (see quick tip, page 272)
- ¼ cup crumbled blue cheese or shredded white cheddar cheese
- ¼ cup bottled balsamic vinaigrette salad dressing

① In a large salad bowl combine greens, cranberries, pecans, and blue cheese. Add salad dressing; toss to coat.

PER SERVING 110 calories; 8 g total fat (2 g sat. fat); 4 mg cholesterol; 206 mg sodium; 9 g carbohydrate; 1 g fiber; 2 g protein

Caesar-Style Salad with Crispy Parmesan Rounds ♥

Once you've tried them, you'll want to make the Crispy Parmesan rounds a regular part of your repertoire—they're absolutely addicting.

MAKES 4 servings **START TO FINISH** 25 minutes
OVEN 300°F

- ½ cup finely shredded Parmesan cheese
- ⅛ teaspoon freshly ground black pepper
- ¾ cup 1-inch cubes whole grain baguette-style bread
   Olive oil nonstick cooking spray
- 2 tablespoons light mayonnaise or salad dressing
- 1 tablespoon lemon juice
- ½ of a clove garlic, minced
- ⅛ teaspoon freshly ground black pepper
- 4 cups torn romaine lettuce
   Freshly ground black pepper (optional)

① Preheat oven to 300°F. For Parmesan rounds, line a large baking sheet with parchment paper or foil. Draw four 4-inch circles on the paper or foil, spacing circles at least 1 inch apart. In a small bowl combine cheese and ⅛ teaspoon pepper. Divide mixture among circles, spreading evenly to edges of circles.

② Bake for 10 to 15 minutes or until cheese is melted and just beginning to brown on the edges. Cool on baking sheet. Carefully remove cheese rounds from parchment paper or foil.

③ Meanwhile, for croutons, place bread cubes in a small skillet. Lightly coat with cooking spray. Turn cubes; lightly coat again with cooking spray. Cook over medium-high heat for 3 to 5 minutes or until bread is lightly toasted, tossing cubes occasionally.

④ For dressing, in a small bowl whisk together mayonnaise, lemon juice, garlic, and ⅛ teaspoon pepper until well mixed. Divide romaine among salad plates. Drizzle with dressing; top with croutons and Parmesan rounds. If desired, sprinkle with additional pepper.

PER SERVING 96 calories; 6 g total fat (2 g sat. fat); 10 mg cholesterol; 256 mg sodium; 7 g carbohydrate; 2 g fiber; 5 g protein

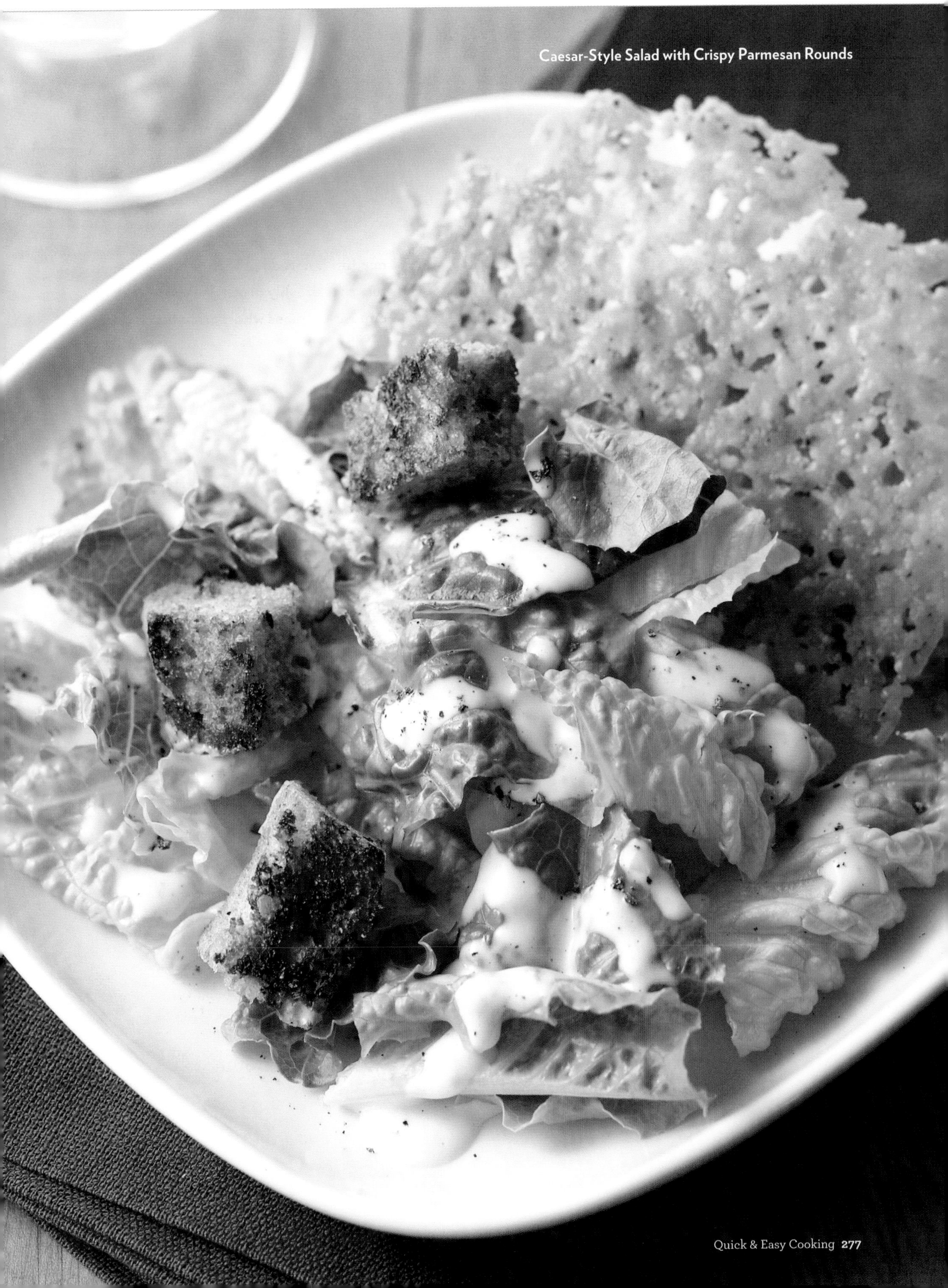
Caesar-Style Salad with Crispy Parmesan Rounds

Spinach Salad with Dijon Dressing

Spinach Salad with Dijon Dressing ♥

Beets, long relegated to grandmothers' root cellars, are making a big comeback on top-notch restaurant menus.

MAKES 8 servings **START TO FINISH** 20 minutes

- ¼   cup lemon or lime juice
- ¼   cup water
- 2   small apples, cored and very thinly sliced
- 8   cups fresh baby spinach (thick stems discarded)
- 4   packaged refrigerated cooked whole baby beets, thinly sliced
- ½   cup bottled light honey-Dijon salad dressing
- 4   ounces soft goat cheese (chèvre), crumbled

① In a large bowl combine lemon juice and the water. Add apple slices to juice mixture; turn slices to coat well. Set aside.

② Divide spinach among 8 serving plates. Drain apple slices. Arrange apples and beets on top of the spinach. Drizzle with dressing and sprinkle with goat cheese.

PER SERVING 106 calories; 5 g total fat (2 g sat. fat); 7 mg cholesterol; 227 mg sodium; 12 g carbohydrate; 2 g fiber; 4 g protein

---

quick tip Should you be unable to find refrigerated cooked whole beets, canned beets will make a perfectly adequate stand-in.

Tomato and Cucumber Salad

Use whole-grain Dijon mustard if you like.

MAKES 4 servings **START TO FINISH** 20 minutes

- ⅓   cup bottled balsamic vinaigrette salad dressing
- 1   tablespoon Dijon mustard
- 3   medium tomatoes, cut into wedges
- 1   medium English cucumber, sliced
- 1   small red onion, halved and sliced
- 4   lettuce leaves (optional)
- ¼   cup crumbled feta cheese

① In a small screw-top jar combine dressing and mustard. Cover and shake well.

② In a large bowl toss together tomatoes, cucumber, and onion. Toss with dressing to coat.

③ If desired, line salad plates with lettuce leaves. Spoon tomato mixture on lettuce-lined plates. Top with feta cheese.

PER SERVING 128 calories; 8 g total fat (2 g sat. fat); 8 mg cholesterol; 435 mg sodium; 12 g carbohydrate; 2 g fiber; 3 g protein

Tomato and Cucumber Salad

Broccoli-Cauliflower-Raisin Salad

Layered salads like this one are a perfect choice for toting to potluck meals.

MAKES 10 servings **START TO FINISH** 30 minutes

- 6 cups broccoli florets
- 3 cups cauliflower florets
- ½ cup golden raisins
- ⅓ cup walnut pieces, toasted (see note, page 272)
- ¼ cup olive oil or canola oil
- ¼ cup cider vinegar
- 1 teaspoon salt
- 1 teaspoon honey or sugar
- ½ teaspoon dried basil, crushed
- ½ teaspoon black pepper
- ¼ teaspoon crushed red pepper (optional)

① In a saucepan bring 2 inches of water to boiling. Add broccoli; return to boiling. Cook, covered, for 2 minutes or until broccoli is crisp-tender and bright green; drain. Rinse with cold water; drain well.

② In same saucepan cook cauliflower in water using same method as Step 1.

③ In 2- to 2½-quart bowl layer half the broccoli, cauliflower, raisins, and walnuts. Repeat layers. Cover with plastic wrap and chill. In a screw-top jar combine olive oil, vinegar, salt, honey, basil, black pepper, and, if desired, red pepper. Cover tightly and shake well. Add dressing just before serving; toss to coat.

PER SERVING 128 calories; 8 g total fat (1 g sat. fat); 0 mg cholesterol; 29 mg sodium; 13 g carbohydrate; 3 g fiber; 3 g protein

Blue Cheese Coleslaw

Choose a less expensive variety of blue cheese, such as Danish blue, for this savory slaw.

MAKES 10 servings **START TO FINISH** 10 minutes

- ½ cup cider vinegar or rice vinegar
- ⅓ cup canola oil or salad oil
- 1 tablespoon sugar
- 1 teaspoon dry mustard
- ½ teaspoon onion powder
- ¼ teaspoon salt
- ¼ teaspoon ground white or black pepper
- 1 16-ounce package shredded cabbage with carrot (coleslaw mix) (5 cups)
- ¼ cup crumbled blue cheese (1 ounce)

① For dressing, in a screw-top jar combine vinegar, oil, sugar, mustard, onion powder, salt, and pepper. Cover and shake well. Chill until serving time.

② To serve, in a large bowl combine shredded cabbage and blue cheese. Shake dressing; add to cabbage mixture and gently toss to coat.

PER SERVING 95 calories; 8 g total fat (1 g sat. fat); 3 mg cholesterol; 115 mg sodium; 5 g carbohydrate; 1 g fiber; 1 g protein

BLT Coleslaw

As they say, bacon makes everything better—and it does wonders for this sensational slaw.

MAKES 8 to 10 servings **START TO FINISH** 15 minutes

- 1 16-ounce package shredded cabbage with carrot (coleslaw mix)
- 6 slices packaged ready-to-serve cooked bacon, torn into bite-size pieces
- 1 pint grape or cherry tomatoes, halved
- ½ cup bottled ranch salad dressing

① In a large bowl combine coleslaw mix, bacon, tomatoes, and salad dressing. Toss to coat.

PER SERVING 110 calories; 9 g total fat (2 g sat. fat); 8 mg cholesterol; 201 mg sodium; 6 g carbohydrate; 2 g fiber; 3 g protein

Blue Cheese Coleslaw

Asparagus-Snap Pea Stir-Fry

Asparagus-Snap Pea Stir-Fry

Stir up this side dish in the spring, when asparagus and snap peas are at their best.

MAKES 6 servings **PREP** 20 minutes **COOK** 6 minutes

- 1 pound asparagus spears
- 1 tablespoon vegetable oil
- 2 teaspoons grated fresh ginger
- 2 cloves garlic, minced
- 1 medium red onion, cut into thin wedges
- 1 medium red sweet pepper, cut into 1-inch pieces
- 2 cups fresh sugar snap peas or frozen sugar snap peas
- 1 tablespoon sesame seeds
- 2 tablespoons soy sauce
- 2 tablespoons rice vinegar
- 1 tablespoon packed brown sugar
- 1 teaspoon toasted sesame oil

① Snap off and discard woody bases from asparagus. If desired, scrape off scales. Bias-slice asparagus into 2-inch pieces (you should have about 3 cups).

② In a wok or large skillet heat vegetable oil over medium-high heat. Add ginger and garlic; cook and stir for 15 seconds. Add asparagus, onion, and sweet pepper; cook and stir for 3 minutes. Add sugar snap peas and sesame seeds; cook and stir for 3 to 4 minutes more or until vegetables are crisp-tender.

③ Add soy sauce, rice vinegar, brown sugar, and sesame oil to vegetable mixture; toss to coat. If desired, serve with a slotted spoon.

PER SERVING 86 calories; 4 g total fat (1 g sat. fat); 0 mg cholesterol; 343 mg sodium; 10 g carbohydrate; 3 g fiber; 3 g protein

Peas Parisienne 🍲 ♥

A finishing touch of nutmeg infuses peas with warm, spicy sweetness.

MAKES 6 servings **PREP** 20 minutes **COOK** 10 minutes

- 1 cup finely chopped onion (1 large)
- 6 cloves garlic, minced
- 2 teaspoons snipped fresh thyme or ½ teaspoon dried thyme, crushed
- 2 tablespoons butter
- 1 16-ounce package frozen peas (3¾ cups)
- ½ cup chicken broth
- ¼ teaspoon black pepper
  Pinch ground nutmeg

① In a large saucepan cook onion, garlic, and thyme in hot butter over medium heat about 5 minutes or until onion is tender and begins to brown, stirring occasionally. Add peas, broth, pepper, and nutmeg. Bring to boiling; reduce heat. Simmer, uncovered, about 5 minutes or until peas are tender and heated through, stirring occasionally.

PER SERVING 108 calories; 4 g total fat (2 g sat. fat); 10 mg cholesterol; 279 mg sodium; 13 g carbohydrate; 4 g fiber; 5 g protein

Peas Parisienne

Artichokes with Herb-Butter Sauce

Artichokes are a great appetizer to serve when there is a chance that dinner may take longer than expected—they take a long time to eat!

MAKES 2 servings **START TO FINISH** 30 minutes

- 2 artichokes (about 10 ounces each)
  Lemon juice
- ¼ cup butter
- 1 tablespoon lemon juice
- 1 teaspoon snipped fresh dill, tarragon, or oregano, or ¼ teaspoon dried dillweed, tarragon, or oregano, crushed

① Wash artichokes; trim stems and remove loose outer leaves. Cut 1 inch off the top of each artichoke; snip off the sharp leaf tips. Brush the cut edges with a little lemon juice. In a large saucepan or Dutch oven bring a large amount of lightly salted water to boiling; add artichokes. Return to boiling; reduce heat. Simmer, covered, for 20 to 30 minutes or until a leaf pulls out easily. Drain artichokes upside down on paper towels.

② Meanwhile, for Herb-Butter Sauce, melt butter. Stir in the 1 tablespoon lemon juice and the desired herb. Turn artichokes right side up; serve with the butter sauce.

PER SERVING 268 calories; 23 g total fat (15 g sat. fat); 61 mg cholesterol; 278 mg sodium; 15 g carbohydrate; 7 g fiber; 4 g protein

Artichokes with Curry Dip: Prepare as above, except thoroughly chill artichokes after Step 1 and omit Herb-Butter Sauce. For Curry Dip, combine ½ cup mayonnaise, 1 teaspoon lemon juice, 1 teaspoon prepared horseradish, 1 teaspoon finely chopped onion, 1 teaspoon curry powder, and ⅛ teaspoon salt. Cover; chill for 2 to 24 hours.

Artichokes with Lemon-Mustard Mayo: Prepare as above, except thoroughly chill artichokes after Step 1 and omit Herb-Butter Sauce. For Lemon-Mustard Mayo, combine ½ cup mayonnaise, ½ teaspoon finely shredded lemon peel, 2 teaspoons fresh lemon juice, and 1 teaspoon Dijon mustard. Season with freshly ground black pepper to taste. Cover; chill until serving time.

PER SERVING 466 cal.; 44 g total fat (8 g sat. fat); 20 mg chol.; 613 mg sodium; 15 g carbo.; 7 g fiber; 4 g pro.

Eggplant Parmigiana

Choose an eggplant that is dark, glossy, and free of scratches and soft spots.

MAKES 4 servings **PREP** 20 minutes **COOK** 13 minutes

- 1 small eggplant (12 ounces)
- 1 egg, lightly beaten
- 1 tablespoon water
- ¼ cup all-purpose flour
- 2 tablespoons vegetable oil
- ⅓ cup grated Parmesan cheese
- 1 cup meatless spaghetti sauce
- ¾ cup shredded mozzarella cheese (3 ounces)
  Shredded fresh basil (optional)

① Wash and peel eggplant; cut crosswise into ½-inch slices. Combine egg and water; dip eggplant slices into egg mixture, then into flour, turning to coat both sides. In a large skillet cook eggplant, half at a time, in hot oil over medium-high heat for 4 to 6 minutes or until golden, turning once. (If necessary, add additional oil and reduce heat to medium if eggplant browns too quickly.) Drain on paper towels.

② Wipe the skillet with paper towels. Arrange the cooked eggplant slices in the skillet; sprinkle with the Parmesan cheese. Top with spaghetti sauce and mozzarella cheese. Cook, covered, over medium-low heat for 5 to 7 minutes or until heated through. If desired, top with basil.

Baked Eggplant Parmigiana: Preheat oven to 400°F. Prepare as above, except in Step 2 place the eggplant slices in a single layer in an ungreased 2-quart rectangular baking dish. (If necessary, cut slices to fit.) Sprinkle with Parmesan cheese. Top with spaghetti sauce and mozzarella cheese. Bake, uncovered, in the preheated oven for 12 to 15 minutes or until heated through. If desired, top with basil.

PER SERVING 250 calories; 15 g total fat (5 g sat. fat); 70 mg cholesterol; 563 mg sodium; 20 g carbohydrate; 5 g fiber; 12 g protein

Corn on the Cob

Corn on the Cob 🍲

With these three terrific toppers, you'll be able to keep corn on the cob tasting new and different all summer long.

MAKES 8 servings **START TO FINISH** 20 minutes

8 **ears of corn**

Butter, margarine, or 1 recipe Herb Butter, Cajun Butter, or Chipotle-Lime Butter

Salt and black pepper

① Remove husks from the ears of corn. Scrub with a stiff brush to remove silks; rinse. Cook, covered, in enough boiling lightly salted water to cover for 5 to 7 minutes or until tender. Serve with butter, salt, and pepper.

PER SERVING 179 calories; 13 g total fat (7 g sat. fat); 31 mg cholesterol; 168 mg sodium; 17 g carbohydrate; 2 g fiber; 3 g protein

Herb Butter: In a small mixing bowl beat ½ cup softened butter, 2 teaspoons snipped fresh thyme, and 2 teaspoons snipped fresh marjoram or oregano with an electric mixer on low until combined. Cover and chill for 1 to 24 hours.

Chipotle-Lime Butter: In a small mixing bowl beat ½ cup softened butter, 1 teaspoon finely shredded lime peel, ½ teaspoon salt, ⅛ to ¼ teaspoon ground chipotle chile pepper, and dash cayenne pepper with electric mixer on low speed until combined. Cover and chill for 1 to 24 hours.

Cajun Butter: In a small mixing bowl beat ½ cup softened butter, 1 teaspoon garlic salt, ¼ teaspoon black pepper, ¼ teaspoon cayenne pepper, ⅛ teaspoon ground ginger, and ⅛ teaspoon ground cloves with an electric mixer on low until combined. Cover and chill for 1 to 24 hours.

Bistro Mushrooms 🍲

A steaming spoonful of these flavor-packed mushrooms takes the simplest steak, chicken breast, pork loin, or fish to the gourmet level.,

MAKES 4 servings **START TO FINISH** 20 minutes

2 **tablespoons olive oil, roasted garlic olive oil, or butter**

3 **cups sliced cremini, stemmed shiitake, and/or button mushrooms (8 ounces)**

⅓ **cup dry red wine, dry sherry, or beef broth**

1 **tablespoon Worcestershire sauce for chicken**

2 **teaspoons snipped fresh thyme**

Salt and black pepper

Snipped fresh parsley

① In a large skillet heat oil over medium-high heat. Add mushrooms; cook and stir for 4 minutes. Stir in wine, Worcestershire sauce, and thyme. Simmer, uncovered, for 3 minutes. Season to taste with salt and pepper. Sprinkle with snipped fresh parsley. Serve with beef, fish, pork, or poultry.

PER SERVING 79 calories; 7 g total fat (1 g sat. fat); 0 mg cholesterol; 210 mg sodium; 3 g carbohydrate; 0 g fiber; 1 g protein

Bistro Mushrooms

Skillet-Browned Broccoli with Toasted Garlic 🍲

In this unusual treatment seared sliced broccoli takes on an appealing nutty taste—without even a hint of bitterness.

MAKES 8 servings **START TO FINISH** 25 minutes

- 3 large heads broccoli with stems attached
- ¼ cup olive oil
  Coarse salt or salt
  Freshly ground black pepper
- 3 tablespoons thinly sliced garlic

① Slice broccoli lengthwise into 1-inch slices. Brush both sides of broccoli with some of the oil and sprinkle lightly with salt and pepper.

② Preheat a very large cast-iron skillet over medium heat. Place broccoli, half at a time, in hot skillet; weight broccoli with a medium heavy skillet. Cook for 6 to 8 minutes or until well browned, turning once (for more tender broccoli, cook over medium-low heat for 10 to 12 minutes, turning once). Transfer broccoli to a warm platter; cover and keep warm.

③ Add the remaining oil to hot skillet; reduce heat to medium-low. Add garlic; cook and stir about 2 minutes or until lightly browned. Drain on paper towels. Sprinkle lightly with salt and pepper. Sprinkle toasted garlic over broccoli.

PER SERVING 84 calories; 7 g total fat (1 g sat. fat); 0 mg cholesterol; 119 mg sodium; 5 g carbohydrate; 2 g fiber; 2 g protein

Skillet-Browned Broccoli with Toasted Garlic

Maple-Glazed Brussels Sprouts and Onions 🍲

Brussels sprouts—a cruciferous vegetable—are packed with vitamins A and C.

MAKES 8 servings **START TO FINISH** 20 minutes

- 3 tablespoons butter
- 2 10-ounce packages frozen Brussels sprouts
- 1 10-ounce package frozen small whole onions
- ⅓ cup maple syrup
  Salt and black pepper
- ¼ cup broken walnuts, toasted

① In a large skillet heat butter over medium heat. Add frozen Brussels sprouts and onions. Cook, covered, about 10 minutes or until vegetables are nearly tender, stirring occasionally.

② Drizzle vegetables with maple syrup. Cook, uncovered, for 1 to 2 minutes more or until vegetables are tender, stirring occasionally. Season to taste with salt and pepper.

③ Transfer vegetables to a serving bowl. Sprinkle with walnuts.

PER SERVING 139 calories; 7 g total fat (3 g sat. fat); 12 mg cholesterol; 83 mg sodium; 18 g carbohydrate; 4 g fiber; 4 g protein

quick tip When cruciferous vegetables such as broccoli and Brussels sprouts are cooked in water, their healthful compounds may create off-putting odors. When quickly sautéed—as the vegetables in these recipes— the good-for-you veggies will smell as good as they taste.

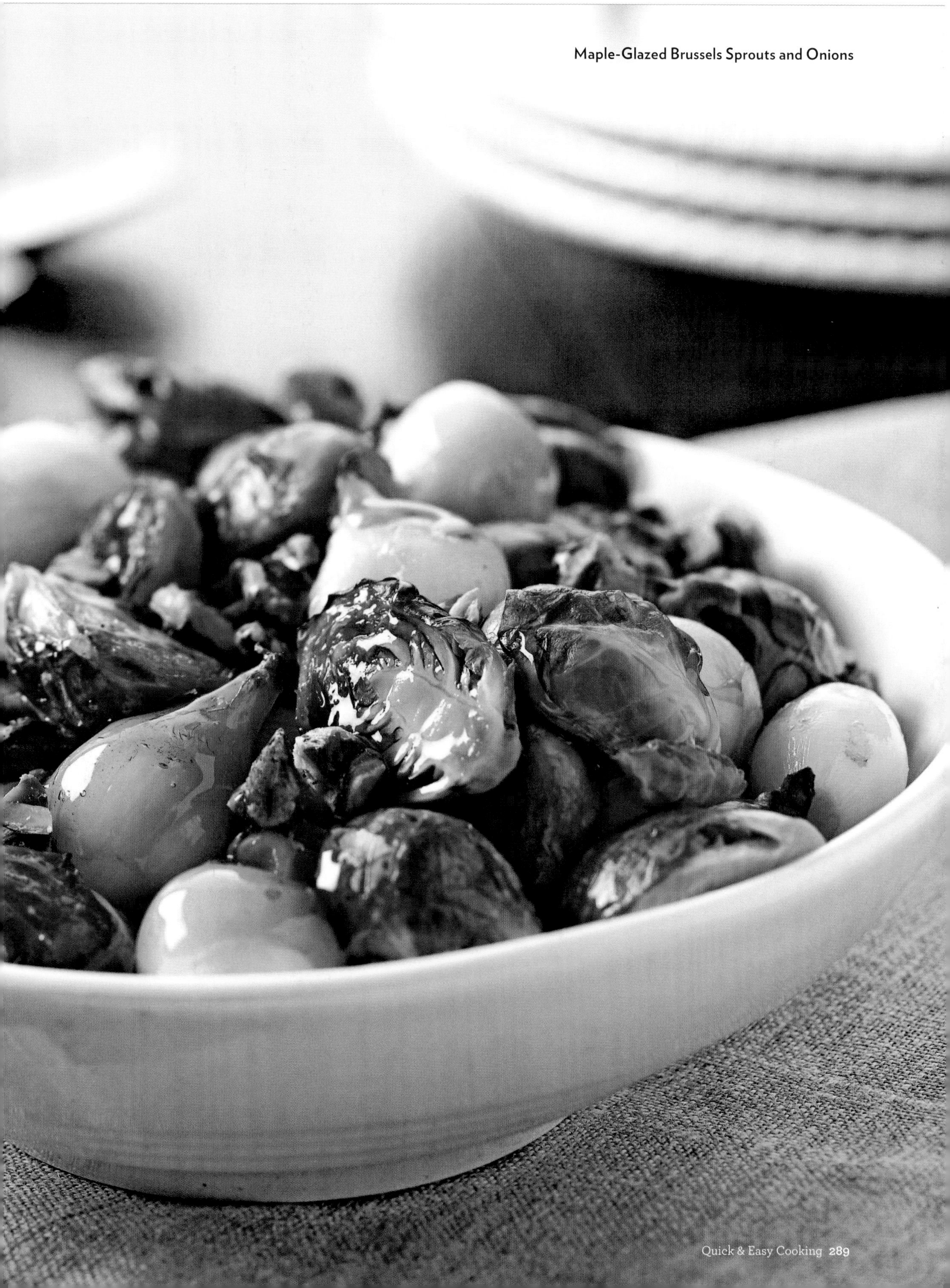

Maple-Glazed Brussels Sprouts and Onions

Cottage-Fried Potatoes

Cottage-Fried Potatoes 🍲

Baby red or new potatoes make wonderful cottage fries and hold together well when turned in the pan.

MAKES 4 servings **START TO FINISH** 30 minutes

- 3 tablespoons butter or margarine
- 2 cloves garlic, minced
- 3 medium potatoes, peeled, if desired, and thinly sliced (1 pound)
- 1 small onion, thinly sliced
- ¼ teaspoon salt
- ⅛ teaspoon black pepper
    Snipped fresh parsley

① In a large skillet melt butter over medium heat. Add garlic; cook and stir for 15 seconds. Layer sliced potatoes and onion in skillet. Sprinkle with salt and pepper. Cook, covered, for 8 minutes, turning occasionally. Uncover; cook for 12 to 15 minutes more or until potatoes are tender and lightly browned, turning occasionally. (If necessary, add additional butter during cooking.) Sprinkle with snipped fresh parsley.

PER SERVING 171 calories; 9 g total fat (6 g sat. fat); 23 mg cholesterol; 214 mg sodium; 22 g carbohydrate; 3 g fiber; 3 g protein

Cottage-Fried New Potatoes: Prepare as above, except substitute 1 pound new potatoes, cut into wedges, for potatoes. Decrease cooking time of uncovered potatoes to 8 to 10 minutes or until potatoes are tender and lightly browned.

quick tip To keep potatoes from sticking to your knife when slicing them, coat the knife with cooking spray before and during the slicing session.

Sweet Potato and Cranberry Sauté 🍲

This colorful one-pan dish brings a little Thanksgiving taste to meals year-round.

MAKES 4 servings **START TO FINISH** 30 minutes

- 1¼ cups apple juice or apple cider
- 1 pound sweet potatoes, peeled, cut into ¼-inch slices (about 3 cups)
- 1 cup coarsely chopped cooking apple (1 large)
- 2 tablespoons dried cranberries
- ¼ cup pure maple syrup or maple-flavor syrup
- ¼ teaspoon salt
- 2 tablespoons chopped hazelnuts (filberts) or walnuts, toasted (see quick tip, page 272)

① In a large skillet heat apple juice to simmering. Add sweet potato slices, spreading evenly. Cook, covered, over medium-low heat about 12 minutes or until potatoes are nearly tender. Stir in apple, cranberries, maple syrup, and salt. Cook, covered, over low heat for 3 to 4 minutes or just until apple is tender. Uncover; boil gently about 4 minutes more or until liquid is syrupy. Sprinkle with nuts.

PER SERVING 238 calories; 3 g total fat (0 g sat. fat); 0 mg cholesterol; 213 mg sodium; 53 g carbohydrate; 5 g fiber; 3 g protein

Sweet Potato and Cranberry Sauté

Glazed Sweet Potatoes

Sweet potatoes are a nutritious addition to dinner.

MAKES 8 servings   **START TO FINISH** 25 minutes

3   pounds sweet potatoes, peeled and cut into ½-inch slices

2   cups coarsely chopped red onions (2 large)

½   teaspoon dried rosemary, crushed

⅓   cup butter

⅓   cup packed brown sugar

¼   cup broken pecans, toasted (see quick note, page 272) (optional)

   Fresh rosemary sprigs (optional)

① In a covered large saucepan or 4-quart Dutch oven cook sweet potatoes in enough boiling, lightly salted water to cover for 10 to 12 minutes or until tender; drain.

② Meanwhile, in a large skillet cook onions and dried rosemary in hot butter over medium heat for 8 to 10 minutes or until onions are very tender, stirring frequently.

③ Add brown sugar to onion mixture, stirring to dissolve. Stir in sweet potatoes. Cook, uncovered, for 5 to 8 minutes or until potatoes are glazed, stirring gently once or twice. Transfer to a serving dish. If desired, sprinkle with pecans and garnish with fresh rosemary.

PER SERVING 239 calories; 11 g total fat (4 g sat. fat); 21 mg cholesterol; 77 mg sodium; 35 g carbohydrate; 5 g fiber; 3 g protein

Hash Brown Potatoes 🍲

Russets, or high-starch potatoes, make the best hash browns. If you are unsure what variety of potatoes you have, slice one in half. If your knife is covered with a moist, powdery liquid, you have a nice starchy potato.

MAKES 4 servings   **START TO FINISH** 30 minutes

4   medium potatoes (1½ pounds)

¼   cup finely chopped onion

¼   teaspoon salt

⅛   teaspoon black pepper

3   tablespoons butter or margarine

① Peel potatoes; coarsely shred to equal 1½ cups. Rinse shredded potatoes and pat dry. Combine potatoes, onion, salt, and pepper.

② In a large skillet melt butter over medium-low heat. Using a pancake turner, pat potato mixture into skillet. Cook about 10 minutes or until bottom is crisp. With the pancake turner, turn potato mixture in large sections. Cook for 8 to 10 minutes more or until golden.

PER SERVING 202 calories; 9 g total fat (6 g sat. fat); 23 mg cholesterol; 214 mg sodium; 30 g carbohydrate; 2 g fiber; 3 g protein

Cheese-Topped Hash Browns: Prepare as above, except before serving sprinkle with ½ cup (2 ounces) finely shredded cheddar cheese. Cover and cook 1 to 2 minutes more or until cheese melts.

PER SERVING 260 cal.; 13 g total fat (8 g sat. fat; 0 g trans fat); 38 mg cholesterol; 301 mg sodium; 29 g carbo.; 2 g fiber; 6 g pro.

❰ Imagine making the delight of American diners in your own kitchen— hash browns are heavenly! ❱

Glazed Parsnips and Carrots

Glazed Parsnips and Carrots 🍲

Parsnips are often coated with a thick layer of paraffin to keep them fresh. Be sure to peel the wax away before cutting the parsnips.

MAKES 6 servings **START TO FINISH** 30 minutes

- 8 ounces parsnips, cut into thin strips (see quick tip, below) (2¼ cups)
- 8 ounces carrots, cut into thin strips (see quick tip, below) (2¼ cups)
- ¾ cup orange juice
- ⅓ cup dried cranberries
- ½ teaspoon ground ginger
- 2 firm ripe pears, peeled, if desired, and sliced
- ⅓ cup pecan halves, toasted (see Quick Tip, page 272)
- 3 tablespoons packed brown sugar
- 2 tablespoons butter or margarine

① In a large nonstick skillet combine parsnips, carrots, orange juice, dried cranberries, and ginger. Bring to boiling; reduce heat to medium. Cook, uncovered, for 7 to 8 minutes or until vegetables are crisp-tender and most of the liquid has evaporated, stirring occasionally.

② Stir pears, pecans, brown sugar, and butter into vegetable mixture in skillet. Cook, uncovered, for 2 to 3 minutes more or until vegetables are glazed.

PER SERVING 213 calories; 9 g total fat (3 g sat. fat); 10 mg cholesterol; 60 mg sodium; 35 g carbohydrate; 6 g fiber; 2 g protein

quick tip If desired, thinly slice parsnips and carrots rather than cutting them into strips.

Brown Sugar-Glazed Carrots 🍲 ♥

Carrots plus sugar equals children eating their vegetables.

MAKES 4 servings **START TO FINISH** 25 minutes

- 1 pound peeled baby carrots or medium carrots, halved lengthwise and cut into 2-inch pieces
- 1 tablespoon butter or margarine
- 1 tablespoon packed brown sugar
  Dash salt
  Black pepper

① In a medium saucepan cook carrots, covered, in a small amount of boiling salted water for 8 to 10 minutes or until crisp-tender. Drain; remove carrots from pan.

② In the same saucepan combine butter, brown sugar, and salt. Cook and stir over medium heat until combined. Add carrots. Cook and stir about 2 minutes or until glazed. Season to taste with pepper.

PER SERVING 85 calories; 3 g total fat (2 g sat. fat); 8 mg cholesterol; 135 mg sodium; 14 g carbohydrate; 3 g fiber; 1 g protein

Herbed Glazed Carrots: Prepare as above, except substitute 1 tablespoon honey for the brown sugar and add 1 tablespoon snipped fresh thyme or ½ teaspoon dried thyme, crushed, to the butter mixture. Sprinkle with snipped fresh Italian parsley before serving.

quick tip Another time, make this recipe using 2-inch cubes of fresh butternut squash.

Caribbean Couscous Salad ♥

If you immerse fresh limes in warm water for about 15 minutes before squeezing, they will release their juices much more generously.

MAKES 10 servings **PREP** 20 minutes
STAND 5 minutes **COOL** 10 minutes

1¼ cups water
1 cup whole wheat couscous
1 15-ounce can black beans, rinsed and drained
2 cups coarsely shredded fresh spinach
1 medium red sweet pepper, seeded and coarsely chopped
1 medium mango, peeled, seeded, and chopped
¼ cup thinly sliced green onions
1 recipe Ginger-Lime Vinaigrette

① In a medium saucepan bring the water to boiling. Remove from heat. Stir in couscous; cover and let stand for 5 minutes. Fluff with a fork. Let stand at room temperature about 10 minutes or until cool.

② In a large bowl stir together beans, spinach, sweet pepper, mango, and green onions. Add couscous and Ginger-Lime Vinaigrette. Toss to coat. Serve immediately or cover and chill in the refrigerator for up to 24 hours.

Ginger-Lime Vinaigrette: In a small bowl whisk together ¼ cup snipped fresh cilantro, 3 tablespoons lime juice, 2 tablespoons canola oil, 1½ teaspoons grated fresh ginger or ½ teaspoon ground ginger, ⅛ teaspoon salt, and ⅛ teaspoon cayenne pepper.

PER SERVING 156 calories; 3 g total fat (0 g sat. fat); 0 mg cholesterol; 142 mg sodium; 29 g carbohydrate; 6 g fiber; 6 g protein

Risotto

Arborio rice is blessed with a super-starchy coating that, when cooked slowly, makes risotto ultracreamy.

MAKES 4 servings **PREP** 10 minutes **COOK** 15 minutes

½ cup chopped onion (1 medium)
1 clove garlic, minced
2 tablespoons olive oil
2 tablespoons butter
1 cup arborio rice
2 14.5-ounce cans reduced-sodium chicken broth
½ cup finely shredded Parmesan cheese
⅛ teaspoon black pepper

① In a large saucepan cook onion and garlic in hot olive oil and 1 tablespoon of the butter until onion is tender; add rice. Cook and stir over medium heat 2 to 3 minutes or until rice begins to brown.

② Meanwhile, in another saucepan bring broth to boiling; reduce heat and simmer. Slowly add 1 cup of the broth to the rice mixture, stirring constantly. Continue to cook and stir over medium heat until liquid is absorbed. Add another ½ cup of the broth to the rice mixture, stirring constantly. Continue to cook and stir until the liquid is absorbed. Add remaining broth, ½ cup at a time, stirring constantly until the broth has been absorbed. (This should take 15 to 20 minutes.)

③ Stir in the remaining butter, Parmesan cheese, and pepper.

PER SERVING 289 calories; 15 g total fat (6 g sat. fat); 22 mg cholesterol; 683 mg sodium; 30 g carbohydrate; 1 g fiber; 9 g protein

Lemon-Asparagus Risotto: Add 1 cup chopped asparagus and 1 teaspoon finely shredded lemon peel to the risotto after half of the chicken broth has been stirred into the risotto.

Spinach-Pea Risotto: Stir 2 cups chopped fresh spinach, ½ cup frozen peas, and 2 teaspoons snipped fresh tarragon or ½ teaspoon dried tarragon, crushed, into the risotto with the butter, Parmesan, and pepper. Cover and let stand 5 minutes.

Mushroom Risotto: Prepare as above, except cook 8 ounces sliced fresh assorted mushrooms (such as button, cremini, and/or stemmed shiitake) with the onion and garlic until tender and all liquid is evaporated. If desired, substitute ½ cup dry white wine for ½ cup of the chicken broth. Stir in 1 tablespoon snipped fresh basil with the butter, Parmesan, and pepper.

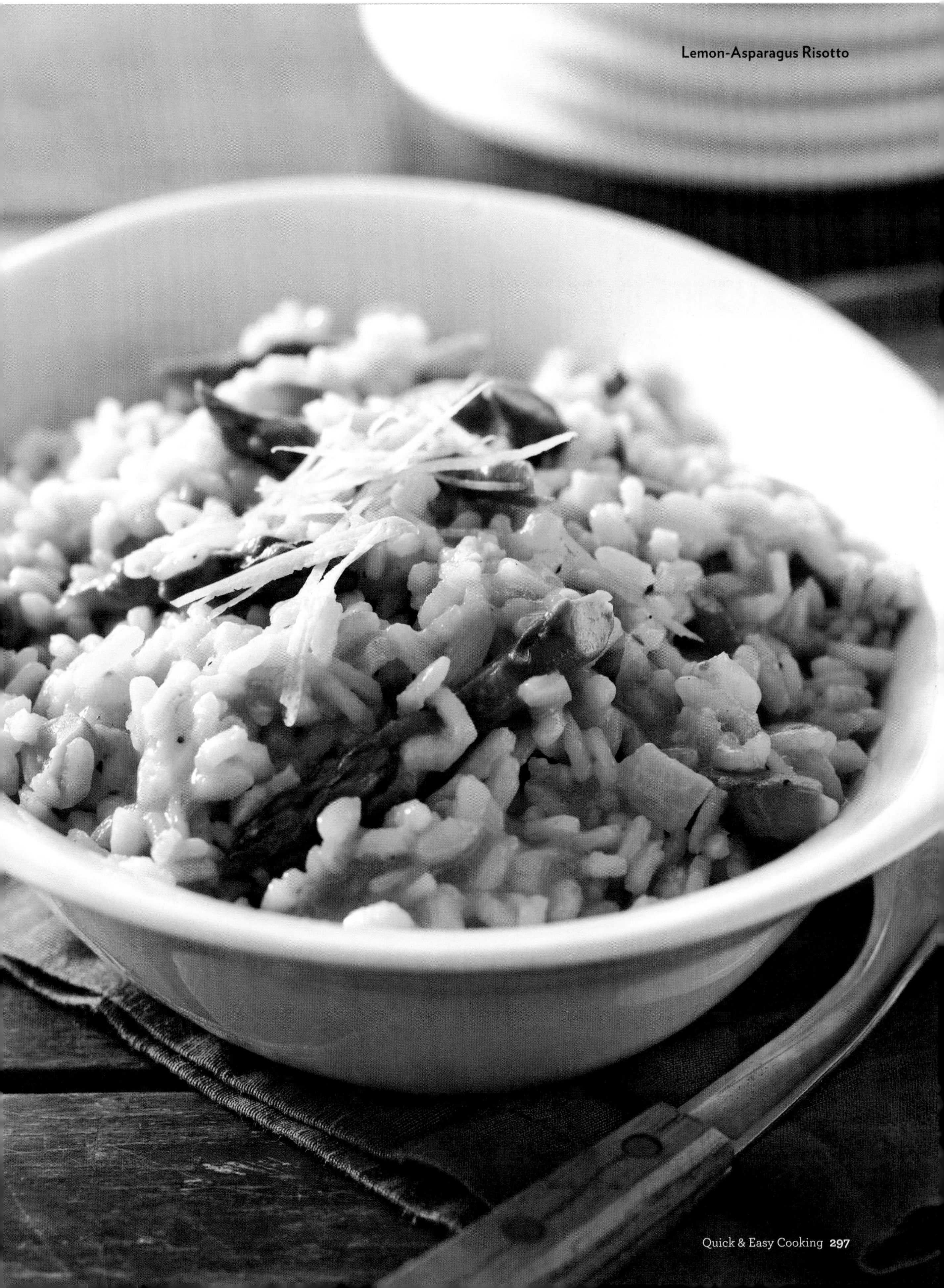
Lemon-Asparagus Risotto

Garlic Bread

Garlic Bread

This lovely loaf will elevate even the quickest suppers of pasta and jarred sauce to new heights.

MAKES 12 servings **START TO FINISH** 22 minutes
OVEN 400°F

1	16-ounce loaf baguette-style French bread
6	cloves garlic
¼	cup packed fresh basil leaves
2	tablespoons fresh parsley leaves
1	tablespoon fresh oregano leaves
¼	teaspoon salt
¼	teaspoon black pepper
½	cup butter, softened
2	tablespoons olive oil

① Preheat oven to 400°F. Using a serrated knife, cut bread in half horizontally.

② In a food processor combine garlic, basil, parsley, oregano, salt, and pepper. Cover and pulse until chopped. Add butter and olive oil. Cover and pulse until combined. Spread mixture on cut sides of bread halves. Reassemble loaf and wrap tightly in heavy foil.

③ Bake for 12 to 15 minutes or until heated through. (To broil, place bread halves, spread sides up, on a baking sheet. Broil 4 to 5 inches from the heat for 3 to 4 minutes or until toasted.)

PER SERVING 200 calories; 11 g total fat (5 g sat. fat); 20 mg cholesterol; 349 mg sodium; 22 g carbohydrate; 1 g fiber; 5 g protein

quick tip Slices of garlic bread—especially from a loaf this lovely—disappear fast. If you're expecting a young or especially hungry crowd, you may wish to prepare a backup loaf. If you don't use the emergency loaf, just pop it in the freezer until you need garlic bread again.

Honey-Nut Corn Muffins

Three ingredients make these muffins out of the ordinary.

MAKES 6 to 8 muffins **START TO FINISH** 25 minutes
OVEN 400°F

1	8.5-ounce package corn muffin mix
½	cup chopped pecans
2	tablespoons honey

① Preheat oven to 400°F. Grease six to eight 2½-inch muffin cups; set aside.

② Prepare corn muffin mix according to package directions, except stir in nuts and honey. Spoon batter into prepared muffin cups, filling each about three-fourths full.

③ Bake 15 minutes or until golden brown. Serve warm.

PER MUFFIN 263 calories; 12 g total fat (1 g sat. fat); 36 mg cholesterol; 297 mg sodium; 36 g carbohydrate; 1 g fiber; 5 g protein

Brandied Blue Cheese Bread

Serve these rich and creamy bread slices on steak night—they're a satisfying stand-in for typical potato side dishes.

MAKES 12 servings **START TO FINISH** 20 minutes
OVEN 350°F

1	12- to 16-ounce loaf baguette-style French bread
½	cup butter, softened
½	cup crumbled blue cheese (2 ounces)
1	tablespoon snipped fresh chives
1	tablespoon brandy (optional)
⅛	teaspoon cayenne pepper

① Preheat oven to 350°F. Use a serrated knife to cut bread crosswise into 1-inch slices, cutting to, but not through, the bottom crust.

② In a small bowl stir together butter, cheese, chives, brandy (if using), and cayenne pepper. Spread butter mixture between slices of bread. Wrap loaf in foil.

③ Bake for 10 to 15 minutes or until bread is heated through and cheese is melted.

PER SERVING 166 calories; 10 g total fat (6 g sat. fat); 24 mg cholesterol; 305 mg sodium; 16 g carbohydrate; 1 g fiber; 5 g protein

Turn the page to discover pastry shop-perfect sweets. But they're not the kind that demand hours slaving over a hot oven. These lickety-split lovelies ask for only as much of your time and patience as you're willing to devote to them.

305

310

321

SWEET TOOTH-DESSERTS

314

Tropical Cookies

A drizzle of white chocolate gives these cookies pastry shop appeal.

MAKES 24 cookies **PREP** 20 minutes
BAKE 11 minutes per batch **OVEN** 375°F

- 1½ **cups flaked coconut**
- 2 **tablespoons milk**
- 1 **18-ounce package refrigerated ready-to-bake white chocolate and macadamia nut cookie dough (12 cookies)**
- 2 **ounces white baking chocolate**
- ½ **teaspoon shortening**

① Preheat oven to 375°F. Line 2 cookie sheets with parchment paper or foil; set aside. Place coconut in a shallow dish. Place milk in a small bowl. Divide each cookie dough piece in half. Using your hands, roll dough pieces into balls. Roll balls in milk, then roll in coconut to coat. Place balls 2 inches apart on the prepared cookie sheets.

② Bake in the preheated oven for 11 to 13 minutes or until set and coconut is golden brown. Let stand for 1 minute on cookie sheet. Transfer to a wire rack and let cool.

③ In a small heavy saucepan combine white baking chocolate and shortening. Heat and stir over low heat until smooth. Drizzle melted chocolate over cookies. If necessary, chill cookies about 15 minutes or until chocolate is set.

PER COOKIE 149 calories; 9 g total fat (5 g sat. fat); 5 mg cholesterol; 77 mg sodium; 16 g carbohydrate; 1 g fiber; 2 g protein

Everything Good Cookies ♥

These cookies—packed with the goodness of whole grain and iron-rich dried fruit—are cookies you can be proud to pack in a lunch box.

MAKES 6 dozen cookies **PREP** 30 minutes
BAKE 8 minutes per batch **OVEN** 375°F

- ½ **cup butter, softened**
- ½ **cup shortening**
- 1 **cup granulated sugar**
- 1 **cup packed brown sugar**
- 1 **teaspoon baking powder**
- 1 **teaspoon baking soda**
- 2 **eggs**
- 2 **tablespoons milk**
- 2 **teaspoons vanilla**
- 2 **cups whole wheat flour**
- 2 **cups regular or quick-cooking rolled oats**
- 1 **cup chopped toasted nuts (see quick tip, page 272)**
- 1 **cup raisins or other snipped dried fruit**
- ¼ **cup toasted wheat germ**

① Preheat oven to 375°F. In a very large mixing bowl beat butter and shortening with an electric mixer on medium to high for 30 seconds. Add the granulated sugar, brown sugar, baking powder, and baking soda. Beat until combined, scraping sides of bowl occasionally. Beat in eggs, milk, and vanilla until combined. Beat in as much of the flour as you can with the mixer. Using a wooden spoon, stir in any remaining flour, the oats, nuts, raisins, and wheat germ.

② Drop dough by rounded teaspoons 2 inches apart onto an ungreased cookie sheet. Bake in the preheated oven about 8 minutes or until light brown. Transfer to a wire rack and let cool.

PER COOKIE 83 calories; 4 g total fat (1 g sat. fat); 9 mg cholesterol; 34 mg sodium; 12 g carbohydrate; 1 g fiber; 1 g protein

❮ This duo makes the cookie jar an even more desirable destination. ❯

Chewy Coconut Macaroons

Chewy Coconut Macaroons ♥

Among macaroons' many admirable qualities—tropical coconut flavor, airy texture, and absolute prettiness—the one that stands out in the minds of dieters is that these exquisite cookies are less than 100 calories.

MAKES 30 cookies **PREP** 15 minutes
BAKE 20 minutes per batch **OVEN** 325°F

- 2 3.5-ounce cans flaked coconut (2⅔ cups total)
- ⅔ cup granulated sugar
- ⅓ cup all-purpose flour
- ¼ teaspoon salt
- 4 egg whites
- ½ teaspoon almond extract
- 2 ounces semisweet chocolate (optional)
- ½ teaspoon shortening (optional)

① Preheat oven to 325°F. Lightly grease and flour a large cookie sheet; set aside.

② In a medium bowl stir together coconut, sugar, flour, and salt. Stir in egg whites and almond extract.

③ Drop egg white mixture by rounded teaspoons 2 inches apart onto the prepared cookie sheet. Bake for 20 to 25 minutes or until edges are golden brown. Transfer to a wire rack and let cool. If desired, in a heavy small saucepan heat and stir chocolate and shortening over low heat until smooth. Drizzle melted chocolate over cooled cookies.

PER COOKIE 55 calories; 3 g total fat (2 g sat. fat); 0 mg cholesterol; 27 mg sodium; 8 g carbohydrate; 0 g fiber; 1 g protein

quick tip Should you opt for bagged coconut rather than canned, store any leftover flakes tightly wrapped in the refrigerator. Coconut is rich in oils that quickly cause the product to become rancid when stored at room temperature.

Cherry-Almond Chews

The flavors of almonds and cherries are a match made in culinary heaven.

MAKES about 36 cookies **PREP** 10 minutes
BAKE 8 minutes per batch **OVEN** 375°F

- 1 16.5-ounce roll refrigerated gingerbread cookie dough or sugar cookie dough
- ¾ cup dried tart cherries
- ½ cup chopped toasted almonds (see quick tip, page 272)

① Preheat oven to 375°F. In a large bowl stir together cookie dough, dried cherries, and almonds until combined.

② Drop dough by rounded teaspoons 2 inches apart onto an ungreased cookie sheet. Bake for 8 to 10 minutes or until edges are light brown. Transfer to a wire rack and let cool.

PER COOKIE 78 calories; 4 g total fat (1 g sat. fat); 4 mg cholesterol; 46 mg sodium; 11 g carbohydrate; 0 g fiber; 1 g protein

Cherry-Almond Chews

Fudge Ecstasies

These rich and fudgy cookies are sure to become a favorite in your family.

MAKES about 36 cookies **PREP** 20 minutes
BAKE 8 minutes per batch **OVEN** 350°F

- 1 12-ounce package semisweet chocolate pieces (2 cups)
- 2 ounces unsweetened chocolate, chopped
- 2 tablespoons butter
- 2 eggs
- ⅔ cup sugar
- ¼ cup all-purpose flour
- 1 teaspoon vanilla
- ¼ teaspoon baking powder
- 1 cup chopped nuts

① Preheat oven to 350°F. Lightly grease a cookie sheet; set aside.

② In a medium heavy saucepan heat and stir 1 cup of the chocolate pieces, the unsweetened chocolate, and butter over low heat until smooth. Remove from heat. Add eggs, sugar, flour, vanilla, and baking powder. Beat until combined, scraping sides of pan occasionally. Stir in remaining 1 cup chocolate pieces and the nuts.

③ Drop dough by rounded teaspoons 2 inches apart onto the prepared cookie sheet. Bake for 8 to 10 minutes or until edges are firm and surfaces are dull and crackled. Transfer to a wire rack and let cool.

PER COOKIE 102 calories; 7 g total fat (3 g sat. fat); 14 mg cholesterol; 12 mg sodium; 11 g carbohydrate; 1 g fiber; 1 g protein

Peppermint-Fudge Brownie Bites ♥

These adorable delights make quick work of filling holiday cookie trays.

MAKES 25 brownies **PREP** 15 minutes
BAKE 21 minutes **OVEN** 350°F

- 1 16- to 18-ounce package refrigerated triple-chocolate cookie dough
- 1 cup tiny marshmallows
- ⅔ cup miniature semisweet chocolate pieces
- ¼ cup crushed striped round peppermint candies or candy canes
- 1 teaspoon shortening

① Preheat oven to 350°F. Line an 8 x 8 x 2-inch baking pan with foil, extending foil about 1 inch beyond edges of the pan. Break up cookie dough and place in the prepared pan. Press dough evenly into the pan.

② Bake for 18 minutes. Immediately sprinkle the marshmallows and ⅓ cup of the chocolate pieces over brownies. Bake for 3 to 4 minutes more or until marshmallows are puffed but not browned. Sprinkle with crushed peppermint candies. Cool completely.

③ Remove brownies from pan, using the foil to lift brownies. Place on cutting board. Using a long sharp knife (see quick tip, below) cut into squares. In a small saucepan heat and stir the remaining ⅓ cup chocolate pieces and the shortening over low heat until smooth. Drizzle brownies with melted chocolate. Let stand until chocolate is set.

PER BROWNIE 125 calories; 5 g total fat (2 g sat. fat); 3 mg cholesterol; 60 mg sodium; 19 g carbohydrate; 0 g fiber; 1 g protein

quick tip A hot knife will cut through the marshmallows easily. Between cuts, run the knife under hot water and pat dry with a paper towel or clean kitchen towel.

Peppermint-Fudge Brownie Bites

Peanut Butter Blondie Bars

Peanut Butter Blondie Bars

Peanut butter lovers will flip over these rich bars.

MAKES 36 bars **PREP** 25 minutes **BAKE** 20 minutes
OVEN 350°F

- 1 32-ounce package (or two 16.5-ounce packages) refrigerated peanut butter cookie dough
- 1⅓ cups graham cracker crumbs (about 19 graham crackers)
- 1 recipe Peanut Butter Frosting
- ⅔ cup candy-coated peanut butter-flavor pieces
- ½ cup chopped peanuts
- ½ cup miniature semisweet chocolate pieces

① Preheat oven to 350°F. Line a 13 x 9 x 2-inch baking pan with foil, extending foil about 1 inch beyond edges of the pan; set aside.

② In a large bowl knead together the cookie dough and graham cracker crumbs until combined (dough will be stiff). Press the dough evenly into the bottom of the prepared pan. Bake in the preheated oven about 20 minutes or until evenly puffed and light brown across the top. Cool in pan on a wire rack (bars will fall slightly during cooling).

③ Spread Peanut Butter Frosting over cooled bars. Immediately sprinkle with peanut butter-flavor pieces, chopped peanuts, and chocolate pieces. Remove bars from pan, using the foil to lift. Place on cutting board; cut into bars.

Peanut Butter Frosting: In a medium saucepan heat and stir ¼ cup peanut butter and ¼ cup butter just until smooth. Stir in 2 cups powdered sugar and 1 teaspoon vanilla. Stir in about 2 tablespoons milk to make frosting spreading consistency.

PER BAR 225 calories; 12 g total fat (4 g sat. fat); 10 mg cholesterol; 154 mg sodium; 27 g carbohydrate; 1 g fiber; 4 g protein

Oatmeal-Apricot Cookies

Sunny-bright apricots give these easy-to-make cookies extra chewiness.

MAKES about 36 cookies **PREP** 25 minutes
BAKE 10 minutes per batch **OVEN** 375°F

- 1 17.5- to 22-ounce package oatmeal-raisin cookie mix
- 2 eggs
- ½ cup butter, softened
- 1 tablespoon water
- ½ cup snipped dried apricots
- ⅓ cup flaked coconut
- 1 recipe Cream Cheese Frosting
  Snipped dried apricots

① Preheat oven to 375°F. Line a cookie sheet with parchment paper; set aside. In a large bowl combine cookie mix, eggs, butter, and the water. Gently stir in the ½ cup dried apricots and coconut.

② Drop dough by rounded teaspoons 2 inches apart onto the prepared cookie sheet. Bake for 10 to 12 minutes or until edges are light brown. Let stand for 1 minute on cookie sheet. Transfer to a wire rack and let cool.

③ Spread cookies with Cream Cheese Frosting. Sprinkle with additional dried apricots.

Cream Cheese Frosting: In a medium mixing bowl combine two 3-ounce packages softened cream cheese, ¼ cup softened butter, and 2 teaspoons vanilla. Beat with an electric mixer on medium until smooth. Gradually beat in 4 cups powdered sugar to make frosting spreading consistency.

PER COOKIE 182 calories; 9 g total fat (4 g sat. fat); 27 mg cholesterol; 115 mg sodium; 25 g carbohydrate; 1 g fiber; 2 g protein

Butterscotch Bars

Butterscotch brings out the kid in everybody. When paired with chocolate—as it is here—it brings out the kind of kid who snitches cookies when Mom's not looking.

MAKES 48 bars **PREP** 20 minutes **CHILL** 2 hours

- 1   9-ounce package chocolate wafers
- 6   tablespoons butter, melted
- 1   cup creamy peanut butter
- 1½ cups powdered sugar
- 1   11-ounce package butterscotch-flavor pieces (2 cups)
- ¼   cup whipping cream
- ¾   cup chopped peanuts

① Crush chocolate wafers to equal 2 cups. In a large bowl stir together butter, peanut butter, and powdered sugar. Stir in chocolate wafer crumbs. Press mixture into the bottom of an ungreased 13 x 9 x 2-inch baking pan.

② In a medium heavy saucepan combine butterscotch-flavor pieces and whipping cream. Stir over low heat just until pieces melt. Carefully spoon butterscotch mixture over crumb mixture, spreading evenly. Sprinkle peanuts over butterscotch mixture. Cover and chill at least 2 hours. Cut into bars.

PER BAR 130 calories; 8 g total fat (4 g. sat. fat); 6 mg cholesterol; 96 mg sodium; 13 g carbohydrate; 0 g fiber; 2 g protein

Butterscotch Bars

Oatmeal-Caramel Bars ♥

Kids who unwrap the vanilla caramels for the baker get to have not one but two of these chewy treats.

MAKES 60 bars **PREP** 25 minutes **BAKE** 22 minutes **OVEN** 350°F

- 1   cup butter, softened
- 2   cups packed brown sugar
- 2   eggs
- 2   teaspoons vanilla
- 1   teaspoon baking soda
- 2½ cups all-purpose flour
- 3   cups quick-cooking rolled oats
- 1   cup miniature semisweet chocolate pieces
- ½   cup chopped walnuts or pecans
- 30 vanilla caramels (9 ounces)
- 3   tablespoons milk

① Preheat oven to 350°F. Line a 15 x 10 x 1-inch baking pan with foil, extending foil about 1 inch beyond edges of pan; set aside.

② In a large mixing bowl beat butter with an electric mixer on medium to high for 30 seconds. Add the brown sugar. Beat until combined, scraping sides of bowl occasionally. Add eggs, vanilla, and baking soda; beat until combined. Beat or stir in the flour. Stir in the oats. Press two-thirds of the oats mixture (about 3⅓ cups) evenly into the bottom of the prepared pan. Sprinkle with chocolate pieces and nuts.

③ In a medium saucepan heat and stir the caramels and milk over low heat until smooth. Drizzle caramel mixture over chocolate and nuts. Drop the remaining oats mixture by teaspoons over the caramel.

④ Bake in the preheated oven for 22 to 25 minutes or until top is light brown. Cool in pan on a wire rack. Remove bars from pan, using the foil to lift. Place on cutting board; cut into bars.

PER BAR 120 calories; 5 g total fat (2 g sat. fat); 15 mg cholesterol; 66 mg sodium; 17 g carbohydrate; 1 g fiber; 2 g protein

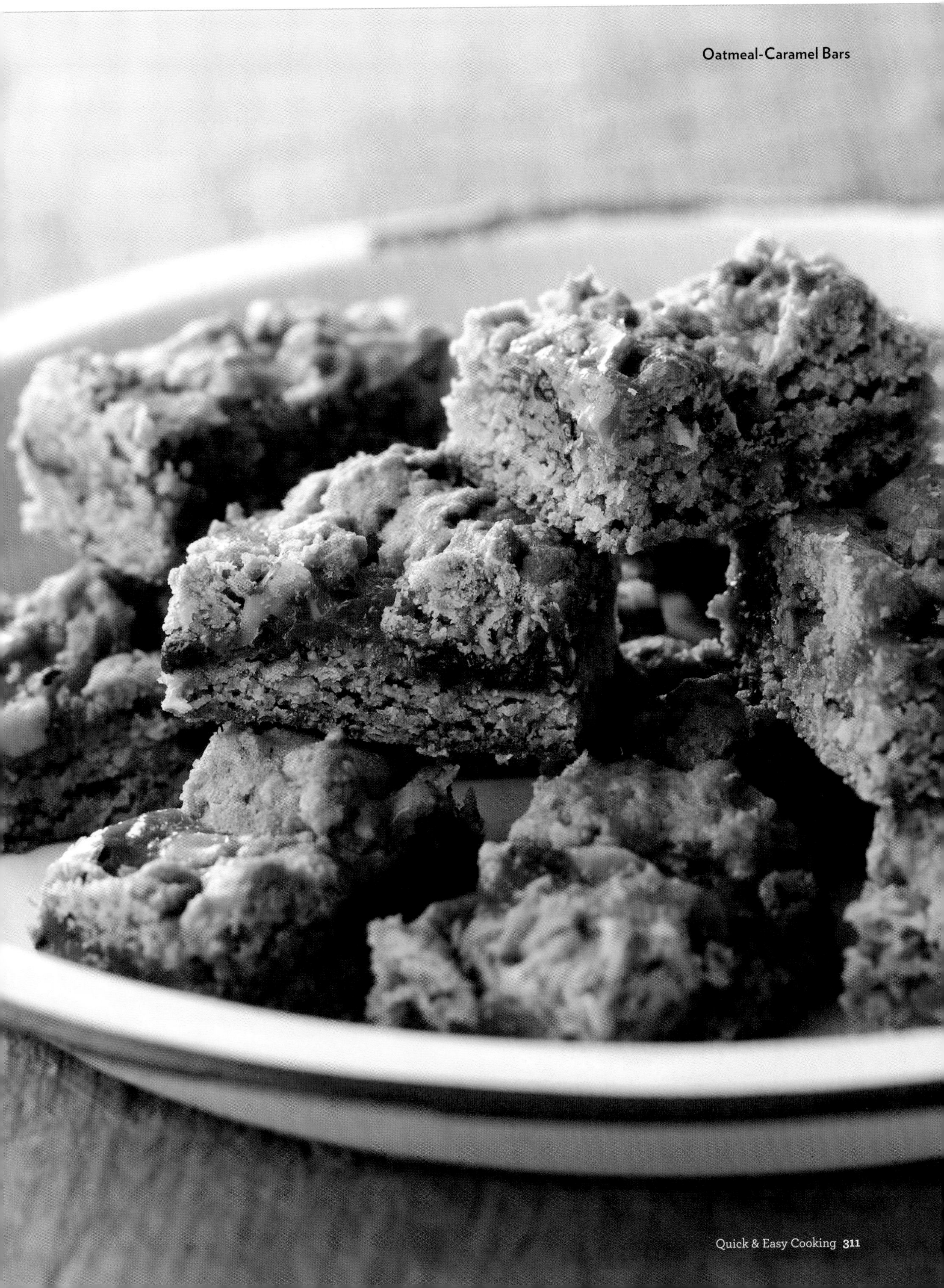
Oatmeal-Caramel Bars

Lemon Curd Bars

Lemon Curd Bars

Another time make these luscious lovelies using lime curd or grapefruit curd.

MAKES 32 bars **PREP** 30 minutes **BAKE** 23 minutes
OVEN 375°F

- 1 **cup butter, softened**
- 1 **cup sugar**
- 2 **cups all-purpose flour**
- ½ **teaspoon baking powder**
- 1 **10- to 12-ounce jar lemon curd**
- ⅔ **cup flaked coconut**
- ½ **cup slivered or sliced almonds or coarsely chopped pecans, toasted (see quick tip, page 272)**

① Preheat oven to 375°F. Line a 13 x 9 x 2-inch baking pan with foil extending about 1 inch beyond edges of pan. Grease foil; set pan aside.

② In a large mixing bowl beat butter with an electric mixer on medium to high for 30 seconds. Add sugar. Beat until combined, scraping sides of bowl occasionally. Add flour and baking powder; beat just until combined and mixture resembles coarse crumbs. Set aside ⅔ cup of the crumb mixture. Press the remaining crumb mixture evenly into the bottom of the prepared pan.

③ Bake in the preheated oven for 5 to 8 minutes or until top is golden. Remove from oven. Spread lemon curd over hot crust to within ½ inch of the edges. In a medium bowl stir together reserved crumb mixture, the coconut, and almonds. Sprinkle crumb mixture over lemon curd.

④ Bake for 18 to 20 minutes more or until edges are golden and topping is brown. Cool in pan on a wire rack. Remove bars from pan, using the foil to lift bars. Place on cutting board; cut into bars.

PER BAR 156 calories; 9 g total fat (5 g sat. fat); 23 mg cholesterol; 18 mg sodium; 20 g carbohydrate; 1 g fiber; 1 g protein

Cookies-and-Cream Cupcakes

Once and for all, the debate over which should be eaten first—the cookie or the filling—is resolved. Eat them both at once in these incredible cupcakes.

MAKES 24 cupcakes **PREP** 20 minutes
BAKE per package directions **COOL** 1 hour **OVEN** 350°F

- 1 **package 2-layer-size white cake mix**
- 1 **cup coarsely crushed chocolate sandwich cookies with white filling**
- 1 **recipe Creamy Cupcake Frosting**
- 24 **miniature chocolate sandwich cookies with white filling**

① Preheat oven to 350°F. Line twenty-four 2½-inch muffin cups with paper bake cups; set aside. Prepare cake mix according to package directions, folding crushed cookies into batter.

② Spoon batter into the prepared cups, filling each about half full. Bake cupcakes in the preheated oven according to cake mix package directions. Cool in pans on wire racks for 5 minutes. Remove cupcakes from pans; cool completely.

③ Using a pastry bag fitted with a star tip, pipe Creamy Cupcake Frosting on each cupcake or spread frosting on cupcakes. Top each cupcake with a miniature cookie.

Creamy Cupcake Frosting: In a large mixing bowl combine ½ cup shortening and 1 teaspoon vanilla. Beat with an electric mixer on medium to high for 30 seconds. Slowly add 1¼ cups powdered sugar, beating well. Add 1 tablespoon milk. Slowly beat in 1 cup additional powdered sugar. Beat in enough additional milk, 1 tablespoon at a time, to make frosting of spreading consistency. Makes about 1¾ cups.

PER CUPCAKE 213 calories; 9 g total fat (2 g sat. fat); 0 mg cholesterol; 193 mg sodium; 34 g carbohydrate; 0 g fiber; 2 g protein

 Either one of these treats is perfect for toting to potlucks or bake sales.

Quick Brownie Surprise

These decadent brownie sundaes benefit from the classic flavor pairing of Black Forest cake (cherry and chocolate) but take just 10 minutes to make!

MAKES 4 servings **START TO FINISH** 10 minutes

- 4 purchased brownies (each about 3 x 2 inches)
- 1 15.10- to 16-ounce carton cherry-chocolate ice cream
- ¼ cup dried cherries
- ¼ cup chopped mixed nuts or nut topping
- 2 tablespoons chocolate-flavor syrup

① Place 1 brownie in each of 4 dessert bowls. Top with a scoop of ice cream. Drizzle with syrup. Sprinkle with cherries and nuts.

PER SERVING 660 calories; 35 g total fat (17 g sat. fat); 81 mg cholesterol; 255 mg sodium; 81 g carbohydrate; 3 g fiber; 9 g protein

quick tip Often, dried cherries—which you expect to find shelved along with raisins, dried apricots, and prunes—are nowhere to be found. Push your cart over to the produce department—you'll likely find them along with the small specialty items there.

Quick Brownie Surprise

Rhubarb and Spice Snacking Cake

When a dessert is called "snacking cake," you are entitled to enjoy small pieces all day long.

MAKES 9 servings **PREP** 25 minutes
BAKE 25 minutes **COOL** 30 minutes **OVEN** 350°F

- ⅓ cup granulated sugar
- ⅓ cup chopped pecans
- 1 tablespoon butter, melted
- 1 teaspoon ground cinnamon
- 1 cup all-purpose flour
- ½ teaspoon baking soda
- ¼ teaspoon salt
- ⅛ teaspoon ground nutmeg
- ¼ cup butter, softened
- ¾ cup packed brown sugar
- 1 egg
- ⅓ cup sour cream
- 1 cup chopped fresh rhubarb or frozen unsweetened rhubarb, thawed, drained, and chopped
- ¼ cup golden raisins
- 1 teaspoon finely shredded lemon peel

① Preheat oven to 350°F. Grease and flour an 8 x 8 x 2-inch baking pan; set aside. In a small bowl combine granulated sugar, pecans, the 1 tablespoon melted butter, and ½ teaspoon of the cinnamon until crumbly; set aside. In another small bowl stir together flour, baking soda, the remaining ½ teaspoon cinnamon, the salt, and nutmeg; set aside.

② In a medium mixing bowl beat the ¼ cup butter with an electric mixer on medium to high for 30 seconds. Beat in brown sugar until well combined. Beat in egg. Add flour mixture alternately with sour cream to butter mixture, beating until combined after each addition (batter will be thick). Stir in rhubarb, raisins, and lemon peel.

③ Spread mixture evenly in the prepared baking pan. Sprinkle with crumb mixture. Bake in the preheated oven for 30 to 35 minutes or until a wooden toothpick inserted near the center of cake comes out clean. Cool in pan on a wire rack for 30 minutes. Serve warm. Or cool completely and serve at room temperature.

PER SERVING 276 calories; 12 g total fat (6 g sat. fat); 45 mg cholesterol; 223 mg sodium; 41 g carbohydrate; 2 g fiber; 3 g protein

Rhubarb and Spice Snacking Cake

Quick & Easy Cooking **315**

Miniature Fruit Tarts

Miniature Fruit Tarts

These could be called Five-Minute Fruit Tarts. Just spread a sugar cookie with cream cheese, sprinkle with coconut, and top with fruit—and they're done!

MAKES 4 tarts **START TO FINISH** 15 minutes

- 4 purchased large (3-inch) soft sugar cookies or chocolate cookies
- ¼ cup tub-style cream cheese spread with strawberries, chocolate-hazelnut spread, or fudge ice cream topping
- 2 tablespoons coconut
- 1 cup sliced fresh fruit, such as kiwifruit, bananas, and/or strawberries

① Spread flat side of each cookie with cream cheese spread; sprinkle with coconut. Top with fruit.

PER TART 164 calories; 9 g total fat (4 g sat. fat); 23 mg cholesterol; 114 mg sodium; 21 g carbohydrate; 2 g fiber; 2 g protein

Grilled Chocolate-Banana Sandwich

Elvis is said to have loved peanut butter and banana sandwiches. He might have really loved these for dessert.

MAKES 1 sandwich **START TO FINISH** 10 minutes

- ½ of a 3.5-ounce chocolate bar, halved
- 2 slices white or whole wheat bread
- ½ of a banana, sliced
- 1 tablespoon butter
  Sifted powdered sugar

① Place the chocolate bar on 1 bread slice. Top with the banana slices and remaining slice of bread. In a skillet heat butter over medium-low heat just until it begins to bubble. Add sandwich to skillet, chocolate side down. Cook, covered, about 1½ minutes or until bread is golden brown and toasted. Carefully flip sandwich and cook until brown. Remove from skillet, slice in half, and dust with powdered sugar. Serve warm.

PER SANDWICH 560 calories; 29 g total fat (17 g sat. fat); 42 mg cholesterol; 473 mg sodium; 70 g carbohydrate; 4 g fiber; 11 g protein

Simple Fudge Tarts

These rich, trufflelike miniature tarts make impressive hostess gifts.

MAKES 24 tarts **PREP** 20 minutes **BAKE** 11 minutes **STAND** 15 minutes **OVEN** 350°F

- ½ of an 18-ounce package refrigerated peanut butter cookie dough
- ½ cup semisweet chocolate pieces
- ¼ cup sweetened condensed milk

① Preheat oven to 350°F. Lightly grease twenty-four 1¾-inch muffin cups; set aside. For tart shells, cut cookie dough into 6 equal pieces. Cut each piece into 4 equal slices. Place each slice of dough in a prepared cup.

② Bake about 9 minutes or until edges are light brown and dough is slightly firm but not set. Remove tart shells from oven. Gently press a shallow indentation in each tart shell with the back of a round ½-teaspoon measuring spoon. Bake about 2 minutes more or until the edges of tart shells are firm and light golden brown. Let stand in cups on a wire rack for 15 minutes. Carefully remove tart shells from cups. Cool completely on wire rack.

③ For filling, in a small saucepan heat and stir chocolate pieces and sweetened condensed milk over medium heat until smooth. Spoon a generous teaspoon of filling into each cooled tart shell. Let stand until filling is set.

PER TART 75 calories; 4 g total fat (1 g sat. fat); 4 mg cholesterol; 46 mg sodium; 10 g carbohydrate; 0 g fiber; 1 g protein

quick tip For the family table, apply cookie toppings right before serving. If transporting Miniature Fruit Tarts when prepared and garnished, carefully arrange tarts about 1 inch apart in a sturdy box lined with a clean terry cloth towel. The towel will keep the tarts from sliding during transport. Serve within 1½ hours of preparation.

Hot Taffy Apple Pita Pizza

This is definitely a different type of apple pie—and it takes just minutes to make. Apple slices bubble in the oven in a rich sour cream-apple sauce on top of pita bread and get a sprinkling of crunchy pecans right before serving.

MAKES 8 servings **PREP** 15 minutes
BAKE 10 minutes **OVEN** 400°F

2	pita bread rounds
½	cup purchased caramel dip for apples
¼	cup dairy sour cream
1	20-ounce can sliced apples, well drained
1	tablespoon butter, melted
2	tablespoons sugar
¼	teaspoon ground cinnamon
⅓	cup chopped pecans

① Preheat oven to 400°F. Place pita bread rounds on an ungreased baking sheet. In a small bowl combine ¼ cup of the caramel dip and the sour cream; spread over pitas.

② Top with drained apples. Drizzle with melted butter. In a small bowl combine sugar and cinnamon; sprinkle over apples. Drizzle with remaining ¼ cup caramel dip (see quick tip); sprinkle with pecans.

③ Bake about 10 minutes or until heated through. Serve warm. If desired, serve with vanilla or cinnamon ice cream.

PER SERVING 233 calories; 10 g total fat (3 g sat. fat); 8 mg cholesterol; 141 mg sodium; 36 g carbohydrate; 2 g fiber; 3 g protein

quick tip If the caramel dip is too thick to drizzle, heat it in a saucepan or microwave oven just until it thins slightly. Spoon the dip into a plastic bag, snip off one corner, and squeeze the bag to drizzle dip.

Whipped Key Lime Pie

For a fun twist to this timeless dessert, try making the Graham Cracker Crust with chocolate graham crackers.

MAKES 8 servings **PREP** 25 minutes
CHILL 1 hour **FREEZE** 2 hours

1	recipe Graham Cracker Crust
1	14-ounce can sweetened condensed milk
1	teaspoon finely shredded Key lime peel or lime peel
½	cup Key lime juice or lime juice
2	cups whipping cream
	Finely shredded Key lime peel or lime peel (optional)

① Prepare Graham Cracker Crust. Cover and chill about 1 hour or until firm.

② For filling, in a medium bowl combine sweetened condensed milk, the 1 teaspoon lime peel, and lime juice. In a medium mixing bowl beat 1 cup of the whipping cream with an electric mixer on medium until soft peaks form (tips curl). Fold whipped cream into lime mixture. Spoon filling evenly into crust-lined pie plate. Cover and freeze for 2 to 4 hours or until firm. Keep remaining cream chilled until ready to serve.

③ To serve, remove pie from freezer. In a medium bowl beat remaining 1 cup cream on medium until soft peaks form (tips curl). Spread whipped cream over filling. If desired, sprinkle with additional key lime peel.

Graham Cracker Crust: In a medium bowl combine 1¼ cups graham cracker crumbs and ¼ cup sugar. Drizzle with ⅓ cup melted butter; toss gently to coat. Press mixture evenly onto bottom and sides of a 9-inch pie plate.

PER SERVING 529 calories; 36 g total fat (22 g sat. fat); 119 mg cholesterol; 266 mg sodium; 47 g carbohydrate; 1 g fiber; 7 g protein

❮ Feather-light and oh-so luscious, Key lime pie provides a cool ending to a warm weather meal. ❯

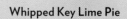

Piled-High Shortcake

Piled-High Shortcake

With a little bit of butter for flavor and a creamy filling made from low-fat cream cheese and yogurt, these homey shortcakes are both fast and healthful.

MAKES 6 servings **START TO FINISH** 30 minutes
OVEN 425°F

- ¾ cup all-purpose flour
- 2 teaspoons sugar
- 1 teaspoon baking powder
- ⅛ teaspoon baking soda
  Dash salt
- 2 tablespoons butter
- ¼ cup buttermilk
- 1 egg yolk, lightly beaten
  Nonstick cooking spray
- ½ of an 8-ounce package reduced-fat cream cheese (Neufchâtel), softened
- 1 cup carton plain low-fat yogurt
- 3 tablespoons low-sugar strawberry preserves
- 1½ cups fresh raspberries, blueberries, blackberries, cutup nectarines, and/or peeled and cutup kiwifruits

① Preheat oven to 425°F. For shortcakes, in a medium bowl stir together flour, sugar, baking powder, baking soda, and salt. Using a pastry blender, cut in butter until mixture resembles coarse crumbs. Make a well in center of flour mixture. In a small bowl combine buttermilk and egg yolk. Add to flour mixture all at once, stirring just until moistened.

② Lightly coat a baking sheet with cooking spray; set aside. On a lightly floured surface pat or roll dough to ½-inch thickness. Using a floured 1½- to 2-inch cookie cutter, cut dough into shapes, rerolling scraps as necessary. Place on prepared baking sheet. Bake for 7 to 8 minutes or until golden. Cool on a wire rack.

③ In a medium mixing bowl beat cream cheese with an electric mixer on medium for 30 seconds. Gradually beat in yogurt and preserves until smooth.

④ Split shortcakes in half horizontally. Divide shortcake bottoms among 6 dessert plates; top each with some of the fresh fruit and yogurt mixture. Add shortcake tops. Serve immediately.

PER SERVING 212 calories; 10 g total fat (6 g sat. fat); 62 mg cholesterol; 232 mg sodium; 25 g carbohydrate; 1 g fiber; 6 g protein

Coffee-Almond Parfaits

Even those who don't drink coffee will enjoy these sophisticated parfaits at the end of a good meal.

MAKES 4 servings **START TO FINISH** 30 minutes
OVEN 350°F

- 2 cups ¾-inch cubes pound cake
- 3 6-ounce cartons vanilla yogurt
- ½ of an 8-ounce container frozen whipped dessert topping, thawed
- 2 tablespoons coffee liqueur or strong brewed coffee
- 4 amaretti cookies, coarsely crushed

① Preheat oven to 350°F. In a shallow baking pan arrange cake cubes in a single layer. Bake for 15 minutes or until golden, stirring twice. Cool.

② Meanwhile, in a medium bowl stir together yogurt and whipped topping.

③ Layer ¼ cup cake cubes in each of 4 parfait glasses. Top with half of the yogurt mixture and remaining cake cubes. Stir liqueur into remaining yogurt mixture; spoon over cake cubes. Sprinkle with crushed cookies. Serve immediately.

PER SERVING 377 calories; 15 g total fat (10 g sat. fat); 62 mg cholesterol; 164 mg sodium; 48 g carbohydrate; 1 g fiber; 8 g protein

Coffee-Almond Parfaits

Rocky Road Malts

Top the malts with marshmallow creme, chopped peanuts, and itty-bitty cookies—absolutely irresistible!

MAKES 4 servings **START TO FINISH** 10 minutes

- 1 quart chocolate ice cream
- ⅓ to ½ cup milk
- ⅓ cup chocolate instant malted milk powder
- ¼ cup creamy peanut butter
  Miniature sandwich cookies (optional)

① Place half of the ice cream, ⅓ cup of the milk, the malted milk powder, and peanut butter in a blender. Cover; blend until smooth, stopping and scraping down sides if necessary. Spoon in remaining ice cream; blend until smooth. If necessary, add additional milk until malts are desired consistency.

② To serve, spoon into 4 glasses. If desired, top with miniature sandwich cookies.

PER SERVING 493 calories; 24 g total fat (11 g sat. fat); 47 mg cholesterol; 252 mg sodium; 66 g carbohydrate; 4 g fiber; 11 g protein

Rocky Road Malts

Chocolate Fondue

Fondue allows diners—bite by luscious bite—to create their own desserts. It's hard to believe that something so fun is so superlatively simple to prepare!

MAKES 8 servings **START TO FINISH** 15 minutes

- 8 ounces semisweet chocolate, coarsely chopped
- 1 14-ounce can sweetened condensed milk (1¼ cups)
- ⅓ cup milk
  Assorted dippers, such as angel food or pound cake cubes, brownie squares, marshmallows, whole strawberries, banana slices, pineapple chunks, or dried apricots

① In a medium heavy saucepan heat and stir chocolate over low heat until melted. Stir in sweetened condensed milk and milk; heat through. Transfer to a fondue pot; keep warm.

② Serve fondue sauce immediately with assorted dippers. Swirl pieces as you dip.

PER CUP FONDUE 306 calories; 14 g total fat (8 g sat. fat); 18 mg cholesterol; 67 mg sodium; 44 g carbohydrate; 2 g fiber; 6 g protein

Chocolate-Liqueur Fondue: Prepare as above, except stir 2 to 4 tablespoons amaretto, orange, hazelnut, or cherry liqueur into chocolate mixture after heating.

Chocolate-Peanut Fondue: Prepare as above, except stir ½ cup creamy peanut butter in with the milk.

Mocha Fondue: Prepare as above, except substitute ⅓ cup strong brewed coffee for the milk.

White Chocolate Fondue: Prepare as above, except substitute white chocolate baking squares for semisweet chocolate and add one 7-ounce jar marshmallow creme to the saucepan with the chocolate. Reduce milk to 2 tablespoons. After fondue is smooth and melted, stir in ¼ cup crème de cacao or amaretto.

quick tip To prevent sliced bananas from oxidizing—or turning brown—slice the bananas directly into a bowl of orange juice. Drain bananas and pat gently dry with paper towels before presenting with fondue.

INDEX Note: Boldfaced page numbers indicate photographs.

In-a-Pinch Substitutions

It can happen to the best of us: Halfway through a recipe, you find you're completely out of a key ingredient. Here's what to do:

Recipe Calls For:	You May Substitute:
1 square unsweetened chocolate	3 Tbsp. unsweetened cocoa powder + 1 Tbsp. butter/margarine
1 cup cake flour	1 cup less 2 Tbsp. all-purpose flour
2 Tbsp. flour (for thickening)	1 Tbsp. cornstarch
1 tsp. baking powder	¼ tsp. baking soda + ½ tsp. cream of tartar + ¼ tsp. cornstarch
1 cup corn syrup	1 cup sugar + ¼ cup additional liquid used in recipe
1 cup milk	½ cup evaporated milk + ½ cup water
1 cup buttermilk or sour milk	1 Tbsp. vinegar or lemon juice + enough milk to make 1 cup
1 cup sour cream (for baking)	1 cup plain yogurt
1 cup firmly packed brown sugar	1 cup sugar + 2 Tbsp. molasses
1 tsp lemon juice	¼ tsp. vinegar (not balsamic)
¼ cup chopped onion	1 Tbsp. instant minced
1 clove garlic	¼ tsp. garlic powder
2 cups tomato sauce	¾ cup tomato paste + 1 cup water
1 Tbsp. prepared mustard	1 tsp. dry mustard + 1 Tbsp. water

FOR A RECIPE TO EARN THIS "HEALTHY" ICON, IT MUST MEET CERTAIN CALORIE, FAT, AND SODIUM REQUIREMENTS.

Maximum levels per serving include:

- Main dish: 400 calories, 13 grams fat, and 480 milligrams sodium.
- One-dish meal: 500 calories, 17 grams fat, and 600 milligrams sodium.
- Side dish: 200 calories, 6 grams fat, and 200 milligrams sodium.
- Dessert: 200 calories, 6 grams fat, and 300 milligrams sodium.

How to Know What You Need

Making a shopping list based on a recipe can be tricky if you don't know how many tomatoes yields 3 cups chopped. Here are some handy translations:

When the Recipe Calls For:	You Need:
4 cups shredded cabbage	1 small cabbage
1 cup grated raw carrot	1 large carrot
2½ cups sliced carrots	1 pound raw carrots
4 cups cooked cut fresh green beans	1 pound beans
1 cup chopped onion	1 large onion
4 cups sliced raw potatoes	4 medium-size potatoes
1 cup chopped sweet pepper	1 large pepper
1 cup chopped tomato	1 large tomato
2 cups canned tomatoes	16-oz. can
4 cups sliced apples	4 medium-size apples
1 cup mashed bananas	3 medium-size bananas
1 tsp grated lemon rind	1 medium-size lemon
2 Tbsp. lemon juice	1 medium-size lemon
4 tsp. grated orange rind	1 medium-size orange
1 cup orange juice	3 medium-size oranges
4 cups sliced peaches	8 medium-size peaches
2 cups sliced strawberries	1 pint
1 cup soft bread crumbs	2 slices fresh bread
1 cup bread cubes	2 slices fresh bread
2 cups shredded Swiss or cheddar cheese	8 oz. cheese
1 cup egg whites	6 or 7 large eggs
1 egg white	2 tsp. egg white powder + 2 Tbsp. water
4 cups chopped walnuts or pecans	1 pound shelled